Measuring the Value of Culture

Jeanette D. Snowball

Measuring the Value of Culture

Methods and Examples in Cultural Economics

Springer

Dr. Jeanette D. Snowball
Rhodes University
Department of Economics
P.O. Box 94
6140 Grahamstown
South Africa
j.snowball@ru.ac.za

Cover Picture: Roman statue of Minerva (Louvre), photo by Warren Snowball

ISBN 978-3-642-09377-7 e-ISBN 978-3-540-74360-6

DOI 10.1007/978-3-540-74360-6

Cover-design: WMX Design GmbH, Heidelberg

Printed on acid-free paper

9 8 7 6 5 4 3 2 1

springer.com

For Warren

Thanks and Acknowledgements

No work of this sort is possible without the help and encouragement of a number of friends and colleagues too numerous to mention here. In particular, I would like to thank Professor Geoffrey Antrobus of Rhodes University, who has been my advisor and co-researcher over a number of years, and I am very grateful for his ongoing support and enthusiasm. I would also like to thank Professor Arthur Webb for his suggestions and helpful comments. Lynette Marais, the Director of the South African National Arts Festival, and her staff, have been unfailingly helpful, both in providing data and comment on festival research. I would also like to thank Professor Ken Willis, of the University of Newcastle-upon-Tyne, for introducing me to choice experiments, and his assistance in applying them to South African case studies. I would like to extend my sincere thanks to those members of the Association for Cultural Economics International who have commented encouragingly on various parts of my work. For friendship and support, I acknowledge the Women's Academic Solidarity Association of Rhodes University.

Table of Contents

Introduction

> "The movie's lesson is: Fight for your country, even if it's a losing battle, and have enough swords and hotel rooms on hand for tourists" (Comment by Greek Deputy Finance Minister, Petros Doukas, on the film, *300*).

The interesting thing about culture, and its expression, the arts, is that it is nearly always contested and a site of struggle. Unlike environmental goods, which can have value not associated with humans, culture and its artifacts are always of value to someone in particular. As pointed out by Brooks (2006) the same piece of art can have both positive and negative values, depending on who is doing the looking. And we are not talking only about developing countries or places where political and social conflict is near the surface. The ongoing struggle of artists for artistic freedom and escape from censorship happens in even the most developed nations, as witnessed by the fierce debate around how funds from the US National Endowment of the Arts are spent.

Counter-factual studies, the science of "what if" which I predict is likely to become an increasingly useful analytical tool, suggest that the deciding moments in history almost always have dramatic cultural consequences. The recent film, *300*, explores such a moment, when 300 Spartan warriors held off the vast invading army of the Persian empire in 480BC for long enough to convince Xerxes to abandon his attack. What if the Spartans had stayed at home? If the Persian empire had conquered Greece, much of present day "western" culture would be vastly different. There would have been no flowering of the Greek culture in the high classical period, no Parthenon, no Socrates. Later on, there would have been no Alexander the Great and consequently, no enormous spread of Greek architecture, poetry, history and philosophy throughout the then-known world. I would probably be writing this is some derivation of ancient Persian, if I was writing it at all, since there would be no universities as we know them.

The point of this flight into fantasy is to illustrate the vast and ongoing influence of culture on our lives. When cultures clash and merge, as they are now doing in the New South Africa, inevitable questions about the value of the arts arise and, specifically, value to whom. Arts and culture, particularly as represented by the "cultural industries," have been shown to have a significant effect on the economies of many countries, both in terms of contributions to GDP and in job creation as shown in the table below from a recent OECD study (Gordon and Beilby-Orrin 2007).

Table 1. GDP and employment contributions of cultural industries

OECD Estimates of Cultural Industries contributions to National GDP			
Country	Reference year	Value in millions	Percent of total economy
Australia	1998-9	17,053 (Aus $)	3.1%
Canada	2002	37,465 (Can $)	3.5%
France	2003	39,899 ( )	2.8%
UK	2003	42,180 (£)	5.8%
USA	2002	341,139 (US$)	3.3%
OECD Estimates of Culture Employment in Selected Cities			
City	Reference year	Employment ('000)	City culture employment as percent of national culture employment
London	2002	525	23.8%
Montreal	2003	98	16.4%
New York	2002	309	8.9%
Paris	2003	113	45.4%

(Gordon and Beilby-Orrin 2007: 6-7)

The availability of such data lends itself towards measuring the "value" of culture in terms of economic impact. The report by Gordon and Beilby-Orrin (2007) on the feasibility of producing reliable measures of the cultural sector to facilitate international comparison also recognized non-market social values. Their recommendation, at least initially, is to focus on measures of revenue, GDP and employment, but a growing number of smaller economic impact studies of cultural goods, events and institutions now also include at least some mention of their social and cultural value. Like the tongue-in-cheek comment by the Greek Deputy Minister of Finance on the "message" of the *300* film quoted at the start, culture and the arts can generate both "intrinsic" and "instrumental" values, to use the terminology of McCarthy et al. (2004). Intrinsic values, like the spiritual or emotional "message" in a work of art are often much more difficult to measure than the instrumental values, which would include increases in tourism and tourist spending.

Economic impact studies are thus one way of measuring the value of the arts, but only *one* way, and its methodology is not unproblematic. A better way of capturing the non-market values of culture might be to use contingent valuation (willingness to pay) studies or their newer relation, choice experiments (also called conjoint analysis). This book sets out to document valuation techniques, both market and non-market, that can be used specifically for the arts and cultural events. These could include arts festivals, museums, community arts centers, non-profit arts industries, libraries, theatres, orchestras and so on. The method, or combination of methods, chosen will depend very much on what the aims of the particular cultural resource or event are and what sort of "value" one is trying to measure.

There are some who find the whole idea of formally "valuing" culture and the arts distasteful, especially when price is used as a unit of account. While we might agree that some things are "priceless" and should not be subjected to a quantifiable valuation process, economics is defined as the study of the allocation of scarce resources to satisfy unlimited wants. The definition implies choices and opportunity costs and the reality is that when it comes to allocating those scarce resources, *some* measure of comparing the value of competing "wants" will be used. In such a situation, why not make the best case possible?

This book is intended to assist arts event organizers, other cultural resource managers and those conducting valuations to place as realistic and unbiased a value as possible on their event or facility. On the other hand, it also aims to inform those making funding decisions about what the most common methods actually measure and where they need to look hardest for misrepresentation and bias.

Secondly, the book aims to provide a review of the current state of the theory of cultural valuation for researchers and a starting point for further investigation. Such theoretical background may also be important to valuation practitioners. Many studies show evidence of having rushed into a particular method without carefully considering the underlying philosophy, with disappointing or misleading results. Discussions include new theoretical developments around ideas of cultural capital as well as debates on currently used methods, like economic impact and contingent valuation.

Finally, for those practitioners who wish to apply valuation theory to a particular cultural good, the book provides a practical "how to". Such issues as which methods are most appropriate, potential problems, questionnaire design and analysis and interpretation of results are all considered.

In addition to being sites of conflict, cultures can also merge and create a wonderful, many layered richness. For example, the photograph on the cover of this book shows the Roman goddess Minerva (derived from the Greek Athena). She is the goddess of wisdom (hence the rather rotund owl), but also of handicraft and war. Some might argue that she is a highly European image to put on a book written by an African, but she has hidden depths. Herodotus was one of the first ancient travel writers, and he tells us that legend states that she was "born" in lake Tritonis in ancient Libya (modern-day Tunisia). It is a story he is inclined to believe because, he says, the local Libyan women wear a cloak very much like the aegis of Athena. She thus seems to me a good choice of guardian for a book about cultural values: fierce, creative, wise and embodying in herself the link between us.

References

Brooks, A. (2006) The Economics of Controversial Art. Paper presented at the Association for Cultural Economics International Conference, 6-9 July, Vienna.

Copetas, C. (2007) Movie catches Sparta unprepared for a craze. International Herald Tribune, Europe. [On line] Available: www.iht.com/articles/2007/05/15/europe/letter.php [Accessed 01/06/07].

Gordon, J. C. and Beilby-Orrin, H. (2007) International measurement of the economic and social importance of culture. STD/NAFS (2007) 1.Organisation for Economic Co-operation and Development (OECD) [On line] Available: http://www.oecd.org/dataoecd/56/54/38348526.pdf [Accessed 08/06/07].

Herodotus: The Histories, Book IV: 180. English translation by De Selincourt, A (1972) Penguin Classics: Hammondsworth, Middlesex

McCarthy, K, Ondaatje, E., Zakaras, L. and Brooks, A. (2004) Gift of the Muse: Reframing the debate about the benefits of the arts. Rand Corporation: Santa Monica, Arlington and Pittsburgh.

1 The Arts, Economics and Valuation

All the terms central to this book, "the arts", "culture", "value" and even "economics" (or at least its scope) are contentious. This chapter outlines the current state of the definition of these terms and their relationships in cultural economics. It is argued that, in addition to the more usual quantitative valuation techniques, which are the focus of this book, a complete measure of value for arts and culture also requires a more qualitative social valuation, probably not based on neoclassical utility theory.

1.1 Defining Culture and the Arts

Most economists would agree that culture and the arts do not operate like normal goods (even normal public goods) in the market. There is something special about culture, but defining what it is can be difficult. Both Klamer (2004a) and Throsby (2001) distinguish between the broader idea of culture as a way of living or "culture as identity" and the expression of culture as art forms. "The arts" as an expression of cultural identity, is what this book is primarily concerned with, in other words, cultural goods. Throsby (2001:4) refers to such goods, in a "functional" definition, as "certain activities that are undertaken by people and the products of those activities, which have to do with the intellectual, moral and artistic aspects of human life". While such a definition may seem almost too broad to be useful, he adds that cultural goods have three characteristics: they have some form of creativity in production, they are concerned with symbolic meaning, which Klamer (2004a) identifies as *the* defining characteristic of cultural goods, and their output is some form of intellectual property.

An interesting shift in cultural economics studies of the arts is evident in these recent, inclusive definitions. Early studies focused almost exclusively on "high" (European) cultural forms, since, as Fullerton (1991) pointed out, "popular" cultural products operated well in the market without the need for intervention. The question of who has the right to define what is "high" culture and its relationship to other cultural forms was first addressed by Antonio Gramsci in the 1920's with his introduction of the theory of hegemony (Turner 1990). Gramsci used this term to illustrate that "high" or dominant cultural forms were imposed on society and given greater perceived value by the economically powerful ruling class, often a minority in terms of numbers, but holding the majority of wealth in terms of both money and leisure time. Many social theory commentators, like Bourdieu (1984), have also noted that cultural preferences are closely linked to education and social origin. Since the social elite had both leisure time and money, they could afford, and thus control, education and intellectual thought – thus valuing "high" culture above other forms.

Popular culture, therefore, was seen as "the battleground upon which dominant views secure hegemony, the parameters of which are partly defined by economic conditions, but that specialize in political struggle expressed at an ideological, representative level" (Turner 1990:211). Seen in this light, the supposed superior value or merit of "high" culture can no longer be assumed. In fact, cultural theorists may argue that by subsidizing "high" culture, one may simply be protecting the dominant view. This is the point made by Peacock (1992:14) when he suggested that the refusal of economists to discuss possible definitions of the arts damaged both our objectivity and credibility since, by passively accepting a particular definition, we may be unintentionally supporting an ideology: "The economist, so it is argued, might become a useful hired gun for the cultural establishment".

As early as 1980, however, commentators like Cwi were protesting against the unwillingness of economists to discuss "the arts" in a broader form. Frey and Pommerehme (1989:6) concluded that, "The question 'What is art?' has been the subject of aesthetics over centuries, but no consensus has been arrived at". They argued that what matters to the economist is not whether an area is multi-faceted and complex, but whether it is possible to observe behavioral regularities among the people concerned; "Whenever such regularities are apparent, the economic concepts of the demand for and the supply of art are appropriate."

This general consensus by economists that they did not have to define precisely the good in order to value it using the market price, still seems to persist, despite (or because of) the more inclusive definitions of the arts now in use. Arjo Klamer, who currently holds the only chair of cultural economics in the world, is at the forefront of cultural economists who argue that, rather than fitting cultural goods into a neoclassical framework, a new kind of economic valuation is needed in the case of the arts.

1.2 Arguments in Favour of Public Support for the Arts

In environmental economics one can distinguish between anthropocentric and non-anthropocentric value; that is, between value to humans and value not dependent on human judgments or uses. In the case of cultural economics, the "good" in question is the product of society and, as such, always related to human value. What this means is that one always has to ask the question, "value to whom?" when talking about the value of arts and culture. Since taste in cultural goods is largely dependent on socio-economic factors, like family origin and education, the debate about the sort of art worth subsiding is inextricably linked to the "value to whom?" question.

A fascinating paper by Lewis and Brooks (2005) uses data from eight General Social Surveys in the US to explore differences in beliefs and values between the general population, artists, arts donors and arts patrons. They find that artists and, to a lesser extent, donors and patrons, differ markedly from the rest of the population in term of being less likely to be religious, more likely to classify themselves as liberal and more likely to uphold individual liberties "when those liberties conflict with traditional morality" (Lewis and Brooks 2005:12). It is thus unsurprising that when the decision as to what sort of art to fund is left to these groups, conflict with the general population is inevitable, especially when the money comes from the government, funded by the taxes of the general population.

There are two distinct streams of thought as to why the arts should be subsidized by the government. The first is based largely on the non-market benefits or externalities that the arts are purported to provide (demand side arguments) and their unique cost structure, as outlined by Baumol (supply side arguments). Both of these are rooted in the neoclassical economic framework. The second stream of arguments is relatively recent and attempts to redefine the framework in which the arts and culture are evaluated; in particular, by introducing the idea of "cultural capital".

1.2.1 Demand Side Arguments

The arts as a public good with positive externalities

Much of the case for the public support of the arts stems from the argument that the arts, while not a purely public good, do have some public good characteristics, along the same lines as education and health. Public goods are defined by Samuelson as "those goods that a number of people can use simultaneously without diminishing their value (non-rivalry) and once these goods are provided it is infeasible to exclude people from their use (non-exclusion)" (Duncombe 1996:31).

The public, or mixed public and private, good aspect of the arts is important because it has been shown in many studies (Morrison and West 1986, Dobson and West 1990, Hendon 1990, Blaug 2001, Borgonovi 2004, Snowball 2005 amongst others) that arts attenders (particularly at "high" culture events) tend to represent the educated, prosperous minority of society. This is hardly surprising, since (as pointed out earlier) taste formation is shaped by education and social origins. If the arts are a purely private good, then government subsidy would be seen as supporting the pleasures of the wealthy minority of society.

Optimal allocation of goods in a free market economy requires that everything can be bought and sold and that those who do not pay can be excluded from the use of the good (Fullerton, 1991). In this way, producers can at least cover their costs and try to make a profit. If, however, the good is not excludable - anyone can consume it regardless of whether they have paid or not - then the market mechanism will fail because of the "free rider" problem. Arrow (1963:945) referred to this problem in his seminal paper on health insurance as the non-marketability problem which he defined as, "the failure of the existing market to provide a means whereby the services can be both offered and demanded upon payment of a price". If too many consumers try to consume a good for which they have not paid, the market will fail regardless of whether the good is generally demanded or not.

Another aspect which is important for the marketability of a good is its rival or non-rival nature. A rival good is one that is used up as it is consumed, while a non-rival good can be used without diminishing it. This characteristic is also found in the market for technological inventions, which Romer (1990: 97) commented on as follows: "A non-rival input has a high cost of producing the first unit and zero cost of producing subsequent units".

As Throsby (1994: 23) pointed out, "The arts exhibit public good characteristics alongside the private benefits conferred by individual consumption", which indicates that there is a non-market demand for the arts which could be filled by public finance. However, insofar as entrance fees and ticket prices can be charged, the arts can be considered a private good which is, at a primary level at least, excludable (Fullerton 1991).

While it is true that a theatre seat, for example, may be regarded as both rival and excludable in that its consumption - the purchase of the ticket - prevents anyone else from being in it at the same time, the social benefits arising from the culture that the arts generate can be regarded as neither rival nor excludable as argued by Abbing (1980). This distinction is also applied to goods like education which, although a place at university for example is rival and excludable, is regarded as having public good characteristics because of the general social benefits that an educated population provides. If one understands the argument in the narrower sense (theatre seats or places in a museum) it is of course true to note that the good is excludable and only non-rival up to a certain maximum capacity. The extent to which the arts show public good characteristics by providing positive externalities from which no one can be excluded is the basis for the public funding arguments.

Externalities refer to the tangible or intangible spillover effects from a particular activity. These unintended costs or benefits affect those who are not direct consumers of the product and cannot, therefore, be efficiently marketed. Such benefits (or costs) are *external* to the market (Swindell and Rosentraub 1998).

Throsby and Withers (1985:1) commented on the fact that art subsidies seem to attract extreme views: "At one extreme are the critics of the arts who assert that theatre, opera, ballet and so on are minority interests, enjoyed only by the rich and well-educated; they argue that it is wrong for public money to be spent in subsidizing such luxury tastes. At the other end of the spectrum are those ... who take the importance of arts to society as a self-evident truth, as if this justifies spending almost unlimited funds...". At the centre of both of these positions is the argument about the degree of excludability of the arts. If the arts are a mainly private good consumed largely by paying customers at market prices, market failure does not warrant public support unless there are large positive spillovers which can be consumed publicly and are, therefore, not excludable.

Early commentators, like Peacock (1969: 330) admitted that, "the author finds it difficult to trace the way in which spillovers from the 'culture vultures' attending live performances to others is supposed to take place." He expressed considerable skepticism about the benefits to the public at large of the upper income members of society attending, for example, subsidized orchestra performances.

Abbing (1980:39) was of a completely different opinion. He argued that the arts are far more of a public good than we realize and that excludability is minimal. In other words, the arts are largely a public good that, if they have positive externalities, should be publicly subsidized. His eloquent argument is worth quoting at some length:

> "At this very moment, I am sitting in the room of a third-rate hotel. The tablecloth is made up of alternating squares, naturalistic and abstract. The former are borrowed from the Japanese art of flower painting; the latter remind one of Braque, however vaguely. The design of the plastic curtain in front of the washbasin is an exact copy of a painting by Vasarely. In front of me are two notepads. The cover of one has a pattern borrowed from Mondrian, but filled in with the present day fashionable colours of green and pink .... The background music is from a synthesizer, and it has an undertone reminding one of the recent German musical formation, *Kraftwerk*. I could go on and on..."

Abbing (1980) argued that art cannot be treated as any other mixed good because it shapes the very way in which society makes sense of and understands events. Even those who have never seen or heard the original work may be affected by it on some level - either through the adaptation of the idea by other artists or through the vaguer channel of the development of social convention. "Matters of consciousness - and that is what it is all about - can be re-expressed and transmitted in every possible way" (Abbing 1980:39). Such broad arguments show the way to the development of ideas like that of cultural capital, which is further discussed below.

The arts as a merit good

Merit goods are defined by Cwi (1980:39) as "goods which some persons believe ought to be available and whose consumption and allocation are felt by them to be too important to be left to the private market" – a definition that will inevitably involve some value judgment being imposed on society. Musgrave (1959:13) defined "merit wants" as public goods which are subject to the exclusion principle and are somewhat satisfied by the market within the limits of effective demand, but which "become public wants if considered so meritorious that their satisfaction is provided for through the public budget over and above what is provided through the market".

Ver Eecke (1998) argues that merit goods are distinct from public goods precisely because they do not take into account the will of the consumer and because their finance is separate from their use (so payment for the good is not related to one's use of it). While merit goods do not thus satisfy consumer needs directly, they lead to or are necessary to achieve the goals of rational citizens. Merit good arguments should thus only be accepted if one can see that they lead to, or are needed for, the fulfilment of some commonly accepted goal. Ver Eecke gives the examples of national defence (needed to achieve security, not charged according to use and requiring some value judgement) and education (needed to achieve rational, informed people to enhance the operation of the free market). Having established that merit goods are a separate class from public goods, he goes on to argue that some goods have both characteristics:

> "Thus in my view it is wrong to ask whether a particular good is a private, public or merit good. The proper question to ask is which aspects of a particular good exhibit characteristics typical for the concept of private good, for the concept of public good and for the concept of merit good" (Ver Eecke 1998:149).

Arguments for public funding should thus, according to Ver Eecke (1998), address all the aspects of the good, not simply class it as one particular thing. Arguments in favour of arts funding could thus be presented in private good terms (economic impact studies), public good terms (contingent valuation studies) and merit good terms (qualitative historical studies including value judgements).

Both Musgrave (1959) and Throsby (1994) recognise that the arguments supporting merit goods are largely normative and involve some value judgement and are thus an interference with consumer preferences. Some of the arguments put forward for regarding the arts as a merit good are: the arts enhance national identity and pride and international prestige, they provide ongoing education for children and adults, they offer a critique of social policy, they foster personal development and they integrate individuals into society (Cwi1980).

Hutter and Shusterman (2006) suggest ten types of non-economic artistic value. These include: art's moral or religious vision; art as a medium though which "the self can be expressed"; art's promotion of "easy, rapid, powerful and widespread communication", which is linked to its social and political value in embodying the ideals (or reactions against accepted ideals) of society. Art can also have experiential value, sometimes related to pleasurable entertainment value, but also to shocking or unpleasant experiences which can, nevertheless, have value. Other values are aesthetic, technical, historical and cult values. What makes such non-economic values problematic is that they are largely intangible and may differ markedly between people or groups of people and are thus difficult to measure.

As Klamer (2004a) points out, neoclassical economists are loath to delve into issues of "value", preferring to defer to the market (or contingent market) as capturing economic value and representing individual preferences. As such, Peacock (1969:323) argued that any attempt at justifying public support of the arts "on the grounds that the community does not know what is good for it" smacks of "cultural paternalism" and represents what someone thinks the community ought to have, rather than what they want. The market allows consumers to vote with their spending, avoiding any sort of big brother approach. Peacock (1992) reiterated this by appealing to the doctrine of consumer sovereignty, in which public funding allows consumers greater access to culture, without choosing the "correct" form of culture for them. This is done by channeling subsidies largely through consumers rather than through suppliers of art, and so preserving the consumer's right to choose; otherwise, once the market is deemed inefficient, some dominant voice or perspective inevitably appears.

Throsby (1994), however, felt there may be a case for subsidy of the arts as a merit good on several grounds. Firstly, consumers may lack the necessary information needed to make informed market choices. In the sense that tastes determine the demand for arts and that, as Peacock (1992) pointed out, the demand for "high" culture is largely dependent on the education which allows one to access it, this point is valid. As early as 1959, commentators like Musgrave (1959:14) agreed, stating, "While consumer sovereignty is the general rule, situations may arise, within the context of a democratic community, where an informed group is justified in imposing its decision upon others".

Throsby (1994) also argued that the notion of consumer sovereignty needed to be expanded to take into account cases where consumers behave inconsistently with their underlying values because of such things as "misperception, weakness of will or the fluctuation of preferences over time". Seen in this light, the guiding hand of the government in selecting cultural products for subsidy in order to prevent them from dying out, could be seen as expanding, rather than limiting, consumer choices in the long run.

Throsby's (1994) view ties in well with the argument that the arts should be protected by subsidy for the benefit of future generations, particularly if it is channeled into child participation in the arts. As Cwi (1980:42) put it:

> "Those concerned about future generations believe that we have a responsibility to assure continuity and access in future years to the produce of current artistic endeavor. It is felt that without subsidy some of that activity will either disappear or be available in only limited quantity, quality and variety."

As he pointed out, however, this assumes that future generations will share our ideas of what is culturally valuable and that once a particular art form is gone, it is irretrievable. A paper by Brooks (2004b) tries to test this theory using an intergenerational model of the perceived benefits of government and private arts sponsorship in the US, taking life expectancy into account. He finds that his model does not enable him to reject the null hypothesis that people are "intergenerationally egotistic" and thus do not take into account future generations when voting for arts subsidies or making private donations. Peacock (1969:331) also pointed out that, considering levels of economic growth, an increase in public investment that redistributes income to future generations from the present one may represent a transfer of wealth from a poorer generation to a richer one.

Throsby's (1994) third argument is that a social welfare function which admits only individual utilities may be too limited in the case of a "socially meritorious" good, such as the arts, and that public financing of social goods which are "irreducible", that is, goods whose utility cannot be ascribed to any one person, should not be constrained by a limited theory. This idea has since been expanded both by Throsby himself (2003) and Klamer (2004b) – that is, that a new theoretical framework is needed for cultural goods whose value is socially constructed.

As Fullerton (1991:68) comments, the fact that the arts may be regarded as a merit good is not enough to justify public funding; "Subsidies are not justified for thousands of profit-making movie theaters ... just because they provide a product which is good". The argument was supported by Rosen (1995) who, in quoting Baumol and Baumol (1981) agreed that "the merit good approach is not really a justification for support - it merely invents a bit of terminology to designate the desire to do so".

The discussion of the arts as a merit good leads very clearly into the notion of cultural capital presented below, but took a long time to be expressed in this form because of the reluctance of economists to discuss "value" as being represented by anything other than market price. However, in order to defend public subsidies for the arts, the merit good argument clearly indicates that one would have to prove that they represented some valuable good that could not be gained through any other means. Also, it is not enough to prove that the arts are a merit good, one must also show why the market is not efficient in providing them, that is, one needs to postulate market failure.

1.2.2 Supply Side Arguments: Baumol's Cost Disease

Baumol's cost disease theory (1965) simply states that, generally, the production costs of the arts will tend to rise more rapidly than those in other industries. While technological advances may significantly and continuously bring down production costs in other sectors of the economy, Baumol and Bowen's (1965) landmark article, followed by their book, published more than four decades ago, argued that productivity in some sectors is stable - the arts being one of them. A much quoted example is that of the performance of a particular piece of music which takes the same amount of time and number of people as it did a hundred years ago, while the time and labour required to produce, for example, a car or a watch, has decreased significantly in the last century (Brooks 1997).

The cost disease has resulted in both the apparent soaring of ticket prices for the performing arts and the relative decline of the wages of artists. Baumol (1995:2) argued that this is true of all the "handicraft" services, such as visits to the doctor and police services, which are labour rather than capital intensive: "As wages go up, there is no productivity offset to rising costs. So the costs and the prices of these things go up far, far faster than the average good or service in any industrialized country". Baumol

(1995) has estimated that the rise in the costs of the arts in the United Kingdom is about two percent higher per year that the rate of inflation.

Baumol (1987) himself pointed out, however, that the fact that the arts have cost problems does not automatically qualify them for public support. However, if taxpayers decide that the arts are worth supporting, as a merit good, because of positive spillovers, for future generations etc., then the cost disease can be used as a strong supporting argument. In a published interview (1995) Baumol reasserted his original point that, without sufficient public support, the arts will decline in both quantity and quality.

Other writers, however, (like Fullerton 1991; Cwi 1980; Peacock 1969, Abbing 2004) have expressed some doubt about the cost disease hypothesis, pointing out that, despite Baumol's logical and neat theory, there has not been a significant decline in the quantity and quality of the arts provided: "While the basic logic of the cost disease is, in its own terms, unarguable, the causal chain linking certain characteristics of production of the live arts to the widening income gap for performing companies is by no means as inexorable as many have supposed" (Throsby 1994:15). Several reasons for this have been put forward.

The first and perhaps most compelling argument against the cost disease theory has to do with the new reproductive technologies. As far back as 1969, Peacock pointed out that access to the arts was greatly expanded by the development of the "new media" of his time such as radio, television and gramophone. This access has vastly increased with the "new media" of today: satellite television, the Internet, Web-casting, video recording, compact discs and MP3 players. Even if one argues that there is no real substitute for live performance, there is no doubt that access to arts products can be greatly increased through new technology. Fullerton (1991) argued that this applies to visual as well as performance arts: "Just as we gain from new technologies that allow sharper musical reproductions ... we can gain from high quality reproductions of art, inexpensive prints, or the safe travel of exhibitions".

According to Abbing (2004) the cost disease has three known causes: 1) technical advances in the arts are less than in other industries 2) artistic production is labour (rather than capital) intensive and 3) wages of those in the arts industry rise at similar rates to those in other industries. Abbing (2005) points out that where research did not show signs of the disease, this was because either technical advances in the arts were faster than expected or the wages of those in the arts industry did not increase by as much as those in other industries. However, he also lays bare some underlying assumptions of the cost disease theory: that preferences are given, that quality is constant and that costs are inevitable. "Even if some of these assumptions and propositions are disproved by the facts, the cost disease theory can still be a consistent theory, but the conclusion that there is a cost disease no longer necessarily follows" (Abbing 2004:8).

For example, Abbing (2004) suggests that the rising costs of artistic production in mainland European countries might be as a result of the cost disease, but might equally be because of increases in quality (which would naturally entail rising costs) or increases in inefficiency which were partly offset by rising subsidies. In general, he argues, the cost disease theory does not take into account fairly large increases in non-market income (donations and subsidies) and issues relating to changing tastes and the price and elasticity of demand as arts consumers change and (at least in developed countries) become wealthier.

Cowen and Grier's (1996) argument is that the arts are not especially labour intensive when compared to other sectors of the economy, and that arts production can involve significant amounts of capital. They also suggested that the arts and industry are far more closely linked than Baumol's theory suggests; for example, the innovations of the 19th century French Impressionists relied heavily on the invention of the tin paint tube which allowed work outside in sunlight, as did their use of new, brighter colours, based on synthetic materials. If one adds to this the costs of the training and traveling of any artist, the production of art may turn out to have a similar capital-labour ratio to other industries.

The new technologies also affect the argument that, as relative wages for artists decline (which they must do in the face of rising costs), would-be artists are more likely to choose other, better paid careers, thus possibly depleting the quality and quantity of the arts (Baumol and Bowen 1965). Cowen and Grier (1996:4) argued that this view is far too simplistic. Firstly, as economic growth increases wages generally, more people will be able to work in those areas, like the arts, in which monetary benefits can be exchanged for personal enjoyment. Secondly, increasing wealth is able to support a growing number of "profitable artistic niches", further increasing non-pecuniary returns, as artists are able to specialize in areas that they find particularly interesting.

Throsby (1994) and Tiongson (1997) mentioned the possibilities of merchandising activities as a substantial way to increase the income of arts organizations, giving as an example the "tremendous income from Broadway shirts, posters and other souvenirs". Tiongson (1997:120) also argued fiercely that Baumol's theory greatly underestimates the importance of the link between the performing arts and the manufacturing technologies and argues that much of the non-rival consumption qualities of the arts depends on the state of technology: "The capacity of technology to extend the consumption of a single performance millions of times needs to be reassessed". Tiongson (1997) cited the ongoing work of Brooks(1997:2), suggesting that, while non-live arts performances are probably always inferior to live ones, broadcastings and recordings of, for example, an orchestral performance may promote the orchestra and make attending its performances more prestigious.

Tiongson (1997) also argued that Baumol's comparison of the performing arts with the manufacturing sector is misleading and inappropriate because of the non-rival nature of the arts. Manufactured goods, like a car, may take an increasingly smaller amount of time and labour to produce, but only a few people can benefit from its use. An arts performance may benefit many more people - either directly, through broadcasts (the magnitude of which depends heavily on the state of technology) or through tangible and intangible spillovers.

Cowen and Grier (1996) conclude that the statistical evidence for the cost disease is doubtful. Like Tiongson (1997:2) they pointed out that it is not accurate to measure a performance as a private good (in the sense that the purchase of a ticket entitles one person's entry), "when in fact performance has become an (excludable) public good through electronic reproduction". They suggested that cost disease studies tended to focus on the segment of the performing arts that is already in decline, like opera, theatre and classical symphonic concerts, while choosing not to study those areas that have grown, like movies and jazz. This argument again focuses attention on the importance of one's definition of "the arts". Baumol's study tends to focus on "high" culture art forms, while Cowen and Grier (1996) suggested that the definition should include popular art forms.

As a result of these and other mitigating factors, Throsby (2001:119) reports that little evidence has been found for the cost disease.

> "These studies have shown that the combined impacts of production adjustments, increased demand and generally rising levels of unearned revenue have countered any tendency towards a secular rise in deficits among arts companies, suggesting that although the cost disease will

> doubtless continue to present such companies with difficult problems, it is unlikely to be terminal."

Given the lack of evidence for and the arguments against the cost disease theory, Abbing (2004) asks why it has remained such a prominent feature of cultural economics. Blaug (2001:124) points out that cultural economics has lacked "a single dominant paradigm or overarching intellectual theme that binds all its elements together" and that this is the reason that Baumol's theoretical work on the cost disease has attracted so much attention. Abbing adds a more contentious idea – that cultural economists tend to be interested in and biased towards the arts and thus naturally seized on a theory that could be used to argue for increased public support for these industries. However, the theory has become less and less credible as technological progress has advanced and arts institutions and activities have, if anything, increased. Perhaps the new theories of cultural capital and value creation will provide a better and more inclusive theoretical framework for the subject.

1.2.3 New Theories of Cultural Capital

Throsby (1999, 2001) first introduced the idea of cultural capital in economics. "Cultural capital, in an economic sense, can provide a means of representing culture which enables both tangible and intangible manifestation of culture to be articulated as long-lasting stores of value and providers of benefits for individuals and groups" (Throsby 2001:44). Like Klamer (2003b), he separates economic from cultural capital, but emphasizes that cultural capital can give rise to both economic value ("ordinary" capital) and cultural value. This distinction is an important one when it comes to valuing cultural goods: "there would be expected to be zero substitutability between cultural and physical capital in respect of its cultural output" (Throsby 2001:52).

The recognition of cultural capital as an economic value can thus produce a whole new set of reasons for the public funding of culture. Throsby (2001) draws a parallel between the preservation of biodiversity (natural capital) and cultural diversity (cultural capital), which generates the kinds of moral arguments that have been used in the case of the preservation of natural capital for years. For example, if the present stock of cultural capital is allowed to decline through lack of investment, one could argue that future generations will be deprived of its benefits, since their interests are not reflected in the current market. Throsby (2001) agrees with Klamer (2002) that the current economic preoccupation with efficiency may be undermining the notion of fairness, that is, "the rights of the present generation to fairness in access to cultural resources and to the benefits flowing from cultural capital, viewed across social classes, income groups, locational categories and so on" (Throsby 2001:56).

Like the arguments for maintaining biodiversity, arguments for maintaining the diversity of cultural capital can also be made, since new capital formation can be shown in both cases to depend crucially on the existing capital stock. Even more compelling is the argument that, as in the natural world, no system is isolated, but all are interconnected and the long term sustainability of our existence depends on the maintenance of all these systems, including natural ecosystems and cultural capital (Throsby 2001). Unlike Klamer, who argues for a complete break away from measuring the outcomes of culture in traditional economic terms, Throsby (2001:58) still sees the link as important:

> "It is becoming clearer that cultural 'ecosystems' underpin the operation of the real economy, affecting the way people behave and the choices they make. Neglect of cultural capital by allowing heritage to deteriorate, by failing to sustain the cultural values that provide people with a sense of identity and by not undertaking the investment needed to maintain and increase the stock of both tangible and intangible cultural capital, will likewise place cultural systems in jeopardy and may cause them to break down, with consequent loss of welfare and economic output".

Klamer (2002) argues that, in addition to economic and social capital, cultural capital should also be counted as part of an individual's wealth. He defines economic capital as "the capacity to generate economic values", usually quite adequately expressed in the market and captured by economic accounting methods. To the extent that human and natural capital allow the generation of economic capital, they are included in this category. The second type of capital is social capital, which is "the capacity to generate social values", like friendship and trust. This is capital in the sense that it needs resources to build it up and maintain it and, while it can also generate economic values, it has some intrinsic value of its own that is not well captured in the market. Finally, cultural capital is defined as "the capacity to inspire and be inspired … to find meaning" (Klamer 2002:465-7).

Streeton (2006) agrees that there has been a shift in development economics from either ignoring culture completely or seeing it as a hindrance to economic growth, to a much more people-centered approach. "The alternative view sees growth as the means to our freedom to live the way we value. And what we value and cherish is a matter of culture. Looked this way, culture is the desirable end: it is what gives meaning to our existence" (Streeton 2006:402)

For McCain (2006) the distinguishing feature of artistic goods is just such a two-way communication between the artist and the meaning-making consumer. For works of art, then, it is not only the artist whose creativity is engaged. "Being a spectator or consumer (interpreter) of art calls on the skills and mental processes characteristic of the artist herself … the creation and consumption of art links the artist and the consumer in a unity of interrelated creative action" (McCain 2006:161). Building on Nozick, he suggests art objects can have three sorts of value: intrinsic value, cultural value (as symbols of a particular cultural group) and economic value (represented by someone being willing to pay for them).

While Klamer (2002) acknowledges the difficulty of measuring social and cultural capital, he argues strongly that this does not mean that they are irrelevant. Rather, they are the very qualities that give meaning and purpose to life and that "wealth" should be measured in terms of all three sorts of capital, not just in the easily measurable economic sense. In fact, Klamer argues that economic capital has no intrinsic value at all, but is valued rather for what it allows individuals to achieve. He (2002:471) does not suggest that markets are useless in measuring economic value, but that we should acknowledge the value of intangible "goods" as well: "When we consider social and cultural values in addition to economic values, the disagreement on an institution like the market becomes a difference of opinion on the weighting of different spheres of value".

However, while their theory of cultural capital provides an important additional (and perhaps the most compelling) reason for public funding of the arts, it is hampered in practice by the difficulty of measurement. Blaug (2001:132) in his review of the development of cultural economics, comments that there is almost "universal consensus" on the question of whether the arts should be publicly funded, "but, of course, the real issue is not whether to subsidize, but how much and in what form…" In order to answer these questions, some sort of valuation of the arts is necessary, be it in the market, the contingent market or some other, more qualitative form.

1.3 Valuing Cultural Goods and the Scope of Economics

As discussed in the previous section, economists have long acknowledged that the arts do not operate well in the market because of their public good characteristics, because they are a merit good and because of their cost structures (Baumol's cost disease). The argument would then be that, in order to argue effectively for government intervention in the arts market, these externalities would need to be proved and measured using a contingent valuation method. However, commentators like Klamer argue that, even when the arts are a private good, their market value is not a good indication of their real value and that this is also the case for contingent market valuations. Thus, rather than refining current market based valuation techniques, an entirely new set of methods and indicators is needed in the case of cultural goods, which, both Klamer and Throsby argue, is closer to the original intention of what the study of economics should include.

Klamer (2003a:3) argues that, "the dominant economic paradigm seriously hampers discussion of values among economists" because it is too focused on the idea of utility and rational choice theory. Goodwin (2006), who traces the historical development of the economics of arts and culture, agrees that a "void" was created by Bentham's emphasis on private utility, which steered economic thinking away from cultural economics for many years. All economists accept the fact that an individual's utility is unknowable – that is, that the satisfaction one gains from a good is highly individual and will be shaped by preferences. However, rational choice theory says that, although one cannot know the reasons for another person's choices, the observation of the choices themselves provides enough information. Since it is assumed that, on average, consumers make choices so as to maximize their utility (whatever it may be), given their budget constraints, one can infer the value they place on various goods by observing their consumption of them. A crucial point is that the idea of "utility" is not affected by this observation – the observer does not presume to draw conclusions about the consumer's motives, morals or reasons for consuming one good instead of another, but, assuming rationality, one can say that the consumed good provides greater utility than the alternative choice of the good not consumed. In other words, consumption and production, which determine market price, are an effective way of valuing a good without having to observe or discuss the reasons behind the choices.

Both Klamer (2002, 2004a) and Throsby (2001) find that rational choice theory is too restrictive a way of "valuing" goods – even private goods that operate well in the market – and that the original scope of economics did not dictate such a narrow field. For example, Keynes referred to economics as a "moral science" and further back, Marshall's definition of economics was "the study of mankind in the ordinary business of life" (Klamer 2002:458-9), neither of which dictates that "value" will be determined only in the market. Throsby (2001:20-23) agrees that early theories of the cost of production and individual utilities, combining to lead to the neat equilibrium market price, led to the belief amongst many economists that, "a theory of price is a theory of value".

McCain (2006:150) however, suggests that the idea that the neoclassical paradigm rejects non-economic values is a misconception: "economics has to do not with any particular realm of values, but with the balancing of different values and different realms of value". The difficulty then becomes defining what cultural non-economic values are.

Does market value, for goods sold in the market, constitute a good measure of value? Proponents of rational choice theory have recognized problems in this area, but have gone about solving them using contingent valuation methods – that is, by constructing a hypothetical market to arrive at a price.

In the case of consumer surplus, that is, the idea that the consumer may be willing to pay significantly more than the market price for a good, price can capture a minimum monetary value that consumers place on the good, but not (even if one accepts that price is value) the total value. For goods not traded in the market, a market structure can still be evoked by creating a market scenario and asking individuals what they would be willing to pay or willing to accept to change or achieve the scenario. Putting aside all the problems related to hypothetical markets for now, would honest, unbiased answers to such willingness to pay questions generate true values? For willingness to pay (WTP) figures, the problem is that an (honest) answer would be constrained by budget, which may not represent a true value at all. For willingness to accept (WTA) figures, not constrained by budget, a true value may still be elusive, since some things are literally "priceless", like health or religion or, it could be argued, culture (Epstein 2003).

For example, suppose one wanted to know the "value" of a child to his or her parents. One could work out the financial cost of the child to the parents, but most parents would probably argue that this was a vast underestimate of the value of the child, since it included a number of non-market externalities that were being ignored. One could then ask what the family would be willing to pay to prevent their child from being taken away from them. An answer might include their whole income and still not be a true value. If one were to ask what they would be WTA as compensation for losing the child, answers are no longer constrained by budget, but they may still not be able to express, in a meaningful monetary amount, how much they value their child.

Of course, the idea is far from new. In his landmark article "Rational Fools" Sen (1977) questioned the assumption of economic agents as rational utility maximisers that underpins welfare economics:

> "The complex psychological issues underlying choice have recently been forcefully brought out by a number of penetrating studies dealing with consumer decisions and production activities. It is very much an open question as to whether these behavioral characteristics can be at all captured within the formal limits of consistent choice on which the welfare-maximization approach depends" (Sen 1977:324).

Sen continues to make arguments against using utility as the measure of value, also arguing that freedom and the available choice sets matter (1985). However, he acknowledges that utility theory does have its uses, but that the problem lies in its being regarded as the *only* theory of value.

Many of the problems associated with the valuation of cultural goods specifically are that the arts, and the cultures they stem from, are very much the product of society rather than the individual around whom marginal utility theory revolves. Both Klamer (2003a) and Throsby (2003) refer to the complex ways in which society values cultural goods, not as individuals, but collectively. Klamer (2004b) puts forward the idea that the arts are a "common" good – that is, not public, because non-members can be excluded from the group in a number of ways, but not private either, in the sense that individual ownership makes no sense where values are socially constructed. The social construction of value or "valorization" (Klamer 2003a) of cultural goods is the crux of the matter.

Klamer gives a number of examples of cases where the evaluation of cultural goods changes their value:

> "If foreigners point out to indigenous people that their piles of old stones are actually cultural treasures and that they are willing to pay to conserve them, the indigenous people change their perception of those stones and may even begin to value them. Get a cultural good listed on the UNESCO world heritage list, and people will value that good more." (Klamer 2003a:11).

Socially constructed values can also change over time. For example, during colonial times, European traders "paid" for African goods in beads, which were valued by Africans because they were foreign and couldn't be produced locally. Since then, however, African beadwork has become an integral part of the culture, beads being used in traditional dress as decoration, but also to indicate such things as rank and tribal affiliations. Klamer (2004a) comments that traditional African beadwork has now become valued by Europeans as "exotic" due to its long presence in Africa.

Klamer (2004a:11) points out that subjecting cultural goods to market valuation may damage them or devalue them. "The rigor of being placed in the sphere of commerce, measured, compared, discussed, priced and treated like any other commodity may very well affect its [the cultural good's] subsequent evaluation". That is, simply by making the market valuation, the value of the good is changed. It may enhance the value of the good, or it may damage it. The example of friendship illustrates this point well: by asking someone what he or she would be willing to pay for your friendship, one may have already lost it.

Interestingly, communitarian theory, developed as a way of explaining the value of leisure activities in sociology, seems to be approaching the same conclusion, but, as it were, from a different starting point; "For communitarians, community is the context of social relationships; it is not simply the utilitarian context for meeting private ends" (Arai and Pedlar 2003: 187). Communitarians value participatory leisure activities, or "focal practices" like the arts, very highly because of the social networks and "shared meanings" they create, not because of the individual utility they provide. "Leisure practice here is described as communal leisure, as a community of people sharing and celebrating a focal practice…which is both created and preserved as a common or public good" (Arai and Pedlar 2003:190).

But far from suggesting that such communal leisure produces unity of voice or widespread consensus, communitarians believe that it is precisely the argument about shared values and goals which such participatory leisure enables, which is so important in developing the "social self" needed for a healthy society. "The crucial point here is that to be truly free, an individual must first care about the society in which he or she exists, for it is within that culture or society that the person is able to acquire and to maintain an identity" (Arai and Pedlar 2003:195).

Having established the problems with market price as a measure of value, the next logical question is how else one might go about measuring such values. Here the theoretical advances have reached a temporary halt. Throsby (2003:279-80) points out that, while economic value, including imputed non-market value, is measurable and expressible in quantitative terms, "Cultural value… is multi-dimensional, unstable, contested, lacks a common unit of account, and may contain elements that cannot be easily expressed according to any quantitative or qualitative scale". Klamer (2002, 2003, 2004) acknowledges the difficulty of measurement, but argues that this is not a sufficient reason to exclude cultural value from economic study. He points out that, "when *De Economist* began its appearance, there was no notion of income and a magnitude like economic growth was not much more than a concept, without numerical content" (Klamer 2002:453).

In fact, there appears to be a significant literature developing on the subject of "cultural indicators", particularly amongst arts policy makers and proponents. Madden (2004), in a study conducted for the International Federation of Arts Councils and Culture Agencies, reports that there are almost 200 articles in English on the subject, exploring many aspects of the value of the arts to society. However, he also finds that the field is "still largely under development" and that the wealth of theory has not been turned into practical arts funding policy.

In discussing possibilities, both in the identification and measurement of cultural indicators, Throsby (2001) does suggest, however, that studying individual responses, if enough consensus arises, might arrive at common indicators of cultural value. A paper by Scott, presented at an international *Fuel4arts* Internet conference (2004), discusses the use of the Delphi technique in arriving at consensus between the public and experts on the social impact of museums. The technique works by asking individuals, chosen because of their knowledge and experience, questions via the Internet. Responses are then circulated to all participants, commented on and used in a second round of "discussion" to "build towards a consensus" (Scott 2004:6). The results of the study on what the purpose of museums is and should be, showed that it is possible to reach agreement on general cultural indicators, even between quite disparate groups.

On another track, Throsby (2001, 2003) suggests that cultural value and economic value have a positive relationship so that, although economic value is recognized as insufficient to capture cultural value, the two could be highly correlated, since both values are "formed by a negotiated process akin to a simple market exchange" (2003:281). For Klamer (2002) this is a sell-out – a retreat into the neoclassical framework he is trying so hard to break out of - but until the theories of cultural capital or value can be made operational, even economists who agree with him are likely to continue using market and non-market valuation techniques because of another definition of economics, namely, that it is the study of the allocation of scarce resources to satisfy unlimited wants. At some stage, a decision on spending on non-market goods has to be made and valuation of these goods, however imperfect, provides one way of making allocative decisions, perhaps a more democratic way than leaving it entirely to politicians and experts.

Although quantitative measurement of cultural value seems unlikely, qualitative valuations may be more fruitful. Throsby (2001:29-30) discusses several ways of doing this, including mapping, attitudinal analysis, content analysis, expert appraisal and thick analysis. The latter is described as "a means of interpretive description of a cultural object, environment or process which rationalizes otherwise inexplicable phenomena by exposing the underlying cultural systems etc. at work and deepens the understanding of the context and meaning of observed behaviour".

An attempt at such a long-term qualitative valuation of a cultural good, the South African National Arts Festival, has been made (Snowball and Webb 2007). The existence of this arts festival from 1974 to the present covers a turbulent period in South Africa's political and economic history and, as such, one is bound to ask whether, or to what extent, it reflected, assisted, or hindered, the process. If culture is at the heart of hegemonic control, it is reasonable to assume that the festival would have had some role to play in the struggle for freedom and equality and such a postulated role would certainly constitute an important value, although it is unlikely to emerge from standard economic valuation techniques and is probably not quantifiable.

1.4 Conclusions

The purpose of this chapter was to introduce the debates around definitions of "value" and "the arts" from a theoretical perspective. Much of the work is still under construction and changing quickly, but provides an exciting agenda for future research.

The remaining chapters deal with valuation methods founded on the very notions of utility and rational choice that much of this chapter has criticized. It will be argued that, understood as partial values, they can still be very useful valuation techniques for the arts and, in some cases, powerful tools in motivating for public funding. Nevertheless, it is important to keep in mind the underlying debates presented in this chapter, particularly when choosing and justifying a particular valuation method.

References

Abbing, H. (1980) On the rationale of public support to the arts. Towse, R. (ed) 1997 Cultural economics: the arts, the heritage and the media industries Vol. 2 Edward Elgar: Cheltenham.

Abbing, H. (2004) Let's forget about the cost disease. Paper presented at the Association of Cultural Economics International, 13th conference, Chicago: 2 – 5 June

Arai, S. and Pedlar, A. (2003) Moving beyond individualism in leisure theory: A critical analysis of concepts of community and social engagement. Leisure Studies 22: 185-202.

Arrow, K. (1963) Uncertainty and the welfare economics of medical care. American Economic Review 53,5:941-973.

Baumol, W. and Bowen, W. (1965) On the performing arts: the anatomy of their economic problems. American Economic Review 55,2:495-509.

Baumol, W. (1987) Excerpt from The New Palgrave: A Dictionary of Economics, Towse, R. (ed) 1997 Cultural economics: the arts, the heritage and the media industries Vol. 2 Edward Elgar: Cheltenham.

Baumol, W. (1995) The case for subsidizing the arts: interview with economics professor William Baumol. [On line] Available: http://web1.infortrac.london.galegroup [Accessed 14/12/99]

Blaug, M. (2001) Where are we now on cultural economics?. Journal of Economic Surveys 15,2123-143.

Borgonovi, F. (2004) Performing arts attendance: and economic approach. Applied Economics 36,17:1871-1885.

Bourdieu, P. (1984) Distinction: A social critique of the judgment of taste. Harvard University Press: Cambridge, Massachusetts.

Brooks, A. (1997) Towards a demand-side cure for cost disease in the performing arts. Journal of Economic Issues 31,1:197-208

Brooks, A. (2001) Who opposes government arts funding? Public Choice 108:355-367.

Brooks, A. (2004a) In search of true public arts support. Public Budgeting and Finance 24,2:88-100.

Brooks, A. (2004b) Do people really care about the arts for future generations? Journal of Cultural Economics 28:275-284

Cowen, T. and Grier, R. (1996) Do artists suffer from a cost disease? Rationality and Society 8.1

Cwi, D. (1980) Public support of the arts: three arguments examined. Journal of Cultural Economics 4,2:39-62.

Dobson, L. and West, E. (1990) Performing arts subsidies and future generations. Journal of Behavioral Economics 19,1:23-34.

Duncombe, W. (1996) Public expenditure research: what have we learned? Public Budgeting and Finance 16,2 :26-59.

Epstein, R. (2003) The regrettable necessity of contingent valuation. Journal of Cultural Economics 27:259-274.

Frey, B. and Pommerehme, W. (1989) Art, the economic perspective. Towse, R. (ed) 1997 Cultural Economics: the arts, the heritage and the media industries. Vol. 1 Edward Elgar: Cheltenham.
Fullerton, D. (1991) On justification for public support of the arts. Journal of Cultural Economics 15,2:67-82.
Goodwin, C. (2006) Art and culture in the history of economic thought. Handbook of the Economics of Art and Culture. Ginsburgh, V. and Throsby, D. (Eds.) North Holland, Amsterdam.
Hendon, W (1990) The general public's participation in art museums. American Journal of Economics and Sociology 49, 4
Hutter, M. and Shusterman, R. (2006) Value and the valuation of art in economic and aesthetic theory. Handbook of the Economics of Art and Culture. Ginsburgh, V. and Throsby, D. (Eds.) North Holland, Amsterdam.
Klamer, A. (2002) Accounting for social and cultural values. De Economist 150,4:453-473.
Klamer, A. (2003a) A pragmatic view on values in economics. Journal of Economic Methodology 10,2:1-24.
Klamer, A. (2003b) Handbook of Cultural Economics. Towse, R. (ed) Edward Elgar.
Klamer, A. (2004a) Cultural goods are good for more than their economic value. [On line] Available: www.klamer.nl/art/htm [Accessed 13/9/04].
Klamer, A. (2004b) Art as a common good. Paper presented at the Association of Cultural Economics International, 13th conference: 2 – 5 June 2004
Lewis, G. and Brooks, A. (2005) A question of morality: Artists' values and public funding for the arts. Public Administration Review 65,1:8-17
Madden C. (2004) Statistical indicators for arts policy. Report for the International Federation of Arts Councils and Culture Agencies. [On line] Available www.ifacca.org/ifacca2/en/organsation/page09_BrowseDart.asp [Accessed 20/09/04]
McCain, R. (2006) Defining cultural and artistic goods. Handbook of the Economics of Art and Culture. Ginsburgh, V. and Throsby, D. (Eds.) North Holland, Amsterdam.
Morrison, W. and West, E. (1986) Subsidies for the performing arts: Evidence of voter preference. Journal of Behavioral Economics 15, Fall:57-72.
Musgrave, R. (1959) The Theory of Public Finance. McGraw-Hill: New York.
Peacock, A. (1969) Welfare economics and public subsidies to the arts. Journal of Cultural Economics 18,2:323-335.
Peacock, A. (1992) Economies, cultural values and cultural policies. Towse, R. (ed) 1997 Cultural economics: the arts, the heritage and the media industries. Vol. 2 Edward Elgar: Cheltenham
Romer, P. (1990) Are nonconvexities important for understanding growth? American Economic Review 80,2:97-103.
Rosen, H. (1995) Public Finance. Irwin: Chicago.
Scott, C. (2004) Museums and impact. Presented at the Fuel4arts Internet conference on Measuring the Impact of the Arts 17 September – 1 October.

Sen, A. (1977) Rational Fools: A critique of the behavioral foundation of economic theory. Philosophy and Public Affairs 6,4:317-344.

Sen, A. (1985) Well-Being, agency and freedom: The Dewey lectures 1984. The Journal of Philosophy 82,4:169-221.

Snowball, J. (2005) Art for the masses? Justification for the public support of the arts in developing countries – two arts festivals in South Africa. Journal of Cultural Economics 29:107-125.

Snowball, J. and Webb, A. (2007) Breaking into the conversation: Cultural value and the role of the South African National Arts Festival from apartheid to democracy. International Journal of Cultural Policy (forthcoming)

Streeton, P. (2006) Culture and Economic Development. Handbook of the Economics of Art and Culture. Ginsburgh, V. and Throsby, D. (Eds.) North Holland, Amsterdam.

Swindell, D. and Rosentraub, M. (1998) Who benefits from the presence of professional sports teams? The implication for public funding of stadiums and arenas. Public Administration Review 58,1:11-21.

Throsby, D. (1994) The production and consumption of the arts: a view of cultural economics. Journal of Economic Literature 32,3:1-28.

Throsby, D. (2001) Economics and Culture. Cambridge University Press: Cambridge.

Throsby, D. and Withers, G. (1985) What price culture? Journal of Cultural Economics 9,2:1-33.

Tiongson, E. (1997) Baumol's cost disease reconsidered. Challenge 40,6:117-123.

Turner, G. (1990) British cultural studies: an introduction. Routledge: London.

Ver Eecke, W. (1998) The concept of a 'merit good': The ethical dimension in economic theory and the history of economic thought of the transformation of economics into socio-economics. Journal of Socio-Economics 27,1:133-154.

2 Using Economic Impact Studies to Value the Arts

Economic impact studies can be used for valuing all sort of cultural goods, but especially those that attract large numbers of tourists (and thus tourist spending) from outside the impact area. This means that, while there are certain exceptions, like the "superstar" museums discussed by Frey (1998) and "blockbuster" art exhibits (Skinner 2006), the economic impact method is most commonly applied to cultural events, but can also include not-for-profit cultural sectors within a particular region.

For example, economic impact studies conducted on cultural goods have included opera, subsidized theatre, orchestras, the impact of local cinema, art and other museums, music institutes, not-for-profit arts and culture organizations, heritage sites and so on. A very useful resource for these kinds of studies is the Impact Database, hosted by the Centre for Cultural Policy Research at the University of Glasgow. While the method can be easily extended to just about any cultural good or service, this chapter gives special prominence to arts festivals because of their spectacular recent growth.

Since the 1980s there has been an explosion of the number of festivals of all types, not just arts festivals, but folk festivals, harvest festivals, food festivals, family festivals, carnivals, literary festivals – the list is endless. It is estimated that there are more than 300 festivals in the UK (British Federation of Festivals 2004), 1300 in Australia (Johnson et al 2005) and more than 5000 in the US (Blumenthal 2002). Quinn (2005) and Liu (2005) suggest that this change occurred because of a change in the way the service sector of the economy was viewed – not simply as a support for, or parasite on, manufacturing any longer, but as an important, wealth-creating sector in its own right. The implication of such a change for festivals, especially arts festivals, has been that many cities see them as a way to put "even mundane places permanently onto the lucrative tourist map" (Liu 2005:3). In other words, arts festivals are increasingly being regarded primarily as generators of financial benefits – the "just add culture and stir approach to urban regeneration" (Gibson and Stevenson 2004 in Quinn 2005).

As the number of arts festivals has increased world-wide, so too has the interest in valuing them through the use of economic impact studies. As Frey (2005) points out, this presents cultural economists with an interesting dilemma: on the one hand, various commentators (Seaman 1987; Madden 2001) have expressed their concern with using such a purely market-based measure to "value" the arts. On the other hand, arts organizations and practitioners have shown little interest in non-market valuation methods (like willingness-to-pay studies) and a growing reliance on economic impact data as a means of arguing for public and private sponsorship.

It is not that the economic impact method itself is particularly complex, as Tyrrell and Johnson (2006) point out. However, the number and extent of the assumptions and decisions made about such crucial inputs as visitor numbers, the size of the multiplier and the data collection time and method leave economic impact results vulnerable to manipulation and bias (Crompton 2006). Non-specialist readers of economic impact reports are seldom equipped to evaluate such methodological niceties and tend to accept the final figure as a "scientific" outcome.

Economic impact studies attempt to answer the question, "If the event had not taken place, what would the loss of revenue to the impact area have been?" In other words, they attempt to calculate all the additional economic activity that takes place in the impact area as a result of the event or facility being studied. These sorts of studies concentrate on the private good aspect of the arts, captured by market transactions, rather than the merit or public good aspects.

As such, commentators are deeply divided on the usefulness of economic impact studies in valuing cultural goods. On the one side are mostly academic arguments that hotly contest the use of economic impact studies, arguing that, in the case of arts advocacy, they are worse than useless and may even be harmful to the cause by encouraging inappropriate comparisons with other sectors and downplaying the whole purpose of culture (Seaman 1987; Madden 1998, 2001 amongst others). On the other side are mostly practitioners and arts organizations who argue that economic impact studies can provide useful information about culture and cultural events and are, moreover, very effective in helping to lobby for public and community support (Vogelsong et al 2001, Heaney and Heaney 2003, Crompton 1995, 1999, 2001 amongst others). Both dissenters and promoters of the method, however, recognize that there are potentially dangerous methodological issues as well.

This chapter introduces the theoretical debates around using economic impact studies in cultural valuation. Chapter three offers practical advice and examples of how to go about conducting a reliable study.

2.1 The Benefits of Using Economic Impact Studies

The case in favour of the use of economic impact studies in arts advocacy rests mostly, as Cohen et al. (2003) suggest, on the pragmatic rather than the ideal. In other words, the fact that such studies can produce a "bottom line" figure, which can be easily understood and compared, is perhaps the most important positive argument put forward. The numbers are important, as many commentators show, because they are the basis upon which funding decisions are often made, "Public officials, boosters and the media accept the quantifiable which appears to represent reality in order to justify a desired project" (Johnson and Sack 1996:370).

Goldman and Nakazawa (1997) agree, stating that, when "hard choices" about which of a number of desirable projects to fund have to be made, economic impact figures can play an important part. When the funds are provided, or partly provided by community residents, "they [expect to] receive a return on their investment in the form of new jobs and more household income" (Crompton 1999:143) and this return can be shown in economic impact figures. For this reason, a vast number of economic impact studies on the arts have been conducted. Madden (2001) reports that, from 1973 to 1993 more than 200 arts economic impact studies were conducted in the United States alone. Since then, the number has continued to grow and, while few academic journals publish the results, the websites of many arts councils provide a long list of arts impact studies and even "Do-it-yourself" kits for arts managers and events organizers wanting to use the technique (Jackson et al. 2005). A number of computerized input-output models are also available, such as IMPLAN and RIMMS II.

On a more specific level, economic impact studies can provide information about how money can best be spent to improve an event. Such improvements can be both in terms of financial gains for the community, for example improving areas in which visitors are shown to spend most (Vogelsong et al. 2001), and in terms of improving event quality and composition in order to attract new visitors and to keep regular visitors loyal (Heaney and Heaney 2003).

Heaney and Heaney (2003) conducted and economic impact analysis on a two week summer music institute in Stevens Point, USA. They argue that direct impact figures of participants can be used to expand or improve those areas of the event that visitor spending flags as important. For example, in the case of the music institute, it was found that visitor spending on travel was large, since Stevens Point is fairly remote and the authors thus suggest that information on travel routes, maps and websites could be improved since this might be an important "decision-making determinant" for visitors and also impact on "customer satisfaction" (Heaney and Heaney 2003:260). They also argue that indirect and induced economic impact figures could be used to gain community support and sponsorship, especially from those industries (like accommodation and food) that are shown by the economic impact analysis to attract significant visitor spending. In addition, they suggest that economic impact figures are useful in increasing the "stature and validity" of the institution and in lobbying for local government support on the basis that the event increases economic activity in the region.

A number of economic impact practitioners (Herrero et al. 2004; Cohen et al. 2003) recognize that they are only measuring a partial value of the good or event in question, that is, that the arts generate other significant benefits as well. Seaman (2003) points out that the arts generate three types of impact: (i) consumption values, made up of use and non-use values best measured by contingent valuation methods, (ii) long run increases in productivity and economic development, best measured by hedonic pricing models, and (iii) short run net increases in economic activity, best measured by economic impact studies. Guetzkow (2002) points out that the impact of the arts on communities occurs in many ways (for example, through direct involvement, audience participation and in simply having artists and arts organizations present) and on both an individual and community level. Economic impact studies, while one of the most popular forms of measuring value, capture only a part of the "impact" of the arts on communities and individuals.

Herrero et al. (2004) conducted an economic impact analysis of the "European Capitals of Culture" festival event in Salamanca in 2002. They found that the festival generated 556.1 million euros for Castilla y Leon, 247.2

million euros for the rest of Spain and 803.3 million euros in total (2004:15). They argue that this is an important way of valuing the festival because a city nominated as a "European Capital of Culture" must be financially sustainable (profitable) in the long run since, "along with the cultural organization itself, there is a need for a remarkable effort in the form of creating new cultural facilities, urban redesign, tourist equipment and communication in the city" (Herrero et al. 2004:3).

A study conducted on the economic impact of the non-profit arts organization in ninety-one American communities by Cohen et al. (2003) showed that, through the spending of audiences and the organizations themselves, they added $134 billion per annum to the American economy. While Cohen et al. (2003) question the validity of using such financial figures to justify government support for the arts, they report that the study was cited numerous times in political debates and led to a new resolution encouraging the support of non-profit arts organization being adopted by the conference of mayors as well as a $10 million increase in funds to the National Endowment for the Arts being passed by the House of Representatives in 2002 – the largest such increase in nearly twenty years. They conclude that, "At this time in history, economic development is perhaps the most persuasive message when making the case for support [of the arts] to local, state and national leaders" (Cohen et al. 2004:31).

There is no doubt that tourism is big business: including transport, it is estimated to be the largest world industry at $4.4 trillion per year (Liu 2005) and to be growing at around 5% per year (McGuigan 2005). In such a context, festivals are seen as a way for cities to raise their profile and differentiate themselves from other places in a competitive market. The unfortunate consequence is that measuring the value of arts festivals has come to be seen as simply an offshoot of "urban tourism research" (Visser 2005), which focuses only on the potential of festivals as economic development strategies, rather than on the value of the product they produce – the arts.

The process was helped along considerably by the work of Richard Florida and his influential book *The rise of the creative class* (2002). Simply put, his thesis was that the concentrated presence of the "creative class" in cities was positively correlated with higher levels of human capital and with faster economic growth. Despite a number of criticisms, his work has remained important and has been shown to be robust in more recent studies (Rushton 2006). On the one hand, as Rushton (2006:10) points out, this offers arts proponents an alternative approach to the "economically dubious economic impact studies" based on visitor spending. However, it reinforces the idea that art and artists mean money and this link, once made in the minds of promoters and policy makers, is difficult to redefine.

A general review of the press reporting of both increases in funding and in funding cuts seems to verify the argument that the arts in many countries are being valued primarily as drivers of economic growth and development, rather than in terms of their intrinsic cultural value. For example, *Back Stage* (2003) published a highly critical report of a big cut in funding to the California Arts Council. The basis for the criticism was almost entirely the expected fall in economic impact as a result of the cut, rather than the loss of any aesthetic or qualitative values that the arts might provide. Similarly, in South Africa, when announcing provincial government sponsorship for the National Arts Festival, spokespeople concentrated their remarks on the economic benefits, increased tourist attraction and job opportunities offered by the event.

A recent article by Crompton (2006) provides a wide range of examples of the successful use of (often inflated) economic impact studies to argue for increased funding of various tourism projects, including cultural events. Ironically, it is the very success of such studies that has encouraged what Crompton refers to as "mischievous" practices (a less diplomatic word would be "dishonest"), discussed in more detail in the next chapter. However, he concludes with a warning that such hugely inflated economic impact figures are beginning to lose their power as advocacy tools because of the skepticism with which they are coming to be viewed. If economists want these studies to be taken seriously, they will have to be conducted with greater integrity.

2.2 The Dangers of Using Economic Impact Studies

Criticism of economic impact studies in arts advocacy can be divided into methodological issues (dealt with in chapter three) and conceptual problems. The latter generally argue that even the most sophisticated impact study would not be a good way to motivate for public funds and that such focus on financial indicators, rather than helping, may harm the arguments of arts advocators.

The first problem is that any economic impact study is highly sensitive to the impact area or regional delineation of the research question. Since economic impact relies on the spending of visitors from outside the region and, in some cases, additional spending of locals within the region, the question of opportunity cost must inevitably arise. That is, where is the money coming from and what other sectors or regions have suffered because this one has gained? As Seaman (1987:731) puts it, "when enquiring as to the source of these quasi-mysterious 'exogenous' increases in overall spending, one often discovers that they may not constitute net increases, but merely changes in the composition of spending demand". The point is not a new one and was also made by Baade and Dye (1988:41) in their analysis of the rationale for the public subsidization of sports stadiums, where they argue that "net new activity" often includes "a reallocation of the preexisting level of local residents' spending".

Madden (2001) elaborates, pointing out that it is not enough to show that there are multiplier effects within the impact region, rather one must show that these effects are larger in the benefiting region or sector than in those industries or areas from which the event has diverted funds. The same argument holds for diverting government funds towards art:

> "Increases in government expenditure must ultimately come from somewhere – either diverted away from alternative policy expenditures, or away from the expenditures of citizens through their taxes. The net effect depends on the 'inverse' impacts of the area from which the extra money is diverted" (Madden 2001:167).

Madden's (2001:172) point is that lobbying for public funds based on projected financial gains for one region by diverting spending away from other regions is not a politically neutral game. In fact, he argues that it smacks of protectionism and "is an invitation to war – event war". Using financial figures to lobby for arts support can be dangerous in that such studies encourage numerical comparisons with other industries or events whose purpose is entirely different from the arts. This is verified by Crompton's (2006:79) personal experience in what he calls "the economic impacts arms race": When the council was presented with an economic impact figure of $16 million for a three week festival, they rejected the results on the grounds that the impact of a 3 day rodeo event was calculated (by another consultant) to be nearly $60 million.

Both Madden (2001) and Seaman (1987) point out that it is unlikely that the arts will ever be shown to have the impact of a "basic industry" like, for example, petroleum and coal products, and that such comparisons are in any case spurious. Even if the arts could be shown to have a comparably large economic impact, this would still not be a good reason to lobby for public support. Gazel and Schwer (1997) show that the impact of three *Grateful Dead* rock concerts on the Las Vegas economy was between $17 and $28 million, but no one would dream of using these figures to argue for the public support of the rock band.

Another problem with focusing on the financial impacts of the arts in regions where there is a large difference between rich and poor residents is that most of the money accrues to the wealthier residents of the community who have some means of capitalizing on the presence of visitors. For example, in the Grahamstown economy (a small host city in South Africa), it was found that household income from the arts festival held there was vastly greater amongst wealthier European-origin (white) residents than in the poorer African-origin (black) communities, although the percentage of retained income in poorer communities was higher (Antrobus et al. 1997). Seaman (1987:746) concludes, "Arts proponents, therefore, are involved in a dangerous game when they resort to impact studies. In a sense, they are choosing to play one of their weakest cards, while holding back their aces". In other words, it is the positive spillovers provided by the arts to society, the primary cause of market failure, which should be used to motivate for public support to the arts and not the more frequently cited economic benefits.

An example of a case where the financial benefits of arts festivals are regarded as more important than the social, is given in McGuigan's (2005) discussion of the selection of cities for the European Capital of Culture competition. His argument is that, although the criteria for the competition might have started out as being cultural, they have come to focus more and more on the potential financial benefits the prize can provide. "It is not at all surprising that Liverpool won the British competition for designation as European Capital of Culture 2008. It is a perfect test case for the efficacy of culture-led regeneration" (McGuigan 2005:239).

Quinn (2005 and 2006) makes an eloquent argument against seeing the arts and arts festivals primarily as drivers of economic growth on two grounds. Firstly, the focus on arts events as commodities for sale to tourists undermines the traditional role of festivals as community gatherings where people could come together to establish new, or re-establish old, networks and connections. Festivals can be places set apart from everyday life where alternative views and values can be shared and considered, where resistance to the dominant regime can be expressed and where cultural capital (Throsby 2001) can be valued and shared. Of course, arts events can also be about "vibe" and atmosphere, good food and entertainment, but as Peter Aspden (Aspden and Clark 2004) suggests, this should not be their *only* or main function.

Quinn's (2006) second argument is that, if arts festivals are treated primarily as commodities, they are likely to lose their capacity to interest and excite and thus to attract tourists and generate economic or cultural benefits. Liu (2005:4) talks about the threat to traditional cultures of "McDonaldization" and the spread of uniform American cultures:

> In the summer of 2002 I was witness to the first time that paraders in Disney costumes appeared at the end of the traditional Nadaam festival in Ulaanbaatar, Mongolia. No doubt, Mickey, Minnie and Donald will become regulars at the annual celebrations, alongside with Genghis Khan's cart, the wrestlers, acrobats and horses. The warning is quite clear. Unless traditional culture is valued and nurtured, it will not survive the next generation brought up with MTV, videogames and survival shows.

Aspden (Aspden and Clark 2004) agrees that many modern arts festivals simply present works already performed elsewhere at higher prices, "it is a sort of supermarket, where the paying public is persuaded to bulk-buy processed culture". Along with the increased competition for audiences and artists and crowding out effects experienced by some festival managers (Blumenthal 2002), it is not difficult to see that a focus on the monetary gains from such events may defeat both cultural and financial ends.

In such a context, Quinn (2006) argues that arts festivals may fail to fulfil the host community's cultural or economic expectations. Preoccupation with short-run financial benefit excludes longer term values, such as the festival enhancing the identity of the place and its development potential (in terms of infrastructure, increases in demand for artistic products year round, increases in social welfare and so on). To illustrate her point, Quinn (2006) reports the results of a study of two festivals in Ireland, Wexford Festival Opera, geared from the start towards providing high quality opera and the attraction of foreign tourists, and the Galway Arts Festival, a much more community based enterprise. The findings, based on an opinion survey of both visitors and local residents, show that at both festivals participants were aware of the non-market values the festivals provided, like creating arts awareness, developing arts venue infrastructure, helping to build the reputation of the host town and creating more arts activities throughout the year.

However, the Galway Arts Festival became more interested in the financial benefits of the festival and focused more attention on tourists, thus moving away from their original aim of being a community-based festival. Local communities began to resent this move, feeling excluded and dissatisfied because the original relationship between the festival and the community was not being maintained. Quinn (2006) argues that, for a festival to be sustainable in the long run, its aims must be clear from the outset and that it needs to be recognized that different aims will generate different returns. For example, a festival that balances local – international orientation is likely to be very useful in developing cultural infrastructure in the host city and increasing appreciation of and participation in the arts, but is not going to be as successful in attracting visitor demand as a festival which focuses on international (rather than local) visitors and artists.

Madden (2001) goes so far as to say that government intervention based on economic impact figures could do more harm than good, since the objectives of government are seldom aligned with those of the arts. Cohen and Pate (2000:109), talking from the perspective of artists, support this view: "Artists have asserted (in conversation with us) that they feel it is absurd to make decisions on their future funding without fully recognizing the aesthetic worth of their product". In a similar vein, Tusa (1999 cited in Reeves 2002:36) states that,

> "Mozart is Mozart because of his music and not because he created a tourist industry in Salzburg or gave his name to decadent chocolate and marzipan Salzburg kugel. Picasso is important because he taught a century new ways of looking at objects and not because his paintings in the Guggenheim Museum are regenerating an otherwise derelict northern Spanish port…Absolute quality is paramount in attempting a valuation of the arts; all other factors are interesting, useful but secondary".

McCarthy et al. (2004), identify two types of cultural value: "Intrinsic" value, which has a direct relationship with the artistic product itself (like pleasure and cognitive growth); and "instrumental" value, including economic impact, which is a by-product of artistic production and can also be generated by substitute goods. They argue that the "culture wars" in America in the early 1990s necessitated "proving" the value of the arts, which increased focus on the instrumental values disproportionately because they are more easily measured than the intrinsic benefits. Matarasso (1997) found the same pattern in the UK, stating that studies of the impact of the arts have tended to focus on the financial, rather than the social, benefits to the exclusion of "the real purpose of the arts".

In addition to such categorical dismissals of the method, there are other, interpretive problems, arising largely from the attempt to extract information from economic impact studies not designed for the purpose. Personal experience of the disbelief and disappointment of event organizers when presented with final reports has prompted further thought about the ways in which such figures are viewed and used. The first anomaly occurs when stated event aims are compared to the use of financial figures in declaring the festival "a success". The more public good characteristics an event has, the smaller will be the benefits captured by an economic impact study and the larger will be the consumer surplus and the value of non-market goods, which has not been measured by an economic impact study at all. Madden (2001) argues that economic impact studies measure spending on the event, in other words, *costs*, not benefits and that if the arts were available for free, they would undoubtedly increase our well-being or utility by a greater amount because of decreased opportunity costs. The usefulness of economic impact studies in these cases, however well they are conducted, is thus questionable.

Another problem area of economic impact study interpretation arises when arts event organizers try to draw conclusions about the relative importance of various activities from data on visitor spending. In 2001, South African National Arts Festival organizers commissioned a consumer research study chiefly in order to establish consumer spending patterns and opinions with a view to using this information to lobby for further sponsorship of the event. Despite the generally good opinion of festival-goers of Main and Fringe shows – an average of 4 out of 5 for quality and price - festival organizers expressed disappointment that spending on tickets was only the third highest expenditure category, accommodation being first and shopping second (Snowball and Antrobus 2001:18). At first glance, this result does appear to be contradictory or to indicate that festival visitors are interested in other aspects of the event more than in shows. However, if one considers that shows at the festival were highly subsidized - on average, ticket prices for the exact same shows outside of the festival were found to be 41% higher (Snowball 2004) - while accommodation and shopping are not, the errors that can be made by using only expenditure data to indicate interest or value become apparent.

Even those who criticize impact studies as a tool for arguing for the public support of the arts, however, do recognize that they can be useful. Seaman (1987) points out that, if economic impact studies are conducted with methodological soundness, they can be used successfully to examine the relationships between various parts of the economy and to make predictions about income and output changes. Madden (1998) agrees, adding that, in addition to financial flows, economic impact studies can provide important information about the effects of demand and supply shocks on regional economies and a way of comparing the financial redistribution that results from different projects. However, both Madden and Seaman point out that economic impact studies are seldom put to only these uses and they both argue vehemently that, in the majority of cases, economic impact studies of arts and culture are an "abuse of economic analysis" (Seaman 1987:725).

2.3 Conclusions

Considering both the advantages and disadvantages of using economic impact studies in arts valuation, one can make two general observations. Firstly, accepted as a *partial* analysis, and especially if conducted in conjunction with some other sort of study better suited to capturing the aesthetic or cultural values of the event or facility, impact studies can be useful to a certain extent, especially in lobbying for funds. Secondly, economists requested to conduct such studies find themselves in a particularly uncomfortable position. On the one hand are commentators like Madden (2001:174) who argue that undertaking such studies is a "prostitution of economics", since economists must know how questionable the reasoning behind such studies is. On the other hand, attempts to convince arts managers of the usefulness of the conceptually more complex contingent valuation methodologies is, as Madden (2001) also admits, slow work.

It is likely that arts practitioners will continue to commission economic impact studies, despite their theoretical problems, because of their effectiveness in arguing for public and private support. In such an atmosphere, economists who argue against their use are likely to be regarded rather like Cassandra of ancient Troy – doomed to speak the truth, but not to be believed. In this situation, practitioners are better served by refining the method and making sure that methodological issues are kept high on the research agenda rather than by rejecting economic impact as a valuation method entirely.

References

Antrobus, G., Williams, V., Fryer, D., Khumalo, B., Streak, J. & Webb, A., (1997) The economic impact of the 1996 Standard Bank National Arts Festival. Department of Economics, Rhodes University: Grahamstown

Aspden, P and Clark, A. (2004) High brow, low blows. Financial Times Magazine 19/06/04

Blumenthal, R. (2002) Festivals, festivals everywhere: Summer arts events multiply, testing the limits of growth. New York Times 30/07/02

Cohen, C. and Pate, M. (2000) Making a meal of arts evaluation: can social audit offer a more balanced approach? Managing Leisure 5:103-120.

Crompton, J. (1995) Economic impact analysis of sports facilities and events: Eleven sources of misapplication. Journal of Sports Management 9:14-35.

Crompton, J. (1999) The economic impact of sports tournaments and events. Parks and Recreation 34,9:142-151.

Crompton, J., Lee, S. and Schuster, T. (2001) A guide for undertaking economic impact studies: The Springfest example. Journal of Travel Research 40:79-87.

Crompton, J. (2006) Economic impact studies: Instruments for political shenanigans? Journal of Travel Research 45:67-82.

Florida, R. (2002) The Rise of the Creative Class. Basic Books, New York

Frey, B. (2005) What values should count in the arts? The tension between economic effects and cultural value. Institute for Empirical Research in Economics, University of Zurich. Working paper no. 253.

Goldman, G. and Nakazawa, A. (1997) Determining economic impacts for a community. Economic Development Review 15,1:48-52.

Gazel, R. and Schwer, K. (1997) Beyond rock and roll: The economic impact of the Grateful Dead on a local economy. Journal of Cultural Economics 21:41-55.

Guetzkow, J. (2002) How the arts impact communities. Taking the Measure of Culture conference, Center for Arts and Cultural Policy Studies, Princeton University Working Paper Series.

Heaney, J. and Heaney, M. (2003) Using economic impact analysis for arts management: An empirical application to a music institute in the USA. International Journal of Nonprofit and Voluntary Sector Marketing 8,3:251-266.

Herrero, L., Sanz, J., Devesa, M., Bdate, A. and Del Barrio, M. (2004) Economic impact of cultural macrofestivals: the case study of Salamanca 2002, European capital of culture. Presented at the 13th International Conference on Cultural Economics, Association for Cultural Economics International.

Johnson, A. and Sack, A. (1996) Assessing the value of sports facilities: the importance of non-economic factors. Economic Development Quarterly 10,4:369-382

Liu, J. (2005) Tourism and the value of culture in regions. The Annals of Regional Science 39:1-9.

Madden, C. (1998) "Discussion paper: The economic benefits of art. Creative New Zealand [On line] Available: www.creativenz.gov.nz [Accessed 13/08/04].

Madden, C. (2001) Using economic impact studies in arts and cultural advocacy: a cautionary note. Media International Australia incorporating Culture and Policy. Feb,98:161-178.

Matarasso, F. (1997) Use of Ornament? The social impact of participation in the arts. Comedia [On line] Available: http://www.comedia.org.uk/pages/pdf/downloads/use_or_ornament.pdf [Accessed 18/05/07]

McCarthy, K, Ondaatje, E., Zakaras, L. and Brooks, A. (2004) Gift of the Muse: Reframing the debate about the benefits of the arts. Rand Corporation: Santa Monica, Arlington and Pittsburgh.

McGuigan, J. (2005) Neo-liberalism, culture and policy. International Journal of Cultural Policy 11:229-241.

Quinn, B. (2005) Arts festivals and the city. Urban Studies 42:927-943

Quinn, B. (2006) Problematising 'festival tourism': Arts festivals and sustainable development in Ireland. Journal of Sustainable Tourism 14:288-306

Rushton, M. (2006) The creative class and urban economic growth revisited. Paper presented at the 14th International Conference of the Associated for Cultural Economics International, Vienna.

Seaman, B. (1987) Arts impact studies: A fashionable excess. Towse, R. (Ed.) 1997 Cultural economics: the arts, the heritage and the media industries Vol. 2 Edward Elgar: Cheltenham.

Seaman, B. (2003) The economic impact of the arts in Handbook of Cultural Economics. Towse, R. (ed) Edward Elgar.

Snowball, J. D. and Antrobus, G. (2001) Consumer Research: A survey of visitors at the 2001 National Arts Festival, Grahamstown. Department of Economics, Rhodes University: Grahamstown. Commissioned by the Grahamstown Foundation.

Tyrrell, T. and Johnson, R. (2006) The economic impacts of tourism: A special issue. Journal of Travel Research 45:3-7.

Visser, G. (2005) Let's be festive: Exploratory notes on festival tourism in South Africa. Urban Forum 16:155-175

Vogelsong, H., Graefe, A. and Estes, C. (2001) Economic impact analysis: A look at useful methods. Parks and Recreation 36,3:28-33.

3 Calculating Economic Impact

In the introduction to a recent special edition of the *Journal of Travel Research* (Volume 45, 2006), Tyrrell and Johnson define economic impact analysis as seeking "to estimate changes in regional spending, output, income and/or employment associated with tourism policy, events, facilities or destinations". As discussed in the previous chapter, there are a number of good reasons that economic impact data may be very useful in valuing an arts event or cultural facility. As long as it is always presented as a partial value, that is, as long as it is always acknowledged that the economic impact figure is not capturing *all* value, such a figure can be a powerful way to demonstrate the worth of a particular project.

Crompton (2006) argues that it is important not to see economic impact studies as a cost-benefit analysis that applies only to the host city council. For example, if the council spends more on the event than it generates directly in revenue, this is not a good argument for discontinuing because it does not take into account the benefits to community residents, who pay the council taxes in the first place. Below (fig. 3.1) is the useful diagram that he provides showing the rationale for conducting studies of cultural events or facilities that attract tourists from outside the impact region.

As mentioned in the previous chapter, while economic impact studies can also be used to value permanent local cultural facilities or arts organizations, they are most often used when "new" spending occurs in the region because of tourists. When the method is used to value the cultural industries or not-for-profit arts organizations of a whole region, it is more often the local economic activity stimulated by the organizations themselves (for example, their spending on equipment and labour) than the, often small, impact of tourists from outside the region that is mainly considered. This is because, as further discussed below, the spending of local residents in the impact area is not usually included, since this spending may have taken place in any case.

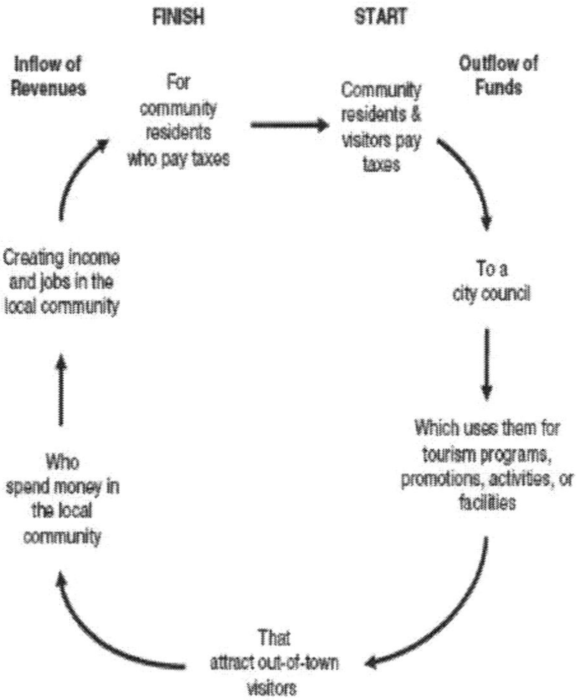

(Crompton 2006:68)

Fig. 3.1. The Economic Impact Cycle of Costs and Benefits

The implication of the above diagram for economic impact studies of cultural events is that it is not enough to track spending and income by organizers or the host city council in question – one also has to take into account the indirect impacts in terms of job creation and income that the event has on local residents. This chapter offers practical advice on how to conduct such as study, with particular reference to cultural events and festivals that draw tourists into the impact region.

3.1 Direct Net Economic Impact

The first step in any economic impact study is to determine the net injections into the impact area as a result of the event, often referred to as direct impact or first-round spending. One way of doing this is to collect visitor spending data using quota or probability sampling and interview or self-completion questionnaires. However, Tyrrell and Johnston (2001) argue that, in addition to visitor spending, spending by producers, the value of the time donated by volunteers and media spending should also be included. The identification of important spending groups will depend on the type of event being valued. For example, an economic impact study of the Edinburgh Festivals in 2004-2005 identified four "strands" of spending, from spectators, performers, journalists and the festival organizers, as shown in the diagram below.

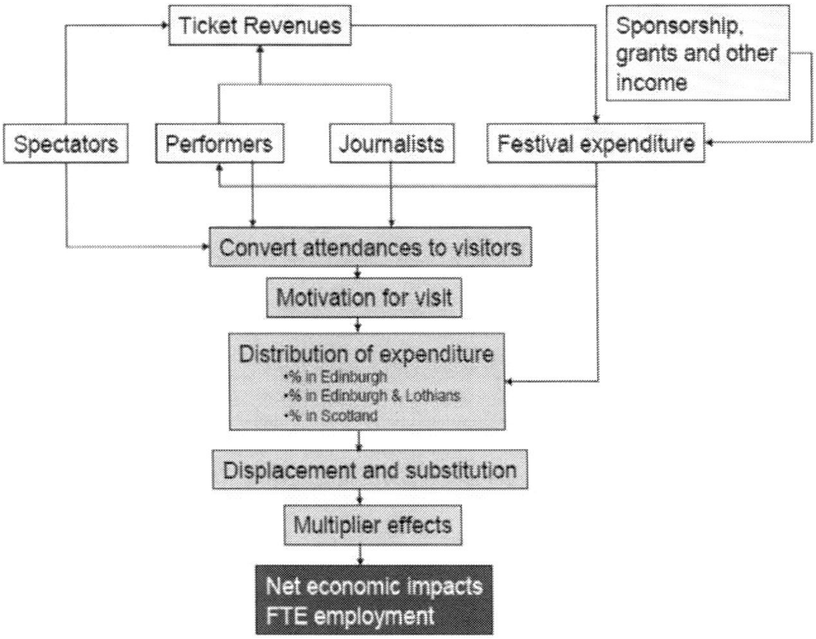

(Edinburgh Festivals Study 2004-2005:6)

Fig. 3.2. Calculating Economic Impact at the Edinburgh Festivals

Net direct spending should not include spending that would have occurred in any case, for example, spending by locals that could be regarded as "diversions of spending" from other goods in the area (Seaman 2003) and spending by "casual" visitors or "time switchers" who would have come regardless of the event. This is why taking into account "motivation for visit" and "displacement and substitution effects" are part of the process of calculating economic impact shown in figure 3.2.

Since short term events sometimes include foreign producers, gross direct impact may be very large, but net direct impact may be negative. This is because of the diversion of local spending away from local goods towards "foreign" producers who take most of their profits away with them. Thus, in the case of arts festivals or events which rely on many performers and vendors from outside the region, it is likely that net and gross direct economic impact will be considerably different. Results are also likely to be affected by how the impact area is defined ("distribution of expenditure" in figure 3.2), as well as the way in which data is collected. The following section discusses methodological issues in calculating net direct impact.

3.1.1 Data Collection Methods and Sampling

The way in which visitor spending data is collected can have a huge effect on the calculation of economic impact, especially if the festival population is highly differentiated in terms of language, number of trips and length of stay. Most studies rely on either interviews with attenders using random or stratified sampling, or self-completion questionnaires returned by mail or at collection points at the event. The advantage of using interviews is that sampling is easier to control and data is generally more reliable and of a better quality. However, this method is expensive and can be supplemented with self-completion questionnaires handed out at, for example, festival shows, restaurants and other facilities near or associated with the cultural resource, art exhibitions, souvenir shops, craft markets and so on. While a cost-effective way of increasing the sample size, combining the two methods (or relying on only one method) can introduce bias.

An example of the difference that data collection methods can make is in the comparison of the economic impact of the South African National Arts Festival (NAF) calculated by two different teams using different methods. One team of researchers had conducted economic impact studies on the NAF for a number of years (Antrobus et al. 1996; 1997; Snowball and Antrobus 2001, 2003; Antrobus and Snowball 2004; Snowball and Antrobus 2006), referred to as the Antrobus method. A second, unrelated team (Saayman et al. 2005), referred to as the Saayman method, conducted a similar study in 2005.

The 2005 Saayman study was based on self-completion questionnaires offered in English. The 2006 Antrobus study (and those preceding it) used both self-completion questionnaires in English and face-to-face interviews with festival goers on a quota basis. The quota was based on past studies and was put in place to prevent interviewers from introducing any unintentional bias. While the Saayman method produced a visitor profile showing that 73% of festival audiences were European-origin (white), English speaking people, the Antrobus method showed only about 64% in this category. It is probable that this is because people who read and write English easily are much more likely to fill in a self-completion questionnaire than second-language English speakers are. In addition, if income is split along racial lines, as it is in South Africa, self-completion data submitted by a higher proportion of wealthier, white people is likely to produce visitor spending data that is upwardly biased. This was shown to be the case in the 2006 study, where the average visitor expenditure per group for the entire stay was R3 204 (about 320), while it was only R2 167 (about 217) on average using interview data. An important finding is thus that, in the situation where groups of attenders show a strong correlation between language and wealth characteristics, self-completion data is likely to be biased unless questionnaires are offered in more than one language where literacy levels are high (Bragge and Snowball 2007).

Loomis (2007) identifies two types of sampling bias that can inflate the final economic impact figure. The first is "avidity bias", that is, people who visit an area where the sample is being selected (like a craft market area or other facilities associated with the event) more often, are more likely to be included in the sample. The second sort of bias is "length of stay" bias – that is, that visitors who stay longer (and who thus are likely to spend more) are more likely to be included in the sample than short duration visitors.

Depending on the type of event being valued, sampling procedures can be used to overcome these forms of bias. For example, using exit intercept interviews may reduce the length of stay bias, but might increase avidity bias (Loomis 2007:43). A way of reducing bias might also be to sample visitors at multiple points. For example, in the case of a festival, sampling could be done at craft markets, show and ticket queues, art exhibitions and other facilities in order to include as many types of visitor as possible. However, those who spent more time on such activities and who stayed longer are still likely to be over-represented.

Loomis (2007:43), adapting from Nowell et al. (1988), suggests correcting for length of stay and avidity bias by weighting visitors sampled by the reciprocal of their length of stay (in days) and number of trips respectively. So length of stay could be corrected by:

$\mu_{LS} = N/\Sigma\ (1/LS_i)$ (1)

where μ_{LS} is the corrected length of stay, N is the total number of visitors sampled, and LS_i is the length of stay in days of visitor i. Similarly, avidity bias could be corrected for using

$\mu_{Trips} = N/\Sigma\ (1/Trips_i)$ (2)

where μ_{Trips} is the corrected number of trips and $Trips_i$ is the number of trips for person i (Loomis 2007:43).

In a case study of rafting trips on the Snake River in Wyoming, Loomis (2007:45) found a significant difference in the corrected and uncorrected estimates of the number of trips per rafter (a 42% overstatement without the correction), the trip length (17% overstatement) and thus the number of visitor days, calculated by multiplying trip length and number of trips (52% overstatement). The cumulative effect of the corrections was that the economic impact of the rafters was 58% lower than the uncorrected figures.

Visitor spending data collection at the South African National Arts Festival

Please estimate how much you intend to spend in total at the Festival on the following items.
(Grahamstown locals, please report only spending in addition to your normal monthly expenses).
Important!
Are these figures for: only yourself? your whole traveling group/family?
Accommodation: R ____________ Shows: R ____________
Food & drinks: R ____________ Shopping: R ____________
Other (please specify)
How many people are you paying for at the Festival?
(Snowball and Antrobus 2006)

The accuracy with which visitors report their spending is also dependent on how the data is collected. For example, it has been shown that visitor spending data is more accurate if it is collected soon after the spending has taken place. A long time lapse between the spending and the reporting can result in bias because of inaccurate recollection and "telescoping" – reporting spending outside of the study area that may have occurred on the same trip (Wilton and Nickerson 2006). These problems are exacerbated for impact studies of permanent tourist attractions, like museums, opera houses and theatres, but are unlikely to occur in event studies because data is typically collected from visitors during their attendance. However, if data for the whole trip is being asked for (as opposed to spending on the day of the interview only), some acknowledgement of "prediction bias" needs to be made, since it is quite likely that visitors will be required to project total spending before their trip is complete.

Crompton et al. (2001) argue that group spending figures are likely to be more accurate than individual spending, especially for accommodation. This is also likely to apply to group ticket sales, especially at events where bookings can be made far in advance. However, it is unlikely that group members would be able to account for other spending categories for all their members (like souvenir spending and spending on food and drinks), so caution needs to be exercised. One way of dealing with the problem is to give visitors the choice of reporting group or individual spending as in the South African National Arts Festival study illustrated above. However, if this is done, it needs to be very carefully recorded which sort of data (group or individual) is being reported.

Visitor spending data collection at Art in the Park, Blackburn

Please can you estimate how much your group/family spent on the following items during your outing to Art in the Park.
(Include all expenditure related to attending the event e.g. staying in Blackburn for a meal/drink afterwards etc.)

Items	Spent of Saturday £	Spend on Sunday £
A. Food (restaurants, take-aways, snacks etc)		
B. Drink (soft drinks, alcohol, tea/coffee etc)		
C. Transport (bus fare, taxi, train, petrol, parking etc)		
D. Gifts/Souvenirs (toys, crafts, programmes etc)		
E. Other items (please specify)		
F. Estimated total cost of day out		

Please can you estimate how much your group/family would spend in Blackburn on a *normal weekend*?

Saturday	£
Sunday	£

(Wood 2005:42)

Finally, the number of spending categories needs to be thought about carefully. Leaving out a potential major category or categories, could result in an underestimation of visitor spending in the impact area. For example, in the 2006 South African National Arts Festival study, a frequently reported "other" category was transport. How much of this spending actually took place in the impact area, however, is doubtful. On the other hand, having too many categories can quickly lead to interviewee fatigue and the possible over-estimation of total spending due to rounding up and imperfect recall. For shorter festivals, like the Art in the Park event in Blackburn, Lancashire (Wood 2005), daily spending figures can aid recall and provide useful information on spending patterns and times to organizers.

3.1.2 The Area of Study and Local Spectators

Crompton (1995; 2006) argues that a failure to define accurately the impact area of the study could lead to widely differing results and is one of the most frequent "mischievous" procedures used to inflate economic impact estimates. As would be expected, the larger the area under consideration, the less would be the "leakages" from the system and thus the greater the multiplier effect and the reported economic impact. Crompton (2006:73) also points out that when one expands the area of study from, for example, one city to the whole province, a great many more "visitors" will count as "local spectators", much of whose spending should be excluded from the analysis.

Despite researchers carefully defining the area of study, media reports may persist in misreporting results. For example, the impact figure for the 2003 South African National Arts Festival (R33 million) was reported as being applicable to the whole Eastern Cape Province in the headline, "Grahamstown festival earns Eastern Cape R33m" (*Daily Dispatch* 2003). This is simply untrue, since the figures were calculated for Grahamstown only, not the whole province. Provincial impact figures would have included fewer "visitors", but also fewer leakages and would have produced substantially different figures. However, since the Eastern Cape government is now a major Festival sponsor, reporting the impact as applying to the whole region made better political sense, but fallacious economics!

Since economic impact studies are attempting to measure the financial difference between a situation with the event versus a situation without the event, only spending that occurs directly because of the event should be included (Tyrrell and Johnson 2006). Spending that would have occurred in any case should be excluded. Thus, only attenders from outside the study area should be included in the study, since the spending of local residents does not represent injections of new money, but merely the "recycling" of money already in the area (Crompton 1995). In small cities and towns, local visitors are unlikely to make up a large proportion of festival goers, but in larger centres, the effect of including local residents can be quite marked. For example, a study of the Melbourne International Festival of the Arts (1996:13) showed that local visitors made up 73% of festival goers and spent $3.14 million, but were excluded entirely from the study on the basis that the spending would have occurred even if the festival had not taken place.

There are two possible exceptions to this rule: firstly, spending by local residents who have stayed in town specifically to attend the festival could legitimately be regarded as new money entering the region. One could estimate this figure by asking local residents to report spending in addition to their normal monthly expenses. "However, these types of estimates are very tenuous and economists invariably recommend that all expenditure by local residents should be disregarded" (Crompton 1995:27). Getz (1991:303) also suggests that if the event keeps local residents of the host community at home, rather than spending their money outside the community, local spending could be included in the impact analysis. Another alternative would be to report economic impact both with and without the additional spending of local attenders.

If additional spending by local residents is going to be included in the impact study, one needs to make careful provision for this in the collection of spending data. Referring to the two examples in section 1.1, note that the South African National Arts Festival survey asks local residents ("Grahamstown locals") to report only spending in addition to normal monthly expenses; the Art in the Park event in Blackburn (Wood 2005:42) asks visitors to "estimate how much your group/family would spend in Blackburn on a *normal weekend*", so that the extent of additional spending as a result of the event can be estimated.

Examples of arts impact studies that did include additional spending by local residents are the 1990 - 1991 Edinburgh Festival study (1991:9) and the Adelaide Festival study (1990:13), which included spending by residents of the region "which is additional to normal economic activity" (Edinburgh Festival study 1991:9). The argument here is that, especially for events of short duration, like a festival, local residents may choose to stay in town and "holiday" at the festival instead of spending entertainment funds outside the area (Adelaide festival study 1990:13).

In a household survey of local residents of the South African National Arts Festival host city (Grahamstown) conducted in 2003 (Snowball and Antrobus 2003), about 87% of the sample reported some spending at the festival. However, of these, 48% claimed that they spent no more than they did in a normal week, while 52% reported some extra spending as a result of the festival. In order for local spending to have a net positive effect on the region, it has to be shown that there is import substitution, in other words, that spending which would have occurred outside the region now occurs in the impact area as a direct result of the event (Seaman 2004). Results show that, for those with additional spending, 53% would have spent it in Grahamstown anyway, 31% would not have spent it (saved) and only 15% would have spent it outside the area.

Furthermore, Seaman (1987:732) points out that it is important to ask how local spending is being funded. "If it is from savings at a local bank, the secondary effect would be a reduction in the available pool of loanable funds for, perhaps, local investment or consumption projects far removed from the arts". In other words, the opportunity cost of diverted local spending should also be considered. All this verifies Crompton's (1995; 2006) point that counting local spending as part of economic impact is problematic.

It is also argued (Crompton 1995, Crompton et al. 2001, Tyrrell and Johnston 2001) that the expenditure from visitors who would have come to the area regardless of the event being measured should not be counted as contributing to the economic impact of the event, since they would have spent money in the area anyway. Crompton (1995) defines "time switchers" as people who may have been planning to visit the area for some time (to visit family and friends or to experience some other feature of the area, like museums and game parks), but have switched the time of their visit to coincide with the festival or event. "Casuals" are visitors who may already have been in the area for whatever reason, and decide to attend rather than do something else. In both cases, these visitors would have spent money in the area regardless of whether there was a festival (or other event) or not.

Another issue is whether visitors to the impact region come primarily for the cultural event or whether they are combining their visit with other reasons for visiting the area. In the latter case, not all spending can be attributed directly to the cultural good in question. For example, the study of the economic impact of the Southern Festival of Books in Memphis (Wallace and Honey 2005) found that, in addition to attending the book fair, a significant percentage of visitors also went to other local attractions like:

Graceland (17.5%), the Memphis Zoo (2.5%), Beale Street (30%), the Peabody Hotel (35%) and other things. Strictly speaking, one could argue that the income from visitor spending (in this study, all attributed to the book fair) should be partly discounted to take into account other attractions. On the other hand, the survey did find that 85% of out-of-town visitors came primarily for the festival and only used these visitor numbers to calculate economic impact, excluding all spending by local residents and the spending of visitors not primarily there for the festival.

The 2004-2005 Edinburgh Festival study found that, after taking into account displacement (spending that would have occurred in the impact area in any case) and leakages (spending outside of Edinburgh), the percentage of total visitor spending that could be attributed directly to the Festivals decreased to 61% of the total.

Table 3.1: Impact Area, Visitor Numbers and the Employment Multiplier

	Grahamstown	**Melbourne**	**Edinburgh**	**Adelaide**
Area definition	Somewhat vague: Albany district included small farming villages, but no bigger cities.	Well defined: separate studies for "city of Melbourne and suburbs" & "greater Melbourne".	Well defined: separate studies done for several areas.	Well defined: 80km radius & separate regional impact.
Including locals	Tickets bought by locals excluded: 21 per cent locals.	Excluded all spending of locals: 73 per cent locals.	Included spending by locals "additional to normal economic activity": 1 million pounds.	Excluded most local's spending except residents "holidaying at the festival".
Including "time switchers" & "casuals"	No check. Did ask foreigners main reason for visiting SA.	Did check: only 24 per cent gave festival as main or only reason for visit.	No check.	Did check: 51,4 per cent of visitors there primarily to attend festival. "Extended stay" also counted.
Employment multiplier	No permanent jobs claimed other than the organizers.	No permanent jobs claimed.	Probable overstatement. 1300 full-time jobs claimed.	No mention of employment created.

(Snowball and Antrobus 2002:1305)

A comparison of economic impact studies conducted at four arts festivals (Snowball and Antrobus 2002) showed that, in general, the area of study was fairly well defined, but that only two of the four studies examined excluded local spending entirely or checked for time switchers and casuals (see table 3.1). However, while these are important considerations, determining visitor numbers, especially for un-gated events with free shows, can be even more problematic and crucial.

3.1.3 Determining Visitor Numbers

Even the best estimates of net economic impact will depend to a great extent on the accuracy of visitor number calculation because, once visitor spending has been determined, it is multiplied by the estimated number of visitors. However, very little on how this figure is arrived at has been written. Crompton et al. (2001) discuss the example of Springfest (a 4 day annual cultural festival held in Ocean City) where they used an hourly and bi-hourly counting method at various access points to arrive at an estimate. Wilton and Nickerson (2006) used counts at highway entry points (traffic counts) and airports to estimate tourist numbers – a useful method particularly when the impact of a long running event or a permanent tourism attraction is being calculated. Estimates from aerial photographs can also be used as estimates when the event in question is held mainly outside.

The National Arts Festival studies in South Africa (Antrobus et al. 1996 and 1997) used two methods for visitor number calculation that relied on having accurate ticket sales data and accurate data of at least one type of accommodation. The first method ("ticket sales method") was to collect data on the average number of ticketed events attended by each respondent for the whole festival. This average number included festival visitors who had attended no ticketed shows and were mainly concerned with shopping at the craft markets and/or attending free shows, street theatre and art exhibitions. The average number of ticketed shows attended was then divided by the total number of tickets sold, excluding those sold to local residents, to arrive at a total number of visitors (21 662 in 1996 and 20 700 in 1997).

The second method ("accommodation method") used the visitor questionnaire to determine the percentage of visitors using university accommodation and the average number of nights festival visitors stayed. Data on the number of bed nights sold during the festival was then obtained from Rhodes University and divided by the average length of stay to give the number of visitors in the university residence accommodation category. Since the percentage of visitors in this category was known from the visitor questionnaire, total visitor numbers, excluding local residents and including day visitors, could then be calculated (25 808 in 1996 and 19 822 in 1997). In both the 1996 and 1997 surveys comparable results were obtained using the two methods. The weak point is that both methods rely heavily on a representative sample of festival goers being drawn from the population to avoid over- or understatement of important figures, like the number of shows attended and the length of stay.

Length of stay bias, discussed in section 1.1, is also mentioned as a problem by Wilton and Nickerson (2006). In additional to a lower probability of being interviewed, short-stay visitors are also less likely to be willing to complete questionnaires because they are generally in more of a hurry than longer-stay attenders (Antrobus et al. 1997). In addition to having a direct effect on spending data and economic impact, such bias may also affect visitor number calculations. At the 1998 South African National Arts Festival (Antrobus and Snowball 1998), a specific attempt to collect data from day and short-stay visitors was made by using a "sixty second interview". The motivation behind it was that, since the interview would take only one minute of the visitor's time, even those who were only staying for a day or two might be willing to help.

Table 3.2. Data Collection and Visitor Numbers at the South African Festival

Category	1996	1997	2003	2004	2006
Method (percentage interview versus self-completion)	84	42	100	41	74
Average number of ticketed shows attended per person	5.2	6	4.9	6	9
Total number of tickets sold	184 761	157 380	95 913	104 617	111 776
Percentage of local respondents	20	21	33	17	7.5
Visitor numbers (* excluding locals)	25 000* (31 250)	20 000* (25 300)	20 000	20 000 (16 600*)	20 700 (17 000*)

Of those interviewed, 12.6% were day visitors. Longer, self-completion questionnaires were also used at the 1998 Festival, but of these respondents, only 5.6% were day visitors. The implication for the average length of stay and thus for the calculation of visitor numbers for use in economic impact studies is great. In particular, the method of data collection (self-completion versus interviews) and the length of the questionnaire are likely to have important effects. In general, visitor number calculations using the ticket sales and accommodation methods are likely to be downwardly biased, especially if only self-completion questionnaires are used and the questionnaire is long. The 2003 and 2004 studies used the ticket sales method of visitor number calculation in conjunction with counting methods (particularly at free events and street shows) done by festival organizers in an attempt to compensate for this possible underestimation (see table 3.2).

As discussed earlier, the economic impact of the South African National Arts Festival (NAF) had been calculated by one team of researchers for a number of years, referred to as the Antrobus method, and was then calculated for one year by an unrelated team referred to as the Saayman method. The results were, unsurprisingly, remarkably different: the 2004 Antrobus method estimate being R38.5 million (about 4 million Euros), while the 2005 Saayman method was R53.5 million (5.5 million Euros). After careful examination of results, it became apparent that, while the Antrobus method was based on estimated visitor numbers of about 20 700, the Saayman method estimated 70 000 visitors. It is not known how the Saayman method calculated the number of visitors, but given reliable ticket sales data for 2005, their figure implies that, over the entire average stay of 4.5 days, visitors attended less than 2 ticketed shows each, which seems implausible given attendance figures from previous studies (Bragge and Snowball 2007).

Another interesting component of table 3.2 is that, when a method of reducing the number of local residents interviewed was introduced in 2006, the percentage of locals dropped from around a 20% average to only 7.5%. However, as can be seen from the visitor numbers excluding locals, the number of outside tourists calculated using the ticket sales and accommodation methods remained roughly the same between 2004 and 2006.

The reporting and interpretation of even very robust visitor number calculation is also far from obvious. Crompton (1999) points out that one of the most contentious parts of any economic impact study is the calculation of visitor numbers because average spending per visitor is multiplied by the number of visitors in order to determine the first round, or direct, economic impact of the event. However, visitor number estimates are also important because there is a prestige component to being able to claim to have many visitors, particularly where the emergence of a number of cultural events in recent years has led to considerable competition.

It is obviously in the interests of the organizers, therefore, to report as many people as possible attending and visitor number calculations are thus quite often based on a certain amount of wishful thinking. Reporting of actual discreet visitors versus visitor days thus needs some clarification since the term "visitor numbers" is not as unambiguous as it sounds. Confusion can lead to many recriminations and disbelief, since it is possible that an obviously smaller event can claim a larger number of visitors, when referring to visitor days, than a much larger one which refers to actual individual people (Snowball 2004).

The confusion arises because of the differing length of time that visitors spend at an event. For example, a festival that is located near large cities is more likely to attract day visitors and short-stay visitors than one that is located in a more isolated area. For example, in 2003 the average visitor at the South African National Arts Festival stayed for about 6 days and there were 20 000 visitors (using the ticket sales and counting methods). However, this figure refers to individual people, so the number of visitor days (i.e. the addition of the number of visitors who were at the festival each day) was in fact around 121 000. The latter figure was, of course, much more acceptable to organizers and also gives a better idea of the size of the event, since it takes into account the characteristics of the particular festival location and makes comparison with other events more meaningful. While a festival located closer to large cities may thus claim to have a larger number of different individuals attending, it is the comparison of visitors per day that is most revealing. However, it must be emphasized that the reporting *method* makes no difference to the economic impact, but (as Loomis 2007 suggests) there may be differences in the spending patterns of shorter-stay and longer-stay attenders that would be reflected in final impact figures.

3.1.4 Producers, Sponsors, Vendors and the Media

Tyrrell and Johnston (2001) argue that, in addition to calculating the spending of visitors or spectators, spending in the impact area by producers, sponsors, vendors and the media should also be included. However, they also point out that, in order to avoid double counting, the source, starting point, destination and reason for the expenditure also needs to be tracked if this method is to be followed.

The implication is that economic impact studies should also include producer surveys – both visiting and local business people and performers – in order to fully capture the economic effects of the event. A survey of local businesses at the South African National Arts Festival showed increased spending of R2.3 million on wages to local residents, materials, site fees, electricity, fuel and living expenses (like accommodation, food and general consumer spending). Visiting traders spent about R38 million in Grahamstown during the 1996 Festival, while visiting performers spent about R1.3 million in 1997, mostly on the provision of accommodation and food for cast members and their families. However, as Tyrrell and Johnston (2001) point out, counting producer expenditure as well as the full value of sponsorship (often used to pay for the costs of artistic productions on the Main program) could result in double counting (Antrobus et al. 1997a).

Surveys of local businesses were also conducted at the 1996 (Antrobus et al. 1997a) and 2003 (Snowball and Antrobus 2003) South African National Arts Festivals. Despite the long time interval, the two business surveys showed very similar results. In both cases, local businesses who provided food and drinks, services (travel agencies, banks) or goods related to festival activities (photography, florists, pharmacies) experienced a significant increase in their monthly income during the event. Both surveys also found that for hardware stores, building contractors and the media (including printing services) business increased directly before the Festival as households and producers prepared for the event. An interesting point from the 2003 survey was that businesses who reported no change in monthly income admitted that, since the festival takes place in the Rhodes University holidays, they would, without the festival, have experienced a fall in income. In other words, events which take place out of season could have an important role in smoothing the cyclical nature of the earnings of local businesses.

Another way of looking at the effects of visitor spending on a local economy is to consider the forward and backward linkages of businesses supplying tourists. Cai et al. (2006) compiled linkage indices for the tourism industry in Hawaii using Leontief and Ghosh supply-driven multipliers. While the backward linkage multipliers are the same for tourist and non-tourist production, there are some interesting differences in the forward linkages. Except for industries specifically geared towards tourist supply, like hotels and air transport, "the web of forward linkages tends to be greater when producing for tourism than for non-tourism consumption" (Cai et al. 2006:43). In other words, tourist related sales may be more beneficial and important for economic activity than non-tourist sales and this could also be a consideration when valuing a tourist event.

However, at most festivals, money-making opportunities are not limited to local traders and the presence of traders from outside the area might have negative implications for local business people. Seaman (1987) argues strongly that, to the extent to which visiting traders provide competition to local stores, the receipts from these activities should be accepted as a substitution for the earnings of those in the local community and thus subtracted from the first round spending in economic impact calculations.

At the South African National Arts Festival the presence of visiting traders was perceived to increase competition in some sectors (particularly amongst clothing retailers) and a cause of congestion and overcrowding that discouraged regular local customers from shopping. If one accepts the Crompton et al. (2001) view that municipal spending on events is expected to generate a financial return for local tax payers, one can understand the frustration of local businesses regarding visiting traders who have paid little or nothing towards the event, but are reaping the benefits, in some cases in direct competition with local businesses.

The value of media coverage, especially in the longer term, could also have a significant effect on the impact area. At the SA National Arts Festival, the Rand value of media coverage of the festival (including newspapers, magazines, online articles, radio and TV) has increased steadily from about R38 million (3.8 million Euros) in 2002 to nearly R80 million (8 million Euros) in 2004. It could thus be argued that the additional publicity has a significant impact on local businesses, private schools, the university, estate agents, game lodges in the surrounding area and other related industries. Such effects would fall into the "long run increases in productivity and economic development" category mentioned by Seaman (2003) and are typically not included in a short run economic impact study.

3.1.5 Supply Constraints and Other Costs

In addition to demand side errors, Seaman (2004) points out that few, if any, cultural economic impact studies have referred to supply side constraints. He argues that if event visitors displace or crowd out visitors who might otherwise have come to the region, then not all event visitor spending can be included as a benefit since, if the event had not taken place, other visitors would have spent in the impact area.

A study of the impact of the Spoleto festival in Charleston, USA actually found that the festival had a negative impact on the local hotel industry (Litvin and Fetter 2006). The authors compared hotel occupancy and daily hotel rates during the festival with those outside of festival times. Despite the fact that the festival is quite long (17 days) and attracts a fairly affluent audience, they found that, on average, Charleston hotels were less full during the festival than in prior and following weeks and that rates were also not higher. They conclude that the festival causes more potential tourists to stay away than it attracts.

The Blackburn study also took into account losses that might have occurred because people who would normally have been in the impact area on non-festival days might have spent more on their normal shopping trip than they did at the festival. However, it is unlikely that such differences would have been large, because 92% of respondents reported that they would not normally have been in the area (Wood 1995:46).

Supply constraints certainly do exist in cities and towns, particularly with regard to accommodation, but Seaman (2004) also gives reasons why this may not occur in certain cases. Firstly, if the timing of the event is annual and well advertised, it is almost certainly known in advance and non-festival tourists could easily reschedule their visit. In fact, some events are specifically scheduled for tourist "low-season" to take advantage of excess capacity. Secondly, some (fairly) small amount of visitor displacement may occur, but this could be offset by additional local spending that would have occurred outside the area, were it not for the festival. In addition, even if there is some crowding out of non-festival visitors, those attending may spend more money than the former group. Finally, it may be that there is enough excess capacity available in the town to cater for both groups.

Crompton (1995; 2006) argues that economic impact analysis should also take into account the opportunity costs of public or private spending on the event as well as any negative impact that the event may have. He points out that local government spending on the event should not be counted as an injection of new funds into the area because the money has come from local residents in the form of taxes, in other words the original "investment" (Crompton et al. 2001). Public funding from outside the region can likewise only be counted as new money (and thus included in the economic impact) if it would not otherwise have been spent in the impact area.

In discussing the economic impact of sports facilities, Johnson and Sack (1986:376) agreed that one needs to ask, "Would a similar or larger amount of state support now be available for a project with more direct economic impact if the tennis complex had not been built?". Although they conceded that this question may be unanswerable, respondents in their study agreed that some of the city's "political capital" had been spent in lobbying for state funds for the project, which, the authors argued, should be acknowledged as a cost (Johnson and Sack 1996:376).

Table 3.3. Benefits and Costs at *Arts in the Park* in Blackburn

Benefits	**Problems**
Local Residents	
Money to the town	Crowds
New visitors to the town	Strangers
Opportunities for family fun	Traffic
Good image for Blackburn	Parking
Bringing community together	Safety on streets
Pride in the area	Litter
Opportunity for new experiences	Vandalism
Something to look forward to	Other crime
Investment in the local area	
Local Businesses	
Money to the town	Demand business can't meet
New visitors to the town	Traffic congestions
Good image of Blackburn	Parking problems
Bringing community together	Litter
Pride in area	Vandalism
New customers to your business	Other crime
Non-local customers for your business	Putting-off regular customers
Greater awareness of your business	
Investment in the local area	
Community Groups	
Community development	Funding
Good image for Blackburn	Traffic congestion
Bringing community together	Parking problems
Pride in the area	Litter
Good publicity for your organisation	Vandalism
Funding for your organisation	Other crime
More involvement in your organisation	Cost of involvement
Awareness of your organisation	
Investment in the local area	
Something to look forward to	

(Wood 2005:43)

While public funds to events might make up a fairly small percentage of the economic impact of the event, studies of whole cultural sectors and non-profit arts organizations in general show that a large percentage of the operating budget comes from government sources. For example, in a study of the economic impact of Florida's arts and cultural industries it was found that 51% of income for these organizations was unearned. Of the total income, federal, state and local government grants made up nearly 19%. In this case, it would be very important to ask questions about how else the money could have been spent and whether it might have been spent in the impact area in any event, especially in the case of local and state grants.

Cost to the host community, in terms of contributions by local government in the form of increased police presence, refuse removal, etc, are also often not subtracted from the total impact figure. An ideal study would consider a wide variety of costs, or negative impacts, such as the pressure on infrastructure, traffic flow problems, overcrowding of the town centre, increased crime, inconvenience to local residents, like lack of parking, crowds, noise and litter, increased competition to local stores and a feeling of antagonism by local store holders to visiting traders (Antrobus et al. 1997, Wood 2005; see table 3.3). Another possible opportunity cost is that of "festival refugees" - those local residents who deliberately leave town when the festival is in progress to avoid the inconvenience. However, in some cases, these residents then let their houses to festival visitors at a profit, so the cost imposed by the loss to the town of the spending of "refugees" during festival may not be significant.

While putting monetary values on longer term benefits and non-market or opportunity costs is often difficult, they could at least be mentioned in the economic impact report in a qualitative way, which would further serve to alert readers to the partial nature of the economic impact figure.

3.2 Indirect Impact

In addition to direct effects, injections of new money into a region generate indirect impact as a result of successive rounds of spending that occur within the impact area: this is known as the multiplier effect. Second round or indirect spending is then added to the estimate of direct spending in order to calculate total economic impact. The following section discusses the use of multipliers, including the importance of the employment multiplier, in calculating this figure.

Once visitor numbers and expenditure have been determined and the direct impact worked out, a multiplier size must be determined in order to calculate indirect impact. The size of the multiplier and thus the effects of successive rounds of spending, will depend on the "leakages" from the economy being considered. Leakages represent the amount of money that is taken out of the host economy in the form of spending by local earners outside the host economy and savings. The amount of leakage (and thus the size of the multiplier) is determined by the level of imports into the impact area, which depends on the size and nature of the host city. For example, in 2003 a business survey was conducted (Snowball and Antrobus 2003) as part of the South African National Arts Festival economic impact study. The impact area, Grahamstown, is a small town with little manufacturing. Local businesses were surveyed to determine the extent to which stock sold in Grahamstown is sourced from outside the region. It was found that, on average, 87% of stock was bought from larger cities in the province. The result suggests that leakages from the area can be expected to be large in second round spending, even if local residents spend festival earnings at local businesses.

Crompton (1995:29) states that, "It is not desirable to take the [multiplier] results of an economic impact assessment from similar studies in other communities and apply it, because the combinations of business interrelationships in communities are structured differently so linkages and leakages will be different". Seaman (2003) reiterates this, but since it is time consuming and expensive to calculate a multiplier from first principles, the tendency in many studies seems to be exactly that, i.e. to use multipliers that have been derived for the region, or for other events, or simply to use an estimate. However, some countries have developed regional input-output models, like Minnesota IMPLAN Group and RIMS II developed by the USA Bureau of Economic Analysis, which can be adjusted to the specific region and help with calculating indirect impact.

One way to estimate multiplier size is to use general rules from meta-analysis. A great deal of literature exists regarding the determinants of regional multipliers, and fortunately, results tend to agree with one another. One very important factor is the size of the region in question and its location. A number of studies (Shahidsaless et al. 1983; Baaijens and Nijkamp 2000 and Greenberg et al. 2002) all found the size of the multiplier to be positively related to both population size and the physical area of the region. Shahidsaless et al. (1983) used the well-known Central Place Theory to further expand on this, finding that the marginal propensity of a region to import is negatively related to the distance to another, larger market. Thus, the closer the impact region to a larger market, the more likely it is to rely on that market for goods and services, the greater the leakages will be and the smaller the multiplier. Greenberg et al. (2002) also find that smaller, rural towns have fewer opportunities for the creation of backward and forward linkages, thus also decreasing multiplier size.

Table 3.4. Variables Included in the Rough-Set Analysis Model

Geographic variables	
Population size (POP)	1. <10,000 2. 10,000 – 100,000 3. 100,000 – 200,000 4. 200,000 – 1,000,000 5. 1,000,000 – 5,000,000 6. no available information
Surface (in km^2) (SUR)	1. <500 (VS = very small) 2. 500 – 10,000 (S = small) 3. 10,000 – 100,000 (M = medium) 4. >100,000 (L = large)
Geographic feature of the area (GEO)	1. island 2. archipelago 3. country (no island) 4. region (no island)
Political autonomy (POA)	1. independent (I) 2. not independent (NI)
Tourist variables	
Number of tourist arrivals (TOA)	1. <10,000 (S) 2. 10,000 – 700,000 (M) 3. >700,000 (L)
Share of arrivals from most important country of origin in total number of arrivals "largest country share" (LCS)	1. <45% (S) 2. 45-75% (M) 3. >75% (L) 4. no available information
Type of tourist attractiveness (ATR)	1. "sun, sand and beach holidays" 2. nature and culture holidays (NC) 3. "mixed" i.e. both "sun, sand and beach holidays" and nature and culture holidays (MI)
Decision variable	
Average tourist income multiplier (TIM)	1. <=0.5 (S) 2. 0.5 – 1.0 (M) 3. 1.0 – 1.5 (L) 4. >1.5 (VL = very large)

(Baaijens and Nijkamp, 1997: 843)

Baaijens and Nijkamp (2000) undertook a very useful meta-analysis of eleven economic impact studies from different countries and developed a "rough-set analysis model. As shown in table 3.4, they provide a means of estimating a multiplier for any region or event based on geographic variables (population size, surface area of the impact area, geographical features of the area and political autonomy) and tourist variables (number of tourists, origin of tourists and tourism type). For example, a small region (less than 500km square) with a population of between 20 000 and 150 000 is likely to have a multiplier of less than 0.5, except where there is a very large (10 000 to 70 000) inflow of people from outside the region.

Table 3.5. Determining the Multiplier Value for Four Arts Festivals

Festival	Year	Multiplier Determination	Direct Impact	Indirect Impact	Implied multiplier value[1]
South African National Arts Festival	1996	"Using a factor of 0,6 for leakages" (1997a:15)	R25.9 million	R4 million	0.18
Edinburgh Festivals	1990 1991	Carried out by Leisure Research Services No discussion of how the "multiplier" was calculated.	43.9m Pounds (Edinburgh and the Lothians)	9.2m Pounds (Edinburgh and the Lothians)	0.22
	1996	Scottish Tourism multiplier study (1996:6)	122m Pounds (Edinburgh)	30m Pounds	0.24
Adelaide Festival	1990	Input-output multipliers generated by Centre for South Australian Studies (1998)	$8.8 million (S. Australia)	$10 million (S. Australia)	1.15
Melbourne Festival	1995	"The derived multipliers for the 1992 Adelaide Formula One Grand Prix have been used to undertake a formal economic evaluation of the 1995 MIFA" (1996:25)	$18.37 million	$20.11 million	1.1

(Snowball and Antrobus 2002:1305)

A second and related method of multiplier estimation is to examine multiplier sizes of similar studies. For example, comparing multipliers used at other arts festivals and taking into account the source of the multiplier (what research it is based on), the size of the impact area and the varying nature of the event can provide a useful starting point. Table 5 below shows such a comparison and can suggest at least upper and lower bounds for other studies. A complication of any such study is that multipliers and their sources are often not explicitly discussed in economic impact reports, leaving them open to misrepresentation and exaggeration, especially where sales multipliers and employment multipliers are used (Crompton 2006).

[1] Except for the South African National Arts Festival, no actual multiplier values were given in any of the festival reports. The above values are thus obtained by inference (comparing direct and indirect income) and may thus be subject to error or over-simplification. However, as a rough comparison, they are still interesting.

Crompton et al. (2001:81) suggest that a sales multiplier, that is, the effect of an extra unit of visitor spending on economic activity, is not actually a very useful measure of economic impact and that it is the personal income multiplier that should be used since "it enables the economic benefits received by residents to be related to the cost they invested". Given the extent of the leakages from local business, turnover in terms of the value of sales is unlikely to be related closely to increases in income. However, specific data on household and business income changes, as a result of the event, is difficult to collect, since respondents are often reluctant to give accurate figures, making the estimation of an income multiplier, in the absence of a pre-existing input-output model, difficult to estimate.

Table 3.6. Edinburgh Festival 2004-2005 Multipliers

	Edinburgh		**The Lothians**		**Scotland**	
	Output	Income	Output	Income	Output	Income
Accommodation	1.52	0.33	1.53	0.35	1.74	0.51
Food and drink	1.70	0.42	1.71	0.45	1.94	052
Entertainment	1.55	0.50	1.56	0.53	1.78	0.67
Shopping	1.54	0.33	1.56	0.35	1.93	0.34
Transport	1.39	0.31	1.40	0.33	1.53	0.36

(Edinburgh Festivals Economic Impact Report 2005:10)

More sophisticated studies provide both sales and income multipliers. For example, the very comprehensive 2004-2005 Edinburgh Festivals report used multipliers from the Scottish Tourism Multiplier Study (1991), which provided sales (output) and income multipliers for various sectors (accommodation, food and drink, entertainment, shopping and transport). As can be seen in table 3.6, the multiplier values vary between sectors, but are generally far smaller for income than for output (taking into account leakages of various sorts from the impact area). In addition, as the impact area increases, so does the size of the multiplier – an expected change, since a larger area generally has fewer leakages.

The employment multiplier shows how many full-time jobs are created as a result of the event or festival. However, as Crompton (1995:22) and Crompton et al. (2001) point out, the employment multiplier is most unreliable because it assumes that, "all existing employees are fully utilized so an increase in external visitor spending will inevitably lead to an increase in the level of employment". Especially for a once a year event, like a festival, it is unlikely that many new jobs would be created. Rather, existing employees would work overtime or "casual" short term help would be hired for the period of the event. An interesting point that other commentators do not seem to take into account, is that not all the jobs created will necessarily be filled by people from the impact area. For example the 1996 South African National Arts Festival study found that, of the 387 temporary jobs created by visiting traders, only 36% were taken by people from the impact area (Antrobus et al. 1996:15). This seems to be largely as a result of the lack of technical skills amongst unemployed local residents, which encourages artists and vendors to bring in their own personnel.

Skinner (2006) argues that the only really reliable way to find out whether the event in question has attracted additional tourists from outside the region (and thus created additional jobs) is to conduct an *ex post* study of the region. Skinner conducts such a study to determine whether three "block buster" art exhibitions in Jackson, Mississippi had any impact on regional income using a time series analysis. The measure of economic growth is the change in employment figures. Taking into account seasonal changes and the business cycle, Skinner (2006:123) finds that, for at least two of the three exhibitions, the estimated job creation from the *ex ante* economic impact studies (721 jobs) is "virtually indistinguishable from the 699 job creation forecast of the filtered time series model". The findings support the idea that, at least in some cases, employment multipliers can give reliable information on the job creation potential of cultural events.

When the cultural good in question is a permanent feature, like the Columbia Museum of Art (CMA), using impact figures to calculate increases in jobs is more feasible. For example, the CMA generates 61 jobs directly from its own operation and 98 jobs indirectly from visitor spending (Miley Gallo and Associates 2006). Since the CMA operates all year round, jobs created directly are likely to be stable, but since tourism is seasonal, the indirect jobs may be an overstatement. As in short event studies, existing staff might be utilized to deal with temporary tourist influxes and so not create "new" jobs.

3.3 Total Economic Impact

The total economic impact of the event can be calculated quite simply by adding the net direct and indirect impact figures. As the preceding discussion has suggested, the method itself is not very complex, but the underlying assumptions that lead to the net direct and indirect figures used in the final calculation are crucial.

Table 3.7 shows the calculation of economic impact at the South African National Arts Festival over a number of years. While the study is not very sophisticated (only one multiplier is used and, owing to data unavailability, an assumption of the size of immediate outflows was made based on past studies), it does serve to show the mechanics of the calculation and give an idea of trends. Total visitor spending (row A) is calculated by multiplying the average spending per visitor by the estimated number of visitors. This figure included only *additional* spending by local residents. The presence of "time switchers" and "casuals" was investigated, but found to be negligible – expected, given the relative remoteness and small size of the host city. The potential negative effects of the "crowding out" of local suppliers and "festival refugees" was not included, but was expected to be small.

To this is added sponsorship (assumed not to have been spent in the region if not for the festival) and rental earnings by local organisations holding shares in the Village Green craft market. In row C, an estimate of the immediate outflows (earnings by non-local traders and performers) is made by extrapolating from the 1996 data (the last time a producer survey was conducted), which showed outflows as approximately 30% of total visitor spending. Row D shows the net direct impact and E the indirect impact, calculated by multiplying direct impact by the estimated multiplier.

Table 3.7. Economic Impact Calculations at the South African Arts Festival

Category (All figures in millions of Rands)[2]	**1996**	**1997**	**2003**	**2004**	**2006**
A. Total visitor spending	25.9	23.5	27	30	33.6
B. Sponsorship and craft market	1.5	1.5	13	13	13
C. Immediate outflows (30% of A + B)	7.6	7	12	13	14
D. Net direct impact (A + B – C)	19.8	15	28	30	32.6
E. Indirect impact (D x 0.18)	3.4	2.7	5	5.5	5.9
F. Total economic impact	23.3	17.7	33	35.5	38.5
Total impact at 2000 prices (Rands)[3]	30	21	27	28.6	25.5

While not as accurate as an ideal study, impact figures over time can provide useful information on the evolution of an event, as well as an indication of its financial value. Noteworthy points of the above table are the fall in ticket sales, visitor numbers and real economic impact from 1996 to 1997, with a slow recovery being reflected in the 2003 and 2006 figures. However, ticket sales of 1996 levels (184 761) have not been seen again, with 2003 and 2004 figures hovering around 100 000, but showing an up-

[2] Where one Rand is equal to about ten Euros

[3] Using the Consumer Price Index from Statistics South Africa

ward trend. The same is true of real economic impact (at 2000 prices), which is now starting to approach 1996 levels again.

The major reason posited for the decline is the emergence in the New South Africa of many other arts festivals, the greatest rivals at present being the *Klein Karoo Nationale Kunstefees* (KKNK), started in 1995 and catering for a mostly Afrikaans speaking audience, and the *Aardklop* Arts Festival that began in 1998. Perhaps the decline is also partly due to the freedom of expression and speech in the New South Africa. During the apartheid era, the National Arts Festival played a very important role as an outlet for otherwise repressed expressions of political and social protest. Once the elections had been held and the New South Africa was underway, its role necessarily had to change and the falling off of ticket sales and economic impact may have been a reflection of this period of uncertainty (Snowball and Webb 2007). The stabilization and growth of the festival in recent years may thus indicate that this tricky period has been successfully negotiated, even in the face of increased competition from other festivals, and that it is finding its place in the new democracy.

3.4 Conclusions

A thoughtfully designed economic impact study can produce credible results that can be a useful way of valuing a cultural event or resource. However, the opportunities for misrepresentation are quite considerable and care should be taken at each stage of the process. While economic impact figures can be useful in arguing for the public and private support of the arts, this relies on their being regarded as believable, particularly where comparisons over time, or with other tourist events, are made.

Quite often, economists may feel pressured to come up with the "right", that is, large, economic impact figure, especially if the study has been commissioned by event organisers or sponsors. Sometimes, it can be very difficult to present figures that may not show such a big financial impact and it is then useful to be able to suggest other ways of evaluating the cultural resource. One of the most popular methods is contingent valuation, or willingness to pay studies, which will be discussed in the next chapter.

References

Adelaide Festival Study, McDonald, S. (1990) The Adelaide Festival: the economic impact. Centre for South Australian economic studies: University of Adelaide, Adelaide.

Antrobus, G., Williams, V., Fryer, D., Khumalo, B., Streak, J. & Webb, A., (1996) The economic impact of the 1996 Standard Bank National Arts Festival. Department of Economics, Rhodes University: Grahamstown

Antrobus, G., Webb, A. and Mather, D. (1997) The economic impact of the 1997 Standard Bank National Arts Festival. Department of Economics, Rhodes University: Grahamstown.

Antrobus, G. and Snowball, J. (2004) National Arts Festival 2004: Festino Survey. Department of Economics, Rhodes University: Grahamstown.

Baaijens, S. and Nijkamp, P. (2000) Meta-analytic methods for comparative and exploratory policy research: An application to the assessment of regional tourist multipliers. Journal of Policy Modeling 22,7:821-858.

Bragge, B. and Snowball, J. (2007) Why arts proponents love economic impact studies and economists hate them. Paper submitted to AIMAC Cultural Policy conference, Valencia, Spain.

Cai, J., Leung, P. and Mak, J. (2006) Tourism's forward and backward linkages. Journal of Travel Research 45:36-52.

Cap Gemini Ernst & Young; Milward Brown Ulster (2005) Study of the economic and social impact of subsidised theatre in Northern Ireland. [On line] Available:http:///www.artscouncilni.org/departs/all/reports/research/subsidised%20theatre.pdf [Accessed 11/05/07].

Crompton, J., Lee, S. and Schuster, T. (2001) A guide for undertaking economic impact studies: The Springfest example. Journal of Travel Research 40:79-87.

Crompton, J. (1995) Economic impact analysis of sports facilities and events: Eleven sources of misapplication. Journal of Sports Management 9:14-35.

Crompton, J. (2006) Economic impact studies: Instruments for political shenanigans? Journal of Travel Research 45:67-82.

Edinburgh Festivals Study (1991) Final Report: Edinburgh festivals study 1990/91. Scottish Tourist Board: Edinburgh.

Edinburgh's Year Round Festivals, 2004-2005 Economic Impact Study (2005). SQW Economic Development Consultants and TNS Travel and Tourism: Edinburgh.

Getz, D. (1991), Festivals, Special Events and Tourism, Van Nostrand Reinhold, New York, NY

Greenberg, M., Lewis, D., Frisch, M., Lowrie, K., and Mayer, H. (2002) The US department of energy's regional economic legacy: special dimensions of a half century of dependency. Socio-economic Planning Sciences 36:109-125.

Johnson, A. and Sack, A. (1996) Assessing the value of sports facilities: the importance of non-economic factors. Economic Development Quarterly 10,4:369-382.

Litvin, S. and Fetter, E. (2006) Can a festival be too successful? A review of Spoleto, USA. International Journal of Contemporary Hospitality Management 18,1:41-49.

Loomis, J. (2007) Correcting for on-site visitor sampling bias when estimating the regional economic effects of tourism. Tourism economics 12,1:41-47.

Melbourne International Festival of the Arts (1994). A report on the economic and social impacts. Ernst and Young, Melbourne.

Melbourne International Festival of the Arts (1996) Evaluation of attendance and economic impact. Commissioned by the City of Melbourne and MIFA: Melbourne

Miley Gallo and Associates (2006) The economic impact of the Columbia Museum of Art on the city of Columbia [On line] Available: http://www.colmusart.org/assets/files/ecoimpact.pdf [Accessed 15/05/07].

Saayman, M., Slabbert, E. and Saayman, A. (2005) The economic impact and profile of visitors to the Grahamstown National Arts Festival 2005. Institute for Tourism and Leisure Studies, North-West University, Potchefstroom.

Seaman, B. (1987) Arts impact studies: A fashionable excess. Towse, R. (Ed) 1997 Cultural economics: the arts, the heritage and the media industries Vol. 2 Edward Elgar: Cheltenham

Seaman, B. (2003b) The economic impact of the arts in Handbook of Cultural Economics. Towse, R. (Ed) Edward Elgar.

Seaman, B. (2004) The supply constraint problem in economic impact analysis: An arts/sports disparity. Presented at Lasting effects: assessing the future of economic impact analysis conference, New York.

Shahidsaless, S., Gillis, W. and Shaffer, R. (1983) Community characteristics and employment multipliers in non-metropolitan counties, 1950 – 1970. Land Economics 59,1: 84-93.

Skinner, S. (2006) Estimating the real growth effects of blockbuster art exhibits: A time series approach. Journal of Cultural Economics 30:109-125.

Snowball, J. and Antrobus, G. (2001) Consumer Research: A survey of visitors at the 2001 National Arts Festival, Grahamstown. Department of Economics, Rhodes University: Grahamstown.

Snowball, J. and Antrobus, G. (2003) Economic valuation of the 2003 Grahamstown National Arts Festival: economic impact, business and household surveys. Department of Economics, Rhodes University: Grahamstown.

Snowball, J. and Antrobus, G. (2002) Valuing the arts: Pitfall in economic impact studies of arts Festivals. South African Journal of Economics 70,8:1297-1319.

Snowball, J. and Antrobus, G. (2006) National Arts Festival 2006 Festino Survey. Department of Economics, Rhodes University: Grahamstown.

Tyrrell, T. and Johnston, R. (2001) A framework for assessing direct economic impacts of tourist events: Distinguishing origins, destinations and causes of expenditure. Journal of Travel Research 40:94-100.

Tyrrell, T. and Johnson, R. (2006) The economic impacts of tourism: A special issue. Journal of Travel Research 45:3-7.

Wessex Group (2000) Virginians for the Arts: The economic impact of arts and cultural organisations in Virginia. [On line] Available: http://www.vaforarts.org/tempdocs/Wessex.pdf [Accessed 23/05/07]

Wilton, J. and Nickerson, N. (2006) Collecting and using visitor spending data. Journal of Travel Research 45:17-25

Wood, E. (2005) Measuring the economic and social impacts of local authority events. International Journal of Public Sector Management 18,1:37-53

4 The Contingent Valuation Method

In addition to the economic or financial benefits that the arts and heritage provide, they also supply us with non-market goods, like pleasure, national pride, building and expressing community identity, etc. (as discussed in chapter one). Such values relate to the public good nature of the arts and are sometimes referred to as positive externalities because they are *external* to the market. Expressing these values in monetary terms is not always possible (or desirable, as Klamer argues), but, as in environmental economics, such value estimates can be a useful indication of public (non-expert) opinions and reveal values not associated with purely financial gains.

There are a number of ways in which the value of externalities provided by public goods may be measured and they can broadly be divided into revealed and stated preference methods. Revealed preference methods involve gathering market data on actual spending, such as how much it cost to travel to a heritage site or how much more the property in a particular culture-rich area costs. Stated preference methods rely on hypothetical scenarios and directly ask respondents what value they place on a good.

The travel cost method measures the access costs of users to a specific site or event, i.e. what consumers are willing to pay in travel costs in order to attend, for example, an arts festival, a heritage site or a museum (Mundy and McLean 1998:292). The hedonic price method assumes that households "migrate into or out of geographic regions based on tradeoffs between quality of life in those regions and differences in housing prices" (Ready et al. 1997:439), i.e. what consumers are willing to pay in increased housing prices (or decreased wages) in order to live in an area that has certain cultural amenities. The contingent valuation (CV) method, so-called because the valuation is contingent upon the given scenario, asks respondents directly what they would be willing to pay, or willing to accept, in a hypothetical market situation to conserve or expand some public good (Ready et al. 1997:439). The CV method also includes stated choice or choice experiment surveys, which ask respondents to choose between various scenarios in which the levels of the attributes making up the good are varied (further discussed in chapter six)[1].

Although not a focus of this book, the travel cost method is becoming more popular as a valuation method in cultural economics and a number of recent studies have used it. For example, Poor and Smith (2004) valued the historic city of St. Mary's, considered to be one of the most significant historical sites in the US, using a zonal travel cost method. Visitor benefits are shown to be extensive, but the authors point out that they are measuring only use values and that non-use value may also be important. Bedate et al. (2004) use travel cost to estimate consumer surplus for cultural goods (two cathedrals, a music event and a museum) in the Castilla y Leon region in Spain. Other examples are Boter et al. (2005) who use the method to value Dutch Museums, and Alberini and Longo (2006) who combine travel cost and contingent valuation to estimate domestic visitors' use and non-use values for cultural heritage sites in Armenia.

The hedonic pricing valuation method has proved not to be very useful in the case of cultural goods because it has been shown that the arts and cultural activities are by no means the most important determinants of either individuals' or firms' decisions to move to a particular area. Also, the particular cultural attraction would have to be very large and well known in order to enter into the decision making process at all (Bille and Schulze 2006). Although the work of Florida (2002) has done much to forge a link between the "creative classes" and economic growth and development, causality has not been conclusively proven. As a result, the hedonic pricing method has not been much used in cultural good valuation.

Contingent valuation (CV) is by far the most popular valuation method, both in environmental economics (where it started) and in cultural economics, because it is currently the only method of measuring non-use values. The National Oceanic and Atmospheric Administration (NOAA) review on the use of CV studies published in the Federal Register in 1993, states that,

> "This [CV] approach allows the valuation of a wider variety of non-market goods and services than is possible with any of the aforementioned techniques (site-specific valuation methods such as travel cost, factor income approach, or hedonic pricing models) and is the only

[1] Both willingness to pay and choice experiments (also referred to as conjoint analysis) are part of contingent valuation or stated preference methods, but the term "contingent valuation" is often used to refer to willingness to pay studies, while "stated preference" often means choice experiments.

method currently available for the express purpose of estimating passive use values" (NOAA 1993).

Passive use values (also referred to as non-use values) are defined by Carson et al. (1999:100) as "those portions of total value (measured by WTP or WTA) that are unobtainable using indirect measurement techniques which rely on observed market behaviour". Thus, while methods like travel cost and hedonic pricing will capture the non-market value of the good to users, this does not include people who, for whatever reason, might be non-users, but who are still willing to pay to preserve or support the public good. In other words, passive use values require no direct involvement of the user with the good at all and "as a result, economists are fond of saying that passive use leaves no behavioural trace" (Carson et al. 2003:258). Diamond and Hausman (1993) outline three types of non-use values: the value of one's own possible future use of the good, the value of one's enjoyment of the use of the good by others (also called bequest value) and finally, values unrelated to human use of the good.

A number of models can be used to estimate willingness to pay (WTP) or willingness to accept (WTA) functions (Johansson 1993; Carson et al. 1999), but the general theory can be presented as follows: if initial utility (U_0) is a function of certain levels of income, prices, private goods and public goods, and an increase in the amount of public good supplied increases utility (U_1), then WTP represents (or exactly offsets) the difference between U_0 and U_1, such that the final level of utility is unchanged. In the WTA case, the decline in utility is exactly equal to the increase in utility due to the compensation amount.

The rest of this chapter discusses the use of WTP studies in cultural economics and some of the problems associated with the method.

4.1 Examples of WTP Studies in Cultural Economics

Willingness to pay studies have been used in the valuation of a wide variety of cultural goods. The appendix table to this chapter gives some examples of studies that have been conducted on the arts, heritage, historical and archaeological sites, museums, libraries, broadcasting and theatre. While it is not possible to discuss all these case studies here, the following section gives a brief summary of some them and others are used as examples in later methodological discussions.

WTP Studies of the Arts and Theatre

One of the earliest arts WTP studies was conducted by Thompson, Throsby and Withers (1983) in Australia. The survey asked a random sample of 827 Sydney residents detailed questions about the arts, including their interests, attendance, participation, perception of benefits or costs, views on public funding and WTP to support the arts under various conditions. Eighty per cent of respondents were interested in at least one of the art forms mentioned and there was wide-spread agreement with the idea that the arts provided "community public benefits", such as national pride, assistance in understanding and interpreting "our country and its culture", as well as general educational value (Throsby and Withers 1985:591). Just under three-quarters of respondents voted for increased arts subsidy at a significantly higher level than government support at the time. The authors conclude that "The notion of the arts as a luxury and as only an elite pleasure foisted on an unknowing or resentful public is simply wrong" (Throsby and Withers 1985:594).

Another early WTP study on the arts was conducted by Morrison and West (1986) in Ontario, consisting of a sample of 463 households, using telephone interviews. In particular, they wished to investigate whether increasing arts subsidies would benefit mainly the wealthy arts attenders, or whether what they refer to as the "external" benefits from the performing arts, justified tax spending even for non-attenders. The Morrison and West (1986:68) survey posed the following question to the relevant portion of their sample:

> "Since you personally do not go to live performances of drama, dance, classical music or opera, what benefits, if any, do you feel you get from these things in return for paying taxes towards them?"

Responses (not suggested by the interviewer) covered many of those proposed by the theory, such as national pride, welfare to future generations and educational importance. However, 40% of respondents claimed that they gained no benefit. It should be noted that, unlike the Thompson et al. (1983) study, which found that public arts funding in Australia was significantly below what the public was willing to support, Morrison and

West (1986:69) found that the majority of Canadians were not in support of an increase in arts funding, suggesting that, "all external benefits have already been internalised or, in other words, that no marginally relevant externalities remain".

Studies which combined willingness to pay with economic impact methods were conducted by Thompson et al. (1998 and 2002) on the impact of the arts on the Kentucky economy. In addition to money spent on tickets, Kentucky households stated that they were willing to pay $21.8 million (1998) and $16.9 million (2002) in order to avoid a 25% decline in the number of arts performances in Kentucky. "The value of these donations [WTP] give a minimum estimate of the difference between the value that Kentuckians place on the arts and the amount they pay for arts performances through ticket prices" (Thompson et al. 1998:7), and thus provide an indication of the monetary value of the public good benefits provided by the arts. The economic impact of the arts in Kentucky was calculated to be $22 million and provided 1 324 jobs (Thompson et al. 1998:18). By including the contingent valuation measure of the value of the arts as a public good, the estimated value of the arts to the Kentucky economy was found to be almost double what it would have been if only the economic impact figures had been used (Thompson et al. 1998:3).

An often-cited study by Bille Hanson (1997) estimated the value of the Royal Theatre in Copenhagen to a random sample of the Danish population using 1843 telephone interviews. Although only about 7% of the population actually use the Theatre, non-use values were found to be quite substantial, with a median WTP of 60 DKK and a mean value of 154 DKK. She concludes that "the citizenry's WTP is of a magnitude which at the least measures up to the public subsidy which is given to the theatre" (1997:18).

Glass et al. (1999) surveyed 515 households in Kansas asking a dichotomous choice WTP question for "a substantial increase in the amount of arts activity in your local area" (Glass et al. 1999:28) to be paid for by an increase in tax. It was found that Kansas households would be WTP $19 million in increased taxes for the rather vaguely defined "substantial increase" and that, as in other studies, participants in arts events or education programmes were more likely to favour the increase. In addition to this, an economic impact study found that expenditure by the Kansas Arts Commission, which provides grants to arts organizations, resulted in an impact of just over $1 million in the region.

In a developing country example, Snowball (2005) conducted a WTP study of two South African arts festivals using telephone interviews of the local populations of the towns in which the festivals take place. In a country with wealth still partly divided along racial lines, a major point of investigation was whether low income African-origin residents perceived the arts festivals as providing as much value as the high income, mostly European origin residents. Results show that, despite lower average attendance at festival events, a higher percentage of respondents from the low income areas were willing to pay to prevent the festivals from getting smaller, although their average WTP amount was lower.

Museums

Sanz et al. (2003) conducted a survey of 1108 visitors to the National Museum of Sculpture in Valladolid, Spain, to find out if they would be willing to contribute to a preservation fund for the museum. They also conducted telephone interviews with 1041 Valladolid households to determine non-use values for the museum. The mean WTP of direct users was between 25 and 40 , and passive use, option, bequest and existence value (i.e. non-use value) was between 27 and 36 .

Maddison and Foster (2003) asked 400 visitors to the British Museum whether they would be willing to pay to reduce congestion (indicated by photographs showing varying numbers of people in the museum). They find that there is a "congestion externality of £8.05 per person" (2003:186) and suggest that, rather than the current free entry, a charge should be made at busy periods. This is particularly feasible, since most visitors are foreign with high household incomes and only 1% of visitors interviewed said that they came to the Museum because it was free.

Historical Sites and Heritage

There have been a large number of willingness to pay studies conducted on historical sites and heritage in general. For example, Willis (1994) used a payment card (listing various willingness to pay amounts) to elicit visitor's WTP an entrance fee to Durham Cathedral, as opposed to a voluntary contribution payment method being used at the time. However, he found that the revenue from voluntary contributions was actually slightly larger than the revenue that could have been collected by charging one price based on average WTP. Using photographs to illustrate various scenrios, Pollicino and Maddison (2001) asked a random sample of residents of Lincoln whether they would be willing to pay to decrease the time between cleaning their Cathedral from 40 to 10 years. Although Lincoln Cathedral is acknowledged to be one of the most beautiful cathedrals in the UK, it suffers significant damage due to air pollution. They found an average household WTP of between £15 and £23 and then calculated the annual damage to the Cathedral as a result of air pollution to be between £0.4 million and £0.6 million.

Examples of other heritage or historical sites that have been valued using WTP studies are Nidaros Cathedral in Norway (Navrud and Strand 1992), the Fez Medina in Morocco (Carson et al. 1997), Warkworth Castle in England (Willis and Powe 1998), Rivoli castle in Italy (Scarpa et al. 1998), the Surrey Archival History Centre in the UK (Ozdemiroglu and Mourato 2001), the historic centre of the town of Noto in Sicily (Cuccia and Signorello 2002), Bulgarian Monasteries (Mourato et al. 2002), historical shipwrecks off the coast of North Carolina (Whitehead and Finney 2003), the restoration of an old Arab pirate tower in Valencia (Del Saz Salazar and Marques 2005) and many others.

A recent interesting advance is the use of WTP studies to place a value on cultural heritage in developing countries, where resources for heritage preservation are typically limited. Kim et al. (2007) use a WTP study to value the Changdeok Palace, a World Cultural Heritage site in Korea. Interviews were conducted with tourists visiting the site, who were given information about the historical and cultural value of the Palace and then asked their WTP to improve services (tourist guides), research and upkeep of the site. They find that the mean WTP of between \$5.70 and \$6 is 2.5 times higher than the current admission price. Dutta et al. (2007) report on a similar study of Prinsep Ghat in Calcutta, India. A random sample of 181 Calcutta residents was interviewed and asked whether they would be willing to pay to renovate the site and develop it as a tourist attraction. They find that the cost of renovation is far below the WTP estimate and conclude that using market figures (i.e. profits from tourism) to value historic sites significantly underestimates their total economic value.

Archaeological sites

Related to studies of heritage sites and historical buildings are those valuing aspects of archaeological sites. For example, Ringanti et al. (1998) interviewed visitors to the Campi Flegrei Archaeological Park in Naples to determine their willingness to pay to conserve parts of, and the whole, site. Maddison and Mourato (1999) used a WTP study to calculate the welfare effect of removing the roads around Stonehenge (placing one in an underground tunnel and closing another). Interestingly, while a greater percentage of those surveyed chose the current scenario, because there were significant positive externalities to drivers on current roads being able to see the sight, the average WTP to provide the tunnel was higher, suggesting greater intensity of preference in the latter case. Mourato et al. (2004) interviewed visitors to the site of Machu Picchu historic sanctuary in Peru to determine their maximum WTP for access to the site. They then show how such data can be used to estimate a demand curve and to analyse the likely effects of various proposed entry fee changes.

Broadcasting

In one of the very first WTP studies, Bohm (1972) conducted some experiments on WTP for a half-hour popular TV programme in Sweden. While the good itself was not very interesting, experimentation with subsamples on the effects of incentives to over- and understate WTP was the foundation of the "Bohm interval" method of detecting hypothetical bias (further discussed later in this chapter). Papandrea (1999) investigated WTP for mandatory local television programming in Australia. The majority of those interviewed were positive about the benefits of Australian programming, but only 12% of the sample thought it should be increased, while 65% felt it should stay at current levels.

Libraries

Willingness to pay studies of libraries have demonstrated their public and private good characteristics – that is, that it is not necessarily only those who use the library directly who benefit. Harless and Allen (1999) surveyed members of the Virginia Commonwealth University to establish their WTP for extended reference desk services. Mean values for 18.5 additional service hours (excluding 10% of the highest and lowest values) were $5.59 per semester for students and $45.76 for faculty. In this case, the benefits exceeded the cost of providing the additional service by a ratio of 3.5 to 1. Holt et al. (1999) conducted a survey of the St Louis Public Library to determine how much users would be willing to pay to avoid library closure and, in a separate sub-sample, how much they would be willing to accept in compensation for library closure. 88% of respondents were unwilling to accept any reasonable level of compensation for library closure, indicating significant non-market values.

Finally, Aabo (2005) attempted to measure both use and non-use values of public libraries in Norway. Findings showed that the benefits are four times higher than the costs. In addition, only 3% of the sample indicated that closing down their local library in order to spend the money on some other local project would increase their welfare.

4.2 The WTP Method and the Exxon Controversy

Contingent valuation surveys were, until about 1990, a little-studied branch of environmental economics. However, on the 24th of March 1989, the Exxon Valdez oil tanker, misjudging its position, crashed into Bligh Reef in Prince William Sound off the coast of Alaska (Carson et al. 2003). The tanker released 11 million gallons of crude oil into the Sound, hugely damaging what had been one of the most environmentally pristine areas on earth. The local newspaper, *Anchorage Daily News* (1999), in a retrospective of the oil spill ten years after the event, termed the accident "one of the worst human-caused environmental disasters in history". The newspaper also reports the slowness of the response to the disaster as a result of not having disaster management programmes in place.

However, all this was to change when it became known that the State of Alaska and the Federal Government intended to use a contingent valuation study to litigate against the oil company, arguing that they were liable for more than just the clean-up costs and lost income, but also for the non-market value of the huge environmental damage caused to the Sound. As a result of this, "the attention paid to the conceptual underpinnings and estimation techniques for passive use value changed rather abruptly" (Carson et al. 2003).

Early in 1990, Carson et al. (2003) were commissioned to run a huge WTP study to determine the value to the American public of the Prince William Sound, the details of which have recently been published in *Environmental and Resource Economics* (2003). After being given a large amount of information, including maps and photographs, respondents were asked to vote for or against a proposal to provide an escort ship programme for oil tankers entering the sound. The results of the survey showed that American households were willing to pay about $2.8 billion for the programme. Although the case was settled out of court, the State Attorney General was reported as saying that the CV study "was the heavy artillery in our briefcase" (*Anchorage Daily News* 1993).

In an attempt to discredit the method, the oil company appears to have funded quite a lot of research into the method. Many of these papers were presented at a conference organized by Cambridge Economics, Inc., held in Washington in 1992 and were published with transcriptions of discussions (Hausman (editor) 1993). Although there are few direct references to it, traces of a violent debate and doubt over the bias of Exxon sponsored research remain. For example, in a 1996 article, Diamond adds a footnote to the effect that, while earlier research may have been funded by the Exxon company, the current article (also on CV criticism) was not. Carson et al. (1993:258-9) comment that "Much of the recent criticism of CV is contained in the Exxon-sponsored conference volume ..." At the conference itself, discussion was often heated, with one non-economist referring to the process during a discussion as "a milieu of duelling economists" (Hausman 1993:458). Despite this, however, the papers presented at this conference set the agenda for contingent valuation research and many of the issues raised are still being debated.

In their 2003 article, Carson et al. conclude that the out of court settlement between the State of Alaska and the Exxon Company approximated the CV value quite well. They also note that, since 1989, there have been no major oil spills in American waters, perhaps suggesting that the inclusion of non-use values in possible litigation, while not uncontested, is still acting as a significant deterrent to oil companies taking risks that may result in pollution.

One of the results of this heated debate was the National Oceanic and Atmospheric Administration review on the use of CV studies (NOAA 1993), chaired by, amongst others, Kenneth Arrow and Robert Solow. The report concluded that, if its guidelines and recommendations were followed, "CV studies can produce estimates reliable enough to be the starting point of a judicial process of damage assessment, including lost passive-use values" (NOAA 1993:24). Another result was that, although CV studies have now been applied in many fields, most of the methodological research has been conducted in the field of environmental economics.

4.3 Criticisms and Defence of the CV Method

Ever since the Exxon case in the early 1990s, there has been a storm of sometimes quite vehement criticism of the CV method (mostly represented by willingness to pay studies) and equally heated defence. The following section reviews some of the major areas of criticism, focusing on the nature of hypothetical markets and the ways in which CV responses have violated the assumptions of neoclassical economic theory.

4.3.1 Hypothetical Markets and the "Free Rider" Problem

One of the first questions many critics of the willingness to pay method ask is how one can be sure that respondents will tell the truth. The NOAA panel (1993:7) raised the issue of "implausibly large responses" and it has since been found in many studies that hypothetical markets tend to overestimate WTP. The current debate has largely shifted from whether or not hypothetical bias, defined as the difference between hypothetical and real WTP, exists to a discussion on how the problem can be detected and controlled. There are two major directions in this field. Firstly, there are those who, by comparing real and hypothetical valuations for the same good, seek to find some method of calibration for hypothetical responses that will bring them more in line with real responses. Secondly, there is ongoing research into how questionnaire design can be used to moderate this form of bias.

There are at least two possible reasons that respondents may overstate their willingness to pay for a good in a hypothetical scenario. Firstly, they may be "free riders" – that is, they are deliberately over-stating their true value of the good (knowing they won't really have to pay the amount they nominate) in order to ensure that it is provided. Secondly, respondents may not be making a realistic market decision, taking into account their budgets. In this case, they are expressing a positive attitude towards the good, rather than an accurate valuation. The following section provides a historical background to the hypothetical bias and related "free rider" problem in contingent valuation and reviews the current debates regarding calibration and questionnaire design.

The Bohm Test for Hypothetical Bias

The liability or free-rider problem in estimating the value to individuals of public or mixed goods was first formally acknowledged by Samuelson (1954). He pointed out that, so long as all goods were private and operated in a perfectly competitive market, there was no incentive for individuals to misrepresent their demand since they all aspired to their highest indifference curve within the constraints of a budget. However, for a public good, voting or signalling other than that of the market must be used: "Now it is in the selfish interest of each person to give false signals, to pretend to have less interest in a given collective consumption activity than they really do" (Samuelson 1954:388). This is the central problem with a social economy or a socially shared public good. By pretending that it is less valuable than it in fact is, any individual may hope to escape personal liability for their consumption of the good.

Samuelson (1954:389) added, however, that the failure of the market did not mean that there was no optimal solution to the provision of public goods:

> "Given sufficient knowledge, the optimal decisions can always be found by scanning over all the attainable states of the world and selecting the one which according to the postulated ethical welfare function is best. The solution exists; the problem is how to find it".

Some of the earliest and seminal research on the existence and control for free riding and hypothetical bias in WTP studies was conducted by Peter Bohm (1972). He argued that the theory of the free rider motive to conceal demand preferences had not been empirically tested and that other, perhaps stronger, motives could result in honest demand revelation. Bohm (1972) thus conducted a series of WTP studies on small groups of paid volunteers. The public good under discussion was a new TV comedy series. Each respondent was asked to state the highest admission fee that they would pay to see a half-hour programme. If the stated cost of showing the programme was smaller or equal to the amount that the group was prepared to pay, the programme would be shown and each person would have to pay something.

The first group were told that, should the programme be shown, they would have to pay the amount they had stated; the second group would have to pay some percentage of the amount they stated; group three, a variable amount; group four, a flat rate; and group five, nothing. The results revealed that there was no significant difference of the stated WTP between any of the groups. This is particularly surprising between groups one and five, since conventional free rider theory would postulate that group one people would have an incentive to understate their WTP, while group five would have an incentive to overstate. A later non-hypothetical study for an actual public good (Bohm 1984) verified these results.

Bohm (1972:125) did not, however, rule out the possibility that differences in stated WTP existed when different liability methods were used, but suggested that the results of the experiment showed that these differences were not very large. Rather than using the conventional cheating strategies which economic theory postulates, he suggested that group one revealed a true WTP because, "people tend to regard their impact on total demand, however small it may be, as important" and that group five did likewise because "they feel morally obliged to do so".

A recent study, using students in a computer-based experiment by Murphy et al. (2005b), also suggests that the "free rider" phenomenon in WTP studies is not as severe as one might think. Using post-decision questions, such as how much the decisions of others affected the respondent's WTP, they conclude that "most respondents were neutral with respect to the likelihood that others would free ride and report that free riding had little influence on their own payment decision" (2005:336).

There is also a stream of recent research that argues that there is no evidence of hypothetical bias at all. In a laboratory experiment with 264 students divided into smaller groups, Vossler and McKee (2006) tested the difference in response to real and hypothetical willingness to pay situations. They found no evidence of hypothetical bias since "voting decisions do not vary systematically when payment is hypothetical versus when it is real". In a similar sort of experiment, Guzman and Kolstad (2006) argue that, in hypothetical markets, respondents are unlikely to incur the opportunity cost of gathering more information about the good in question. Since willingness to pay tends to increase as information about the good increases, this suggests that contingent valuation estimated in hypothetical markets might actually be *downwardly* biased. Murphy et al. (2005a and 2005b) find that hypothetical bias does exist, but is much more prevalent at higher willingness to pay amounts.

Morrison and West (1986:63), in their study of the performing arts in Canada, agree that other motives may counteract the free rider problem, but argue that it is the very *unimportance* of individual answers that would ensure honesty; "The fact that respondents may perceive their views to have little or no weight is likely to induce true preferences and to reduce strategic bias rather than encourage false or inaccurate responses". They also argued that those who do not want to be part of the study could more easily refuse the interview than provide untrue answers.

What Bohm (1979) suggested was that economic motives to over- or understate demand and WTP may (or may not) be overcome by other, perhaps moral, motives, and that these motives may change depending on factors such as the issue under discussion and questionnaire design. Given that the motives for over- or understating WTP may be different in each situation, he proposed what came to be called "the Bohm interval method" as a way of verifying the results of the study.

Bohm (1979) argued that if two similar sample groups were given the same questionnaire, but differing liabilities, and that the directions of the likely misrepresentation of demand for the two groups were known, then they could act as controls for each other. This effect could be further enhanced because there may be unknown reasons for the participants to reveal their preferences accurately, as suggested above. For example, two population samples were asked to reveal their preferences for a particular public good project. If the project was to be carried out (i.e. the WTP for the project exceeded or was at least equal to its cost) then the first group would have to pay the amount that they stated (or some related sum), while the second group would be asked to pay only a nominal amount or nothing at all. In this case, there was a clear economic incentive for the first group to understate, and for the second group to overstate their WTP.

If the average WTP for both parties was not significantly different, then one could assume that no serious misrepresentation had taken place and that motives to reveal true preferences had dominated. Even if there was a (fairly small) difference between the WTP of the two groups, the responses of the first group could be regarded as a bottom limit and those of the second group as a top limit - the true WTP occurring in the interval between the two. However, the larger the interval, the less accurate the study could be (Bohm 1979).

A number of studies since have used some version of the Bohm interval with largely similar findings to Bohm's original tests. The Thompson et al. (1983) study of the arts in Australia used the Bohm interval method to control for the free-rider problem, but differed from the Bohm method by asking both the liable and non-liable questions in the same sample. Respondents were asked the following two questions (amongst others) directly after each other:

> (a) What is the maximum you would want paid out of your taxes each year to support the arts at their current level, if your taxes were adjusted so that you would actually have to pay the amount you nominated?
>
> (b) Now, suppose that there would be no change in your total taxes. What is the maximum you would want paid out of your taxes each year to support the arts at their current level?
> (Throsby and Withers 1985:32)

In order to check that the question order was not significant, half the sample were asked these questions in the above order and the other half in the reverse order. In any event, no significant difference in response was noted. Where some difference between the liable and non-liable response was found, it was not as great as would have been expected. For example, 14.5% of the sample nominated a WTP of $61 - $100 per year when not liable which decreased to 13.4% when liable.

Throsby and Withers (1986) estimated that about 65% of respondents to their survey gave honest WTP answers, i.e. their WTP did not differ between the liability and non-liability questions. Of the remaining 35%, only one third were "strong" free riders (those who give a positive WTP under non-liability and zero WTP under liability), the rest being "weak" free riders (those who give non-zero responses, but lower responses under liability). A difficulty which Throsby and Withers (1985) considered was the hypothetical nature of the WTP questions, both liable and non-liable. This differs from both the Bohm experiments (1972 and 1984) in which some real payment had to be made.

The Morrison and West (1986:66) study followed the Bohm method more closely. Two separate samples were asked the following question: "Do you think that \$3,35 a year in taxes is too little, too much or just right?". The first sample was asked the question on the understanding that their taxes would not change, while the second sample's taxes would increase or decrease accordingly. Again, no significant difference between the stated WTP of the two samples could be found.

A survey at the South African National Arts Festival (Snowball & Antrobus 2001) used the Bohm interval method in a very similar way to Throsby and Withers (1985) except that a once-off WTP amount of R5 was used (dichotomous choice yes/no response), rather than a bidding system asking for a maximum WTP amount. Respondents were told that, "The Festival costs between R8 and R10 million each year which is paid by the sponsors, mainly the Standard Bank. 2001 will be the last year that the Standard Bank will pay for the Festival. If no new sponsor is found, the Festival will end". They were then asked the following questions:

> "Supposing that there would be **no change in your monthly taxes**, would you be willing to allow R5 of your taxes each month to be spent on supporting the Festival?
>
> Now suppose that **you would actually have to pay** the R5 extra in taxes each month. Considering your monthly expenses, would you still be willing to pay R5 a month towards supporting the Festival?" (Snowball 2000:92).

Of the 80 telephone interviews conducted, 9.4% of the Grahamstown West sample, (largely populated by European-origin residents who have high income and education levels), and 20.6% of the Grahamstown East sample (which has a largely African-origin, low income and education population) responded "yes" and then "no" or "don't know" to the non-liability and liability questions. This suggests that, on average, only 13.6% of the sample were free riders.

Table 4.1. Differences between Liable and Non-liable Willingness to Pay

Study	**Result**
Bohm (1972)	No significant difference
Morrison and West (1986)	No significant difference
Throsby and Withers (1985)	35% (12% "strong" free riders; 23% "weak" free riders)
Snowball and Antrobus (2001)	13.6% (9.4% in high income area; 20.6% in low income area)

However, in the Grahamstown study, not all those who answered "yes" to the non-liable questions and "no" to the liable question can automatically be regarded as free riders, because of the extremely low levels of income recorded (less than R500 a month) for some respondents in Grahamstown East. In these cases, it is quite possible that the refusal to pay extra is the result of honesty about an income constraint, rather than because of free rider behaviour. This would also explain why there appear to be more than twice as many free riders in the low-income, township area compared to the more affluent west side of town. This conclusion is supported by Booysen's (2001:695) article on the major reason for the non-payment for services in South Africa. He concludes that, "the problem of non-payment of services appears to be a problem of ability-to-pay, rather than willingness-to-pay."

Although there have been few studies that have used the Bohm interval as such, his experimental work gave rise to two distinct streams in hypothetical bias research. One stream consists of a growing literature comparing real with hypothetical values in an attempt to find some general rule of calibration, in other words, the ratio of mean hypothetical to mean actual WTP (List and Gallet 2001; Murphy et al. 2005a). Studies range in size and type from tiny samples conducted in laboratory conditions (Botelho and Pinto 2002) to larger mail surveys (Nestor 1998) and face-to-face interviews (List and Shogren 1998).

Experiments with Calibration between Real and Hypothetical Bids

A study in cultural economics comparing real and hypothetical bids was conducted by Willis (1998) who asked visitors to an historical site, Warkworth Castle, who seemed to have decided not to enter the site when they discovered the ticket price, what their WTP for a ticket would be. The tickets were then offered to respondents at their stated WTP. Willis argued that the use of a private good to test the validity of the WTP method, usually used for public or mixed goods, is justified because, if the WTP method cannot closely approximate the real value of private goods (which are often easier to define and better known) then it is unlikely that the method will be more accurate for public goods.

Willis (1998) found that, of the 43 respondents who considered themselves potential visitors, only 17 accepted the tickets to the site at their stated

WTP price. Responses to questions about why respondents would not accept the tickets at their nominated price were not clear. This seems to suggest that, "a substantial proportion of CVM [contingent valuation method] values are neither very robust nor reliable and are subject to considerable ambivalence" (Willis 1998:616).

List and Shogren (1998) conducted first a hypothetical and then a real within-sample WTP study at a collectable baseball card auction. Respondents were first asked to bid hypothetically for a card or a group of cards and the sealed bids placed in a voting-style box without the interviewer seeing the amount. They were then asked to bid in reality for the cards, the highest bidder to be notified by telephone and, on sending the money, receiving the cards. The results showed a ratio of hypothetical-to-actual overbidding of between 2.2 to 3.5, suggesting that the NOAA Panel report proposed "divide by two" rule might be justified (List and Shogren 1998:203). However, they also found that hypothetical bias was highly context specific (so that adding or subtracting substitute cards from the set being bid on changed calibration significantly) and that overstatement was significantly higher for non-dealer respondents who were less familiar with the good and its usual market price.

Nestor (1998) argues that there are great advantages in combining hypothetical or stated preference data with real market or revealed preference data, such as reducing multicollinearity between site or good characteristics and extending the data analysis beyond the range available, using one sort of study only. Using a study on waste disposal options, where some households were already paying an optional tariff for sorted recycling, while others did not yet have the option available to them, she showed that, although hypothetical bias was present, it was not of a very high magnitude. While results were "mixed", she did not find, in contrast to List and Shogren (1998), that experience with the "good" being valued (in other words, more information) had any effect on WTP amounts or hypothetical bias.

Whitehead et al. (2000) conducted a similar analysis, combining revealed preferences from travel cost methods with stated preference data for quality improvements in outdoor recreational facilities. They also found that, by including stated preference techniques, they are able to comment not only on the value of such quality improvements to current users, but also to potential users. Botelho and Pinto (2002) conducted a laboratory experiment comparing real and hypothetical WTP for the provision of an information leaflet on the otter. While hypothetical responses were higher than real responses in a split-sample survey, the hypothetical data could be used to predict, given the demographic characteristics of the respondent, "what they would have responded if they had been placed in the real treatment" (Botelho and Pinto 2002:995). They thus conclude that, while hypothetical bias is present, the valuations of the hypothetical survey still convey useful information, especially if they can be calibrated to real data.

There is thus growing evidence that, although hypothetical bias probably exists, the data from such surveys can still be used to inform decisions. However, the search for a general calibration ratio does not appear promising for various reasons. Firstly, it is only really possible to conduct such tests where a real market situation for the good exists – mostly limited to private goods (Lusk 2003). Carson (1997) argues that, for some classes of goods, in particular, public goods to be provided by voluntary contributions and private goods to be purchased, it is impossible to design a survey in which the dominant incentive strategy will be to tell the truth because, "the survey response must provide the possibility of strictly altering the respondent's choice set without strictly expanding or contracting it ..." On the other hand, WTP surveys on public goods provided through the use of coercive payment mechanisms and quasi-public goods appear to equal or underestimate real market valuations. "Thus, a single private good, rather than representing the "best" case for a successful CV, represents one of the worst cases" (Carson 1997:1503)

The second problem with calibration experiments is that they appear to be good and context specific. A meta-analysis of 29 real and hypothetical WTP calibration experiments, covering a wide range of goods, methodologies and elicitation techniques, comes to this conclusion, as well as arguing that, in general, calibration is relatively small: 1.26 to 1.30 (List and Gallet 2001). The study also finds evidence, as in the baseball card example, that the more subjects know about the good, usually a private good, the smaller will be the hypothetical bias. A related study, a recent meta-analysis of 28 WTP studies by Murphy et al. (2005a) found a calibration factor (median) of only about 1.35, with 70% of their 83 observations having a factor below 2. However, they note that the sample shows significant positive skewness, with the calibration factor for the top ten observations being a mean of 10.3, compared to 1.54 for the rest. Research in this area thus seems to be moving toward the NOAA panel's conclusion that "No automatic or mechanical calibration of responses seems to be possible" (NOAA 1993:25).

"Cheap Talk" Questionnaire Design

The other proposed way of controlling for the hypothetical bias is through questionnaire design. Research in this area has mostly focused on the "cheap talk" design first suggested by Cummings and Taylor (1999). They experimented with questionnaire design that explicitly made respondents aware of hypothetical bias before asking them the WTP questions.

> "The cheap talk script makes three general points: it describes the hypothetical bias phenomena; it discuses possible explanations for this phenomena; and it requests that subjects vote in the upcoming hypothetical referendum as if it were a real referendum" (Cummings and Taylor 1999:651).

While the cheap talk design produced results for hypothetical surveys that were statistically indistinguishable from surveys that required some real payment, the authors admitted that the method had some problems. The most important problem is that the length of the cheap talk explanation is unrealistic for use in most surveys and particularly in telephone surveys. Tests using much shorter versions of the format were unsuccessful (Cummings and Taylor 1999:656).

However, Aadland and Caplan (2003) conducted a 1000 household WTP study of curbside recycling using a cheap talk questionnaire design significantly shorter than that of Cummings and Taylor (1999), but conveying similar information. They find that the design significantly reduces willingness to pay amounts and, by comparing WTP amounts with real market data, are able to conclude that it reduces hypothetical bias.

A WTP mail survey was conducted by Lusk (2003) for genetically modified "golden rice" using a longer cheap talk script for half the sample. He found that the cheap talk design did significantly reduce WTP bids, but that it was most effective amongst respondents who were inexperienced and had no knowledge of the subject (genetically modified foods) prior to the survey. For those with prior knowledge, the cheap talk design reduced WTP, but not by a statistically significant amount.

A study conducted by List (2001) using a cheap talk design in a split-sample field experiment at a collectable sports card auction found very similar results. While List found that the cheap talk design significantly reduced hypothetical bias amongst inexperienced bidders, it had no effect on traders and experienced bidders. He comments that this result represents a challenge for future CV research design in eliminating hypothetical bias for all subject types, but that recognizing the importance of the link between "reliability of stated values and the experience with the good" is an important step forward (List 2001:1504-5).

In a recent study, Murphy et al. (2005b) conducted experiments which included both hypothetical and real WTP scenarios. They found that including a cheap talk section in a hypothetical WTP questionnaire reduced the number of positive responses, compared to the hypothetical situation without the cheap talk design. However, there was still a significant difference between hypothetical and real results, especially at the lower bid amounts ($3 or $6). At higher payment amounts, the cheap talk design did appear to be able to align the hypothetical and real bids.

Related to this is an innovative paper by Champ and Bishop (2001) who use both stated and revealed preference data from two large studies on the purchase of wind-generated electricity. They found that, by asking respondents how certain they were that their WTP responses reflected their true values, where 1 represented "very uncertain" and 10 "very certain", they could identify those respondents likely to be overbidding in the hypothetical market. Simply by recoding "yes" WTP responses from respondents who rated themselves less than 8 on the certainty scale to "no", they found that WTP results replicated those of real market data for the same good and statistically significant hypothetical bias vanished.

Despite the different directions that research into hypothetical bias in contingent valuation studies has taken, it does seem possible to draw some general conclusions. Firstly, the better informed respondents are, or the more familiar they are with the good, perhaps also reflected by their certainty that their WTP bids reflect their true preferences, the less likely it appears that they will be prone to overstating WTP. Secondly, it appears that the Diamond and Hausman (1994) claim that calibration could lie anywhere between 1 and 10 is overly pessimistic and that Bohm's original idea, that hypothetical bias in properly designed surveys is not likely to be large, stands. The crucial issue in controlling for hypothetical bias, therefore, appears to be the information that is provided to respondents (along with their personal previous experience of the good, where applicable) and the way in which the questionnaire is designed.

4.3.2 The Embedding Effect and "Warm Glow" Hypothesis

One of the major ways in which hypothetical bias is detected in WTP surveys of goods without direct market parallels is in inconsistency of the results with what economic theory predicts. Foremost amongst these is the insensitivity of willingness to pay bids to the scope or amount of the good being valued.

> "Usually, though not always, it is reasonable to suppose that more of something regarded as a good is better so long as an individual is not satiated. This is in general translated into a willingness to pay somewhat more for more of a good … Also, if marginal or incremental willingness to pay for additional amounts does decline with the amount already available, it is usually not reasonable to assume that it declines very abruptly" (NOAA 1993:6).

Initially, a number of WTP studies were cited as demonstrating such insensitivity to scope. For example, Kahneman (1986 cited in NOAA 1993:4) found that WTP for the cleanup of all the fishing lakes in Ontario was "only slightly more" than the WTP to clean the lakes in one region. A similar case is the now infamous "birds" study (Desvousges et al. 1993), which showed that the WTP to preserve 2000, 20 000, or 200 000 birds was the same. Diamond's later (1996) analysis in fact argues that, given certain Neoclassical assumptions about the utility function, WTP to save 100 000 birds, for example, must be at least 100 times bigger than the WTP to save 1000 birds in order for the study to pass the scope test.

Positive Attitudes and "Warm Glow"

The explanation for scope insensitivity and related phenomena put forward by critics of the WTP method, like Diamond and Hausman (1994) and Kahneman and Knetsch (1992), was that respondents were not really valuing the good in an economically rational way, but were merely expressing a positive attitude to the good in question, or "purchasing moral satisfaction" from giving to some worthy cause. This "warm glow" hypothesis argues that, since individuals are only showing support for some composite good (like the arts or the environment), there is no reason to suppose that their WTP would vary much with the amount of the specific good in question. The NOAA report (1993:8) notes that, if warm glow does occur, the WTP results "should not be taken as reliable estimates".

Diamond (1996) argues that, if the process of, for example, giving money to save 1000 birds, provides utility in addition to the actual birds saved (the good), then the WTP estimate is, at least in part, capturing some moral satisfaction or warm glow. In other words, 1000 birds are not a perfect substitute for 1000 birds *saved*. This could lead to a situation in which the government could, for example, propose the development of a wilderness area where no development is really intended, and increase welfare by announcing that the results of a WTP study to block the development had been successful. "In other words, if we are not willing to restrict analysis to preferences defined over the state of the environment, rather than also including the process resulting in that state, then we need a new welfare economics ..." (Diamond 1996:346).

Interestingly, this ties in well with the work of Sen (1985) who argues that neoclassical utility theory and welfare economics are flawed in that they do not take into account the process by which the final outcome is reached or consider the role of the choice set available to the individual who made the choice. Sen would undoubtedly agree with Diamond that we need a new welfare economics, but in Sen's case it would be a theory that included utility derived from the process (taking into account the limitations of the other available choices) rather then excluding it. Carson et al. (2001:177) agree with this view, stating that, "It is utility, whatever its source, that matters to total value" and that the motivations behind increases in utility are irrelevant as far as economic theory is concerned.

Some of the most interesting theoretical work on CV has been done by Kahneman et al. (1999). They argue that attitudes are much more closely linked to WTP bids than the economic concept of preferences and that this poses a problem because attitudes violate many of the assumptions of rational choice theory. Preferences are assumed to exist already and imply a choice of one good over another that can be linked to a budget constraint and quantified. However, attitudes do not imply choice and are thus not easily fitted into choice theory. For example, preferring bagpipes to opera implies a choice of one over the other. Having a positive attitude to bagpipes does not imply a negative attitude towards opera. Diamond and Hausman (1993:27) comment that, "Our conclusion is that people do indeed care about preserving wilderness areas, but we infer that standard CV questionnaires do not generate a description of preferences but, rather, elicit responses that generally express concern about preserving wilderness". That is, they argue that CV responses capture attitudes ("general concern") not preferences.

In several experiments, Kahneman et al. (1999) find that attitudes, expressed on rating scales, are highly correlated with valuations expressed in dollar terms. For example, ratings on numerical scales were elicited in the case of a proposed intervention to protect the peregrine falcon being threatened by pollution. Measures used were willingness to pay, degree of political support for the proposed intervention, personal satisfaction from contributing to the scheme and rating of the importance of the problem as a public issue. All the rating systems showed a high degree of correlation (Kahneman et al. 1999).

One of the expected results of the theories of Kahneman et al. (1999) is that WTP studies will inevitably be insensitive to the size or amount of the good being valued because respondents will be using "judgment by prototype" to make decisions and to express an attitude, rather than focusing on the specific situation described. Using a number of examples and with reference to well-known psychological theories, they show that "judging by prototype" is inevitably prone to "extension neglect", that is, unless the attention of respondents is specifically drawn to issues of size or number, they will have little or no effect on the valuation of the good. For example, in the Desvousges et al. birds study, Kahneman et al. (1999:212-3) suggest that the scenario brings to mind a mental image of "an exhausted bird, its feathers soaked in black oil, unable to escape" and that this image is likely to dominate expressions of the respondent's attitude to the problem, including their willingness to pay for a solution, which will not be much affected by the *number* of birds saved. They apply a similar theory to the "add-up test" (or individual valuation and summation).

Adequate Responsiveness and Studies that do Show Scope Sensitivity

The issue of scope sensitivity is a vital one, since the NOAA report (1993:5) sets this measure of internal consistency or rationality as a minimum requirement of proof that the WTP responses "corresponded to some reality". As such, it falls into the panel's "burden of proof" subset, "... if a CV survey suffered from any of the following maladies, we would judge its finding unreliable" (NOAA 1993). However, the NOAA panel, after the initial report was published, noted that the "adequate responsiveness" mentioned in the report did not necessarily mean a statistically significant responsiveness to scope, which may depend crucially on the context and was ultimately a "judgment call" (Arrow et al. 1994, reported in Smith and Osborne 1996:288).

While critics of the method argue that WTP studies will never be able to produce responses consistent with the economic theory of rational choice, however responsiveness to scope may be measured, this is hotly contested by a number of other commentators, whose main argument is usually that it is the survey design and/or method that is at fault.

Hanemann (1994) is the foremost of such defenders. In terms of the case studies often cited in the case for scope insensitivity, he argues that the Kahneman (1986) lakes study actually found a 50% difference in WTP for lake cleanup in one region as opposed to all of Ontario and that the survey itself was not well run, consisting of only a brief telephone interview using an open ended WTP question (1994). In the case of the "birds" study, he argues that the results *were* consistent with what economic theory would predict, given that changes in bird population were described to respondents as "much less than 1 percent" (2000), "less than 1 percent" (20 000) and "about 2 percent" (200 000). Presented in this manner, it would have been surprising if such tiny percentage changes in bird population size had elicited much difference in WTP. However, when this was pointed out to William Desvousges at the Exxon conference, he countered that focus group studies had shown that respondents understood the questions and that respondents were not faced with more than one scenario, so that the relative change in bird population size between scenarios may not have been significant (Desvousges (discussion session) in Hausman, 1993:161):

> "Now, what we were trying to do in the focus groups- keep in mind that we're not asking the same respondent 2000 versus 20 000 versus 200 000 – so I think that that is a difference here. What we did was to take the three versions and give a respondent one of those three versions".

Hanemann (1994) also argues that if one takes into account that birds or lakes may be regarded as substitutes for each other and that saving or cleaning them has a declining marginal utility, one would not expect WTP to increase proportionately with an increase in the good. Randall et al. (1981 in Dupont 2003) agree that sequencing can be understood in terms of economic theory, that is, as the list progresses, budget constraints become increasingly limiting and substitution effects set in.

In a follow up study by Schkade and Payne (1992, cited in Carson and Mitchell 1993), using the Desvousges et al. survey instrument, respondents were asked to "think aloud" as they made their WTP decision. While the study revealed that respondents thought of a strikingly large number of irrelevant factors, indicating the difficulty of the task (as Diamond and Hausman (1994) point out), it also forced respondents to concentrate more and results showed a 100% difference in median WTP to preserve 2000 and 200 000 birds (Carson and Mitchell 1993).

Carson (1997:1505) supports this view, arguing that "specific, avoidable survey problems can mimic the impression of insensitivity to scope" and that these are mostly associated with studies using mall intercepts and short telephone interviews and which have vague descriptions of the good, the provision and/or the payment mechanism.

> "If there is a central problem with contingent valuation it is that people will try to answer whatever question is put to them. The quality of the response is crucially dependent on the information provided to and perceived by the respondent, and the seriousness with which the respondent takes the survey interview" (Mitchell and Carson 1993: 1266-7).

An example of a cultural economics study that did show scope sensitivity is the WTP to preserve the Campi Flegrei conducted by Ringanti and Scarpa (1998). Using face-to-face interviews, they asked respondents' WTP to preserve the Campi Flegrei, an ancient Roman archaeological site near Naples. The WTP questions were designed specifically to test whether bids were significantly different for the whole site versus parts of the site. The WTP to conserve the whole site was $28.81, while conserving only parts of the site had significantly lower WTP results: $10.18 for the part of the Campi Flegrei not open to the public and $6.99 for the Bagnoli. The authors conclude that, with proper questionnaire design, WTP bids are sensitive to the scope of the good being valued.

A growing number of WTP studies conducted in accordance with the NOAA panel guidelines are showing sensitivity to scope. Further research into the theoretical reasons behind those studies showing scope insensitivity is also advancing. Carson et al. (1996) conducted a study looking at four large-sample environmental quality willingness to pay studies, including the original Exxon study, done in 1991, and a follow up study in 1993, all of which conformed to the NOAA panel's guidelines. All studies showed sensitivity to scope, with studies valuing more inclusive public goods producing higher WTP estimates than those valuing "smaller" goods. In a later review (2001) Carson et al. reinforce their claim that the vast majority of modern CV studies do show sensitivity to scope, and that those that don't generally did not follow NOAA guidelines on questionnaire design and survey administration.

Using a meta-analysis of five studies conducted on the WTP for improvements in visibility (air quality) at national parks, Smith and Osborne (1996:290) tested for scope sensitivity and the context-specific a priori expectations dictated by economic theory. They found that, "Regardless of the sample composition or model specification, there was a statistically significant, positive relationship between willingness to pay and proportionate improvement in the visibility range" (1996:295). They also found that when differences between studies in the economic commodity being valued are included, for example, the base visibility conditions, the amount of time the changes in visibility were to occur for, etc., the differences in WTP results were economically plausible.

Possible Reasons for Apparent Scope Insensitivity

On a more theoretical level, Bateman et al. (2004) show that scope sensitivity is significantly affected by whether the "visible choice set" is revealed to respondents before they are asked to bid, or not and that this, rather than the warm glow hypothesis, can account for the variation in scope sensitivity in WTP studies. When testing for scope within a single interview, the amount of the good is varied (quantitative nesting) or the type or quality of the good is changed (qualitative nesting) and respondents are asked their WTP for each scenario. In an experiment and field study, Bateman et al. (2004) found that, where respondents were told in advance what all the possible choices were, the studies were far more sensitive to scope. Furthermore, in the studies with visible choice sets, the order in which the good was varied, bottom-up or top-down, was not a significant factor – in contrast to many studies reporting the so-called sequencing effect, where the order of questions makes a vast difference to the WTP bid.

Bateman et al. (2004:89) offer some suggestions as to why removing the element of surprise should have such a dramatic effect on scope sensitivity. Firstly, they point out that they are not claiming to have solved the issue of strategic bidding, but that by revealing all options before a vote, they have held "strategy space constant" and achieved internal consistency, in that responses are sensitive to scope and do not vary with list direction. This result is as predicted by choice theory: "different strategy spaces result in different valuations". A second suggestion is that reported sensitivity to list direction is as a result of the gains/losses asymmetry (also relevant to the difference between WTP and willingness to accept), which postulates that gains are worth less than losses because of loss aversion, also known as the "endowment effect". Finally, they suggest that the element of surprise can produce negative reactions in respondents, resulting in a lowering of stated values.

Related to this, Dupont (2003) found strong evidence that sequencing effects depend very much on how familiar respondents were with the good in question. In a WTP study used to value improvements to swimming, fishing and recreational boating in Hamilton Harbour in Ontario, she found that WTP bids for passive users and potentially active users were significantly affected by question ordering, while those for current users were not. She concludes that, "If respondents are not familiar with the environmental good/activity (passive users) or are uncertain as to the enjoyment they will obtain from it (potentially active users) then they may be more subject to order effects than active users" (Dupont 2003:336).

One of the few cultural economics WTP studies designed to test specifically for scope sensitivity was conducted by Whitehead and Finney (2003). In a study of the willingness to pay to protect submerged maritime cultural resources like shipwrecks, Whitehead and Finney (2003) find that WTP bids are insensitive to scope, but suggest that this is because of the way the WTP question was asked, rather than unrealistic valuations. Using telephone interviews of residents of North Carolina, respondents were asked their WTP to protect shipwrecks off the North Carolina coast from treasure hunters. In the first version, a single bounded WTP question was asked, for protecting 50 or 100 shipwrecks at a particular price, to which respondents could vote yes or no. If they voted yes, the number of shipwrecks protected and the price was increased and if they voted no, a lower number of shipwrecks and a lower price was suggested.

An interesting aspect of the study was that, no matter what their first vote (yes or no) was, respondents were reluctant to change in the second round. Whitehead and Finney (2003:323) suggest that this is because of "incentive incompatibility": If, after voting yes, respondents are offered the good at a higher price, they may assume that the higher priced good is a waste of money, and vote "no" in the second round, regardless of real willingness to pay. If, after voting no, respondents are offered the good at a lower price, they may assume that the good is of lower quality and still vote no in the second round.

Despite changing the amount of the good offered as well as the price, Whitehead and Finney (2003) found significant incentive incompatibility. That is, less that 10% of respondents voted "no" on the first question and "yes" for a lower price and quantity, while less than 20% voted "yes" for the first question and "no" for a higher price and quantity. As a result, willingness to pay did not show sensitivity to the size of the good being valued. They also suggest that an increase from 50 to 100 shipwrecks out of a total of 5000 (information that was supplied to respondents) represents an increase from 1% to 2%, which may not have been perceived as significant – similar to the Desvouges et al. "birds" study discussed earlier.

Although not the focus of their research, this sort of incentive incompatibility is also evident in the Alberini et al. (2005) study which uses a double-bounded willingness to pay question to place a value on the conservation of S. Erasmo Island in the Lagoon of Venice. As the table below shows, only 5.95% of respondents changed a "no" vote to "yes" in the second round (offered at a lower price) and 17.17% changed a "yes" vote to "no". The evidence thus suggests that, in some studies at least, apparent scope insensitivity may in fact be as a result of questionnaire design issues.

Table 4.2. Double-bounded dichotomous choice responses in two cultural goods studies

WTP	Whitehead & Finney: % WTP to protect 50 wrecks	Whitehead & Finney: % WTP to protect 100 wrecks	Alberini et al. % WTP to conserve S. Erasmo Island
No-no	46.14	46.40	53.54
No-yes	6.59	7.88	5.95
Yes-yes	28.64	29.05	23.34
Yes-no	18.64	16.67	17.17

(Whitehead and Finney 2003:235; Alberini et al. 2005:165)

Further evidence of this is found in the Bateman and Brouwer (2006) survey conducted to measure the WTP to reduce the risk of skin cancer in New Zealand. They specifically tested for scope sensitivity by first eliciting individual WTP and then broadening this to household WTP. They also tested question formats: open-ended (OE) versus dichotomous choice (DC). They find that the DC format WTP question shows statistically significant sensitivity to scope of a magnitude that conforms to *a priori* expectations, while the OE format question does not. "Consequently, we cannot reject the hypothesis that the DC responses are consistent with standard theory" (2006:210).

Another general finding that appears to be emerging is that WTP studies are not sensitive to changes in scope when these changes are small or seen to be too small to matter. A study by Bateman et al. (2005) measuring the WTP to change the acidity level in a large sample of mountain lakes illustrates this point. They find that respondents' WTP did vary depending on the number of lakes being valued, but decreased significantly once a threshold level had been reached. Thus, while willingness to pay to protect five lakes was estimated to be between £16.39 and £20.29, the maximum values for protecting all 400 lakes were only between £22.40 and £30.18. Bateman et al. (2005) argue that this finding does not indicate scope insensitivity, but rather that, once the threshold has been reached, marginal WTP to protect additional lakes is very small.

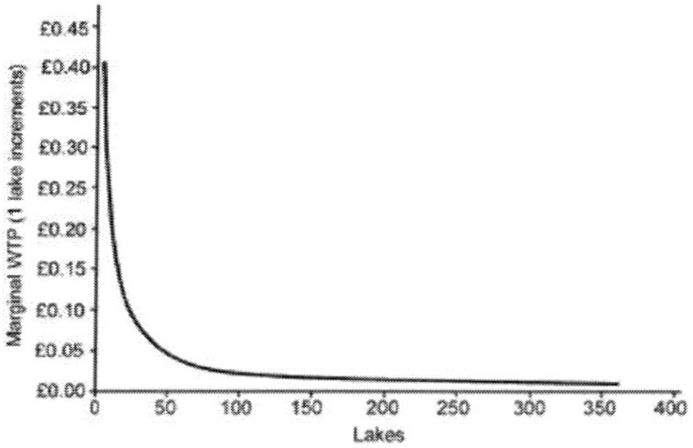

(Source: Bateman et al. 2005:289)

Fig. 4.1. Marginal WTP for Lakes Protected from Further Degradation

Sensitivity to scope will continue to be the acid test of internal consistency in WTP studies. Kahneman et al. (1999:217) conclude that, "Insensitivity to scope is the inevitable result of general rules that govern human judgment. It is naïve to expect broad psychological laws to be overcome by minor methodological adjustments". However, the general consensus seems to be that insensitivity to scope is as a result of poor survey design, rather than proof that contingent valuation itself does not conform to economic theory.

4.3.3 Disparities Between WTP and WTP

Another important way in which contingent valuation surveys violate the standard assumptions of economic theory is in the large difference in the outcome of the survey depending on whether respondents are asked their willingness to pay to avoid a decline in some good or service or if they are asked their willingness to accept (WTA) compensation for the same proposed decline. The Expected Utility Hypothesis, put forward by Willig in 1976 and extended by Randall and Stoll in 1980, implies that, when income effects are small (which most studies suggest they are), then differences between WTP and WTA measures will be small (Inder and O'Brien 2003; Hanemann 1991; Boyce and Brown 1992:1367).

In other words, the theory suggests that, when goods are sold in a competitive market with no transactions costs, they take on the properties of money. In this case, not only can WTP be shown to be equal to WTA, but these can also be shown to approximate the average market price of the good, with straight line indifference curves resulting (Shogren et al. 1994). However, as several authors have noted (Boyce and Brown 1992; Morrison 1997; Hanemann 1991; Shogren et al. 1994) this has not proved to be the case - WTA usually exceeds WTP by a factor of anything from two to ten and sometimes more than this.

Given that income effects have usually been shown to be small, two distinct theories have emerged as possible explanations for the WTP-WTA disparity, namely the substitution effect first put forward by Hanemann (1991) and the loss aversion or so-called endowment effect, proposed by Kahneman et al. (1990). The following section reviews these two theories and their possible combination (Morrison 1997a and 1997b) as well as some other later suggestions.

The Substitution Effect

Hanemann (1991) argues that the implications of the Randall and Stoll model have been misunderstood. He points out that, for changes in the quantity of a good, there is no presumption that WTP must equal WTA, especially if the good has no close substitutes. He develops a model showing that, if income effects are held constant, WTP and WTA measures will become increasingly divergent as the number of substitute goods is reduced. "In the limit, WTP could equal the individual's entire (finite) income, while WTA could be infinite" (1991:625-6). Shogren et al. (1994) use the example of the trade-off between health and wealth to illustrate this, showing that, with no perfect substitutes, indifference curves will take the usual shape, which is convex to the origin. This argument is supported by Amiran and Hagen (2003) who show that, if utility is asymptotically bounded, full compensation for the loss of a public good, which has no perfect or close substitutes, may be impossible because the extra income from compensation (WTA) cannot purchase an equivalent good. It is thus possible for WTA to be infinite without violating any fundamental neoclassical assumptions.

Adamowicz et al. (1993) used two private good experiments to test for the presence of the substitution effect in WTP-WTA disparity. The first experiment obtained WTP and WTA responses for a movie ticket, where the film was also available on video. The second regarded tickets to a live hockey game that would also be shown on TV. The sample was split in each case, one half being informed of the substitutes (the video and TV coverage) the other, not. While the movie/video experiment (using open-ended questions) showed no sensitivity to the presence of substitutes, the hockey experiment (using close-ended questions) did. "Using the mean value welfare measure, the difference between the WTP and WTA was $13.40 (40 percent) smaller for the substitute sub-sample than for the no-substitute subsample" (1993:425). The authors conclude that the availability of substitutes does have a significant effect on the difference between WTP and WTA.

Brown (1994) however, disputes the findings of Adamowicz et al. (1993). He points out that, while both WTP and WTA declined in absolute terms when substitutes were offered (as one would expect), the ratio of WTP to WTA did not change much at all, the WTA/WTP ratio being about 1.86 with or without the substitute.

An interesting test for the effect of substitute goods in cultural economics (and one of the few studies of a public good) was undertaken by Kling et al. (2004). Their study investigated the value of preserving the Northern Hotel in Fort Collins, Colorado. The hotel is a local landmark, originally built in 1866 and host to a number of famous personalities in the past, including President Franklin Roosevelt. However, the hotel had deteriorated seriously and, if not restored, might have become irreparable. Kling et al. (2004) set out to examine the WTP-WTA disparity specifically by splitting the sample between two valuation scenarios: one in which respondents were offered a refund of tax revenue surplus or the building restoration (WTA), and one in which building restoration was coupled with an added tax payment (WTP). They found that WTA bids were significantly higher than WTP amounts and concluded that, in the case of such cultural heritage, there is a significant non-substitutability effect, since there are no close substitutes for unique heritage.

The same seems to apply to a study of the St Louis Public Library (Holt et al. 1998, 1999), which asked library users how much they would be willing to accept to give up some library services and also their willingness to pay ("dollar value") for these services. The findings show that 88% of respondents refused to consider closing the library "at any price", with WTA bids beyond any reasonable level and far exceeding WTP - $136 million (WTA) compared to $15 million. Reasons included that the library was "Important / needed / priceless / too valuable" (Holt and Elliott 1998:43).

The Endowment Effect

The other main argument put forward to explain why WTP and WTA can differ so much is a form of loss aversion or the "endowment effect". In a number of experiments, Kahneman et al. (1990) found that initial ownership, or endowment, affected significantly what subjects would be willing to accept to part with the good. For example, in one of the experiments, one group of subjects was given redeemable tokens to trade while another was given consumer goods (coffee mugs or chocolate bars) and told that, if they could arrive at a mutually agreeable price, they could trade. The expected volume of trade (V*) was about 50% in both markets, in other words, with randomly assigned goods or tokens, about half the goods would change hands. However, in the token market, where tokens had no value, other than that imputed by the researcher, the ratio of actual trade (V) to expected trade was 0.91, while in the consumption good market, V/V* was only 0.31. This pattern persisted even when a number of iterations of the market simulation were run with the same subjects. All eight experiments produced robust results, implying that "the observed undertrading of consumption goods may be largely due to a reluctance to part with entitlements" (Kahneman et al. 1990:1339).

The result contradicts the Coase theorem, which argues that, where there are no transactions costs, the allocation of resources amongst bargaining individuals should not be affected by initial property rights or endowments. "However, if the marginal rate of substitution between one good and another is affected by endowment, then the individual who is assigned the property right will be more likely to retain it" (Kahneman et al. 1990:1340). Kahneman et al. (1990) conclude that the market asymmetry observed in the WTP-WTA disparity is thus not likely to be some kind of cognitive mistake that will disappear with the use of a different survey method or repeat iterations, but that theorists need to accept that utility depends strongly on starting point. In a later study Thampapillia (2000:510) illustrates that "the shape of an individual's underlying utility function, and hence the indifference curves, changes when an individual's endowment changes".

Thompson et al. (1998 and 2002), in their WTP studies of the value of the arts to Kentucky households, also recognise "loss aversion", in that mean WTP per household to avoid a 25% loss was found to be significantly more ($11.44) than the WTP to increase arts performances and exhibitions by the same amount ($6.21). Considering that the costs of increasing arts performances and exhibitions in Kentucky by 25% would cost $12.6 million, a WTP to avoid this loss of $16.9 million indicates a net benefit of $4.3 million. Thompson et al. conclude that the relatively small net benefit indicates that current levels of support are relatively efficient.

Aabo (2005) used a split sample to value public libraries in Norway. One sub-sample was asked their WTA compensation in the form of a tax rebate for closing the library down and the other was asked their WTP to prevent library closure. WTA estimates were found to be five times higher than WTP. However, Aabo argues that, where respondents feel that they have "an inherent right to the good, WTP measures will underestimate welfare impacts" (2005:492). In this study, it was found that 94% of Norwegians felt that they had such rights and Aabo thus suggests that the WTP estimate will be biased downwards, the "true" value being closer to the WTA estimate.

In stark contrast to this, Shogren et al. (1994) ran a number of Kahneman-like tests (coffee mugs and chocolate) and discovered no significant difference in WTP and WTA after the first iteration. In other words, for private goods, with no transactions costs, they found that respondents do learn what reasonable values to place on goods as they gain more market experience and that this equalizes WTP and WTA. However, when the same set of tests were conducted for a good for which there are few substitutes (health in the form of reduced risk of food contamination), they found that WTA is always greater than WTP and conclude that Hanemann's (1991) argument is correct.

One of the major differences between the Shogren et al. (1994) experiments and the Kahneman et al. (1990) tests, however, is that Kahneman et al. used a Becker-DeGroot-Marschak auction, while Shogren et al. used a Vickery auction. Shogren and Hayes (1997) argue that the Vickery auction is far more realistic and like a real market, thus encouraging market-like learning, while the Kahneman et al. method is not. "Is the endowment effect a fundamental part of choice or simply an artefact of a weak exchange environment? The weaker the exchange institution, the weaker the socialization of rational behaviour and the stronger the potential hold of asocial anomalies on choice" (Shogren and Hayes 1997:243).

The idea that market discipline encourages learning is supported by a later study by List (2003) using information from two field studies – a tradable sports cards auction and a collectable pin auction. Using a method similar to that of Kahneman et al. (1990), List finds that, while a significant endowment effect does appear in pooled data (indicated by the low percentage of respondents who were willing to trade their "endowed" good for an alternative good of similar value), the picture changes dramatically when the sample is divided up according to trading experience. In this case, professional traders and experienced non-traders show no endowment effects, while inexperienced traders show a huge effect.

Morrison (1997a and 1997b), however, points out that the possibility that both the income and substitution effects are present, and their possible joint effect on differences between the two contingent valuation methods (WTP and WTA), has not yet been adequately addressed. On conducting an experiment, first allowing both endowment and substitution effects to vary, and then controlling for substitution effects, Morrison (1997a) finds first no significant difference between WTP and WTA and then, in the latter experiment, a significant difference. She thus argues that the Shogren et al. (1994) results, which show that no endowment effect exists, are unjustified.

Psychological Theories for the WTP-WTA Disparity

In addition to these two main streams of thought (that is, the substitution and endowment effects), a few commentators have also suggested rather more psychological theories as to why WTP and WTA often differ so much. Boyce and Brown (1992) suggested that "intrinsic" values may be important in valuing a complex good such as the environment or some aspect of culture. "If an environmental commodity has intrinsic value, we argue that kinked or inflected indifference curves between the commodity and other money expenditures result when intrinsic values are included in WTA measures of value but (at least partially) excluded from WTP measures of value" (Boyce and Brown 1992:1367). In other words, the moral responsibility of preserving a species or an art form or cultural heritage may be captured in a WTA measure, thus inflating it beyond WTP.

Biel et al. (2006) confirm this hypothesis with their WTP-WTA experiment, using a real payment situation amongst students who were paid to participate in the study. Using a split sample, respondents were asked whether they were willing to pay, or willing to accept a reduction in payment, to support a World Wildlife Fund otter protection project. Only 9 out of 48 participants were willing to pay to support the project, while 23 out of 51 were willing to accept a payment reduction. In addition, follow-up questions exploring the emotional responses to the WTP or WTA questions found that, for those who chose not to donate, emotions such as annoyance, self disgust, discomfort, self dissatisfaction and shame were of a much higher intensity in the WTA scenario. They conclude that WTP-WTA disparities "are largely a result of asymmetric emotional experiences and moral perceptions" (2006:10)

Inder and O'Brien (2003) suggest that the unpleasant psychological uncertainty caused by having to make a choice, either as a seller (WTA) or a buyer (WTP), may cause the wide range of disparities observed. They argue that loss aversion is not adequate to explain differences in WTP and WTA because it looks at only one side of the equation – the seller who is willing to accept compensation for a loss – and does not take into account the psychological effect of the sale on the buyer, who might be unsure about what the asset is worth to them, the utility it will generate and what price the buyer will accept. Band and O'Brien suggest that, to compensate for such uncertainty, sellers (WTA measure) will tend to overstate their values, while buyers (WTP measure) will understate theirs, resulting in wide and varying disparity between WTP, WTA and market price.

The NOAA Panel (1993:18) recommended that only the WTP method should be used, "because [it] is the conservative choice". Many commentators (Cummings in Shogren et al. 1994 and Boyce and Brown 1992, amongst others) agree that only the WTP method of contingent valuation studies should be used when attempting to value a non-market good with possible "moral" values because of the likelihood of eliciting infinite WTA even where WTP is small or zero. "It is difficult to see how such infinite individual WTA values can be incorporated into benefit-cost analysis..." (Boyce and Brown 1992:1371). While some commentators, like Mansfield (1999), still argue that compensating value is the correct measure of welfare loss rather than WTP, in practice most studies have stuck to the WTP recommendation.

4.3.4 The Mixed Good Bias

The arts, as a mixed good, have both private and public good characteristics. Some parts of the arts, like concerts and exhibitions, are excludable and have private good characteristics in that those who do not pay an entrance fee are prevented from consuming the good. However, the arts also have public good characteristics, such as the externalities which they generate - usually not excludable and in most cases, non-rival. The following section discusses the difficulty of separating the pure non-market externalities from the market or financial benefits of a mixed good in WTP studies.

Attenders versus non-attenders

Throsby (1984) suggests that there should be separate demand functions for the public and private components of the good and that this may reveal an incentive for the misrepresentation of demand preferences. He is supported by Morrison and West (1986:69) who point out that "horizontal inequity" (differences in benefit between people of similar income levels) may make the idea that it is the wealthy, well educated people that benefit most from arts subsidies too simplistic: "The theatre attender [as opposed to the non-attender of similar income] will enjoy the benefits of subsidy to the direct use of theatres as well as the external benefits".

This idea was later articulated as the distinction between total value and passive use value that Carson et al. (1999) made. They point out that WTP consists of two parts, passive use value (externalities that accrue to users and non-users) and direct use value (that accrues only to users). The main point of Throsby's (1984) argument is that those people who attend the live performing arts will thus have a (logical) reason to overstate their

WTP for the service, even where conventional free rider behaviour is absent. Consider an economy which has a mixed good (x) with two users, A and B. User A demands only the public parts of the good (non-attender) and user B demands the private good component as well (attender). Looked at simply, if there were an increase in subsidy to good x, B would gain more from the decline in price than A (since B is an attender), even though the tax shares of A and B would be equal. There is, therefore, an incentive for B to overstate WTP, since an increase in subsidy would benefit B more than A, while the costs would be shared equally (Throsby 1984:280 - 282).

> "The essence of this analysis is that an incentive for overstatement of preferences exists if the individual's gain from the increase in his or her consumption enabled by subsidisation of the private [part of the mixed] good exceeds his or her perceived share of the tax necessary to finance this increase in output" (Throsby 1984:282).

In applying this theory to their study on the level of public finance for the arts in Australia, Throsby and Withers (1986) found a strong correlation between users (i.e. attenders) and higher WTP; "A downward adjustment of about 40% in average stated WTP is required to eliminate this source of bias". Once this had been done, the results of the study could be used to provide information on the determinants of demand for the public part of the good, such as income, taste and education (Throsby 1984).

These results are confirmed in a number of later cultural economics valuation studies, as shown in table 4.3. Without exception, all the studies show that users or potential users of the resource are willing to pay more than non-users. The mixed good bias fits well with the Thompson et al. (2002) suggestion, which states that, for those who frequently attend the highly sponsored shows, willingness to pay may represent some sacrifice of consumer surplus, or an avoidance of travel costs, rather than purely a valuation of positive externalities.

A particularly interesting study is that of the Surrey Historical Centre (Ozdemiroglu and Mourato 2001), which proposed two valuation scenarios: In the first case, the Centre would remain operational and open to the public as it is presently. In the second case, the Centre would remain operational, but would not be open to the general public. The findings show that, for users, the two scenarios have significantly different values; non-use value being £24, use-value (open to the public) being £34. However, for current non-users, the average WTP for both scenarios was £13, clearly illustrating differing values depending on use.

Table 4.3. Use-value Bias in WTP Studies

Source	Case Study	Findings
Carson et al. (1997)	Preservation of the Fes Medina	Visitors to the site are willing to pay $70 each on average, while visitors to Morocco who did not visit the Fes are willing to pay about $30 each. WTP amongst the European population in general was $2.15
Ozdemiroglu and Mourato (2001)	Surrey Historical Centre archive	An average user's WTP to prevent closure and collection loss was £34 per person per year and £24 to prevent loss of access. Non-users were willing to pay £13 per year for both scenarios.
Snowball and Antrobus (2001)	National Arts Festival, South Africa	56% of low/no attendance respondents were willing to pay, 76% of medium attenders and 100% of frequent attenders.
Snowball and Antrobus (2003)	Oudtshoorn Arts Festival, South Africa	Average WTP of respondents who attended 0-3 shows was R3.33; 4-7 shows was R11.60; 8-12 shows was R13.80; 13 or more shows was R15.22
Del Saz Salazar and Marques (2005)	Old Arab Tower restoration, Valencia	Mean WTP higher for those with "high consumption" of cultural goods
Alberini et al. (2005)	S. Erasmo Lagoon, Venice	Percentage of "no" WTP responses is 49% amongst recent visitors, 50% amongst potential future visitors and 79% amongst non-users.
Del Saz Salazar and Menendez (2007)	El Parque Central, Valencia	Respondents who lived closer to the proposed urban park were willing to pay more than those who lived further away.

Such results are also found in studies of arts festivals (Snowball and Antrobus 2001; 2003) and heritage sites (Del Saz Salazar and Marques 2005; Alberini et al. 2005 and Carson et al. 1997), where willingness to pay was positively correlated with the number of shows attended or visits to the site. In fact, the Del Saz Salazar and Marques study (2005) found that WTP to restore an old Arab tower in Valencia was 133% higher for those respondents who were categorised as "high consumers" of cultural goods in general than those who were low/average cultural good consumers. This suggests that appreciation of cultural goods in general, as well as use of the specific good being valued, could be biasing WTP results upwards. When generalising WTP results to a whole population, therefore, it is very important to examine the extent to which users, or "high" cultural goods consumers, may be influencing the average values.

Mixed Good Characteristics and Earnings

In addition to the consumer surplus of attenders, Seaman (2003a:13) suggests that what a WTP study may also be capturing is a willingness to pay for expected economic benefit. This could be reflected not only in present earnings, but also in the long-term growth of the area. "Would not a very real component of the "bequest" motive of a parent of a 13 year old child be the possibility that that child could possibly manoeuvre into a position to be a direct beneficiary of the higher income and expanded job opportunities that the event would provide?" Such benefit might particularly apply to a cultural event or attraction that would result in an increase in visitors to the area, like an arts festival, a major museum or the restoration of a major heritage site.

Studies conducted by Thompson et al. (1998 and 2002) added WTP estimates to economic impact figures to measure the total value of the arts to the Kentucky economy ($43.8 million a year). However, this method was criticized by Seaman (2003a) on two grounds. Firstly, he argues that part of what the WTP estimate may be picking up is the projected current or future earnings of the respondent or their household due to the arts. In other words, the WTP estimate includes, to some extent, economic impact and that simply adding them leads to double counting. Secondly, he argues that, rather than giving a total value, the WTP figure measures only one scenario (that of a 25% decrease in arts events), not the value of the externalities provided by 100% of Kentucky arts events.

In the study conducted at two South African arts festivals (the Grahamstown National Arts Festival and the *Klein Karoo Nationale Kunstefees* in Oudtshoorn), respondents were asked a follow-up question to the WTP question, probing the reasons for being willing or not willing to support the Festival (Snowball 2005). Respondents, who were local residents in the town where the festival took place, were also asked about their earnings from the festival as a result of additional employment or providing accommodation to tourists. Both the amount of money earned at the festival and the respondent's views on the economic benefits that the festival can or could provide (often cited as a reason for positive willingness to pay) were positive and highly significant determinants of willingness to pay.

Despite much lower average festival earnings, citing economic benefits as a reason for positive WTP was particularly statistically significant in the lower income areas. This suggests that, in areas where cultural events are associated with increases in tourism and thus earnings, where there is a high level of unemployment or low average income, willingness to pay figures will also be capturing some of the value of expected future financial gains. In the higher income areas of the two South African festival towns, actual earnings from festival tourists were statistically significant positive determinants of WTP, and are thus also likely to be biasing the WTP figure upwards (Snowball 2005).

Table 4.4. Festival earnings and spending at two arts festivals in South Africa

	Grahamstown		**Oudtshoorn**	
	High income	Low income	High income	Low income
Average current festival earnings	R390 ($60)	R106 ($16.31)	R833 ($128.15)	R341 ($52.46)
Percentage of respondents who cited financial gains (current or future expected) as a reason for willingness to pay.	19%	53%	35%	40%

(Source: Snowball 2005:118)

If one could establish the extent to which the WTP figure reflects the value of non-market externalities versus market benefits, the ideal situation, as suggested by Seaman (2003a), would be to run both a WTP and accurate economic impact study at the same event. One could then combine the two results, appropriately weighted, in order to arrive at a true economic value for the festival. However, simply adding WTP and economic impact figures would result in some double counting.

4.3.5 Other Categorical Critiques of the CV Method

Sunstein (2002) and Sunstein et al. (2001) argue strongly that the contingent valuation method, especially in the case of cultural goods, will produce incoherent valuation estimates. Their point is that WTP will vary sharply with the category of goods being considered, that is, estimates will be "category bound". For example, for cultural amenities being considered in isolation, it is quite likely that a significant WTP amount will be elicited, but that if other categories were included, like some aspect of health care, the WTP for the cultural amenity would drop sharply. "When people explore particular problems in isolation, they normalize them by comparing them to a cognitively accessible comparison set consisting of cases from the same basic category. When cases from other categories are introduced into the picture, people's judgments can be greatly affected, because the process of normalization is disrupted" (Sunstein 2002:1). Thus, WTP estimates obtained in isolation, particularly for cultural goods, which appear fairly low on most people's public goods rankings, are judged unreliable.

Sunstein (2002) poses two solutions to the problem, both of which he rejects. Firstly, one could include as wide a range as possible of other public goods (health care, education, environment, etc) in the WTP questionnaire. Sunstein rejects this on the grounds that the task would be incredibly complex and result in "cognitive overload". An alternative would be to include at least some other categories, but this would allow for serious manipulation, since the categories chosen would certainly affect the WTP result. Epstein (2003:267-8) supports this position, arguing that, even for private goods, if removed from a specific context where price comparison with similar articles is possible, WTP responses are likely to be "haphazard and of limited reliability".

A second problem, raised by Sunstein et al. (2001), is that of the validity of assuming that WTP responses are a monetary expression of utility. Like Kahneman et al. (1999), they argue that even when people can produce "coherent and consistent moral intuitions", they are not easily translated into numbers. They consider the example of a jury deciding on the penalty (number of years in jail) for a particular crime, which when considered in isolation, appears just, but when considered along with penalties for other crimes, is not coherent. Sunstein (2002) concludes that, while the market mechanism is not suitable for making judgments about the provision of cultural goods, WTP surveys are not a solution either, particularly when one considers income constraints.

Recalling somewhat the endowment theory discussed above, Epstein (2003) argues that, even for private goods, value is not well defined, consisting of a market value and (an often divergent) subjective value. He argues that, even if subjective value is ignored, market values (for example, quotes from various builders for adding to a house) can vary quite a lot. If market values for private goods are unreliable, how much more unreliable will be stated preferences for public goods in hypothetical markets?

Epstein (2003) also points out that there are a number of biases introduced into WTP studies by, for example, assuming that non-use or existence values are always positive and that the lower bound of the WTP response is zero. There may be cases where existence value may in fact be negative. A second point is that existence value can apply to many goods, some of which may exclude others. "To ask whether people attach existence value to redwood trees does not tip the scales in favour of their preservation. It is necessary to pose a second question: do they also attach existence value to redwood furniture. But one cannot have both" (Epstein 2003:272).

In fact, there is one early WTP study that does acknowledge both the possible positive and negative externalities of the good. Maddison and Mourato (1999) conducted a study of the WTP to run one of the roads around Stonehenge underground and to close the other in order to restore the peace of this ancient mystical site. However, after being shown maps and pictures of the current and alternate scenarios, respondents were asked, without financial considerations, which scenario they preferred. This allowed those who preferred the current two roads scenario to the tunnel scenario to state their positive value. Regardless of which option they chose, respondents were then asked their WTP in order to secure their preferred option.

While about half the respondents considered the site to be "disfigured" by the roads, a similar number attached a positive value to being able to see the stone circle when driving past or not liking to drive through long tunnels. This suggests that, at least for some respondents, there is a cost associated with running the road through a tunnel. However, WTP for the tunnel scenario was still considerably higher (£12.80) than the current scenario (£4.80), suggesting a much stronger preference amongst those who chose the tunnel scenario. The net heritage benefit of building the tunnel was calculated to be £149m.

Even the most ardent supporters of CV studies do however recognize their limitations. Carson et al. (2001), while concluding that many of the problems of CV can be overcome, mention two areas in which the method is limited. Firstly, WTP studies are limited by wealth. In developed countries, this is less of a problem, but in the developing world, where government policies are often designed specifically to provide public goods to the poorer parts of the population, this can be a significant handicap. The second limitation is that, like all real or hypothetical markets, only the preferences of the current generation and perhaps those imputed for future generations are taken into account, leaving the true preferences of future people unknown and essentially unknowable.

Throsby (2003) also identifies areas where WTP will not capture the full value of the good, particularly if the good is cultural. For example, if the respondent does not personally value the good, but recognizes that value may accrue to others, either as individuals or society as a whole, and is thus willing to pay for it. Throsby (2003:279) argues that such societal values are particularly relevant to cultural goods because of their nature:

> Culture can be defined as the set of beliefs, traditions, customs, etc. which identify a group and bind its members together ... So the value of cultural goods that I am discussing here is a value identifiable in relation to the group rather than to the isolated characteristics of individuals. It is apparent that the perception of this sort of value is not going to be captured by an expression of individual WTP".

Thus, Throsby (2003) argues that, while WTP studies can certainly capture some of the economic value of a cultural good, the relationship will never be perfect and that even the best studies will tend to undervalue the cultural good in question.

4.4 Conclusions

The above review has given examples of how willingness to pay studies have been used to value cultural goods. Using case studies, the chapter outlines the debate around the major ways in which the results of contingent valuation studies have been criticized and shown to be inconsistent with neoclassical economic theory, that is, by being implausibly large, by showing insensitivity to scope and by demonstrating a large disparity between WTP and WTA measures, as well as other general criticisms. As the NOAA Panel (1993) suggests, many of these problems can be controlled for through rigorous and conservative questionnaire design and much of the CV debate has shifted to this arena. The NOAA recommendations, as well as the results of later research, are discussed in the following chapter, focussing specifically on the practical problems of questionnaire design, result interpretation and validity testing.

Appendix 4.1

Examples of WTP Studies in Cultural Economics[2]

YEAR	AUTHOR	AREA	GOOD	SOURCE
1972	Bohm	Broadcasting	TV programme	*European Economic Review* 3:111-130
1980	Throsby, O'Shea	Arts	Mildura Arts Center, Australia	Research Paper 210, Macquarie University
1983	Thompson et al.	Arts	Tax support for Australian arts	Research Paper 261, Macquarie University
1983	Scheider, Pommerehne	Theatre	Swiss municipal theatre	Book: *Economics of Cultural Decisions,* Hendon and Shanahan (Eds)
1986	Morrison, West	Arts	Performing arts and culture, Ontario	*Journal of Behavioural Economics* 15:57-72
1989	Frey, Pommerehne	Museums	Purchase of two Picasso paintings by Swiss city	Book: *Muses and markets*
1990	Ehrenberg, Mills	Broadcasting	TV viewing	Supplement to *Broadcast* (November)
1992	Navrud, Strand	Historical site	Nidaros Cathedral, Norway	Book: *Pricing the European Environment* Navrud (Ed)
1994	Willis	Historical site	Durham Cathedral, England	*Journal of Environmental Planning and Management* 37,3:267-278
1994	Grosclaude, Soguel	Historical site	Building maintenance, Neuchatel, Swiss	*Journal of Environmental Planning and Management* 37,3:279-287
1994	Martin	Museums	Quebec museums	*Journal of Cultural Economics* 18,4:255-270
1995	Schwer, Daneshvary	Broadcasting	PBS TV in Las Vegas	*Journal of Media Economics* 8,3:95-109
1996	Garrod et al.	Historical	Building renovation, Newcastle	*Cities* 16,6:423-430
1996	Longwood et al.	Heritage	Grazing, Australian alps	*Journal of Environmental Planning and Management* 39,3:357-370
1996	Beltran, Rojas	Archaeological sites	Mexican archaeological sites	*Annals of Tourism Research* 23,2:463-478
1997	Carson et al.	Historical site	Fes Medina, Morocco	World Bank Report, Washington
1997	Bille Hansen	Theatre	Royal Theatre in Copenhagen	*Journal of Cultural Economics* 21, 1:1-28

[2] The above table is largely adapted from, with some updating and additions, the very useful annotated bibliographies of Noonan (2002) and EFTEC (2005). While it includes some actual referenda (which are not part of hypothetical market valuation) the major focus is on the willingness to pay method, not including conjoint analysis (choice experiments) that is discussed in chapter six.

1998	Willis, Powe	Historical site	Warkworth Castle, England	*Journal of Environmental Planning and Management* 41,5;611-619
1998	Chambers et al.	Historical site	Building in St. Genevieve, MO	*Public Finance Review* 26:137-154
1998	Scarpa et al.	Historical site	Rivoli Castle, Italy	Book: *Environmental Resource Valuation: Applications of the CV method in Italy* Scarpa, Sirchai , Bravi (Eds)
1998	Pagiola	Historical site	City of Split, Croatia	World Bank website
1998	Bravi, Scarpa	Museums	Italian museums	Book: *Valuing cultural heritage* Bravi, Scarpa, Sirchia (Eds)
1998	Riganti, Scarpa	Archaeological sites	Campi Flegrei, Italy	Book: *Economic resource valuation* Bishop, Romano (Eds)
1999	Glass et al.	Arts	Local area arts in Kansas	University of Kansas Institute for Public Policy and Business, Research report 257
1999	Maddison, Mourato	Historical site	Road options for Stonehenge	CSERGE Working Paper GEC 99-08 (Available on internet)
1999	Papandrea	Broadcasting	Domestic TV	*Journal of Cultural Economics* 23,3:147-164
1999	Harless, Allen	Libraries	Services at University Library	*College & Research Libraries* 60:56-69
1999	Holt et al.	Libraries	St Louis public libraries	*Public Libraries* 38,2:98-108
2000	Santagata, Signorello	Historical site	Napoli Musei Aperti, Italy	*Journal of Cultural Economics* 24,3:181-204
2000	Creigh-Tyte	Heritage	Historical environment in Britain	Paper presented at the *Association of Cultural Economics International* conference in Minneapolis
2000	Begin et al.	Broadcasting	Filmmaking in Quebec and France	*International Journal of Cultural Policy* 7,2:355-368
2001	Pollicino, Maddison	Historical Site	Cleaning Lincoln Cathedral, England	*Journal of Cultural Economics* 25,2:131-148
2001	Ozdemiroglu, Mourato	Heritage	Surrey History Centre	Paper presented at Economic Valuation of Cultural Heritage Conference, University College, London
2001	Jennings	Broadcasting	Irish public radio	M. Lit. submitted at Trinity College, Dublin University
2001	Snowball, Antrobus	Arts	Arts Festival in South Africa	*South African Journal of Economics* 69,4:752-766
2002	Cuccia, Signorello	Historical site	Visits to Noto, Italy	Book: *The economics of heritage* Rizzo, Towse (Eds)
2002	Willis	Historical site	Bosco di Capodimonte	*Journal of Cultural Economics* 26:307-324
2002	Aabo, Strand	Libraries	Norwegian libraries	*Journal of Librarianship and Information Science* 34,1:5-15
2002	Thompson et	Arts	Arts in Kentucky	*Journal of Cultural Economics*

	al.			26:87-113
2002	Mourato et al.	Heritage	Bulgarian monasteries	Book: *Valuing Cultural Heritage* (Navrud, Ready Eds.)
2003	Maddison, Foster	Museums	Congestion in British Museum	*Oxford Economic Papers* 55:173-190
2003	Whitehead, Finney	Heritage	Submerged maritime heritage, North Carolina	*Journal of Cultural Economics* 27, 3-4:231-240
2003	Sanz et al.	Museum	National Museum of Sculpture, Valladolid, Spain	*Journal of Cultural Economics* 27:241-257
2004	Mourato et al.	Historical site	Access to Machu Picchu	*World Economics* 5, 3
2004	Kling et al.	Historical site	Hotel in Fr Collins, CO	*Urban Studies* 41,10:2025-2041
2004	Alberini et al.	Heritage	Value of S. Erasmo in the Lagoon of Venice	*Journal of Environmental Planning and Management* 48,2:155-175
2004	Brown	Heritage	National Trust properties in England	PhD dissertation, Imperial College London
2005	Del Saz Salazar, Marques	Historical site	Restoring old Arab tower, Spain	*Journal of Cultural Heritage* 6:69-77
2005	Aabo	Libraries	Norwegian public libraries	*New Library World* 106, 1218/1219:487-495
2005	Snowball	Arts	Arts Festival in South Africa	*Journal of Cultural Economics* 29:107-125
2006	Jim	Heritage	Heritage trees in cities	*Environmental Monitoring and Assessment* 116:53-80
2006	Tuan, Navrud	Historical site	World Heritage site in Vietnam	*Environmental and Resource Economics*
2007	Kim et al.	Historical site	Changdeok Palace, Korea	*Tourism Management* 28:317-322
2007	Dutta et al.	Heritage	Prinsep Ghat, Calcutta	*Tourism Management* 28:83-95

References

Aabo, S. (2005) Are public libraries worth their price? A contingent valuation study of Norwegian public libraries. New Library World 106, 1218/1219:487-495

Aadland, D. and Caplan, A. (2003) Willingness to pay for curbside recycling with detection and mitigation of hypothetical bias. American Journal of Agricultural Economics 85,2:492-502.

Adamowicz, W., Bhardwaj, V. and Macnab, B. (1993) Experiments on the difference between willingness to pay and willingness to accept. Land Economic 69,4:416-427.

Alberini, A., Rosato, P., Longo, A. and Zanatta, V. (2005) Information and willingness to pay in a contingent valuation study: The value of S. Erasmo in the Lagoon of Venice. Journal of Environmental Planning and Management 48,2:155-175.

Alberini, A. and Longo, A. (2006) Combining the travel cost and contingent behaviour methods to value cultural heritage sites: Evidence from Armenia. Journal of Cultural Economics 30:287-304.

Anchorage Daily News (1999) Hard Aground: Disaster in Prince William Sound Special feature published form 21-24 March. [On line] Available: www.and.com [Accessed 18/09/02].

Bateman, I.J., Cole, M., Cooper, P., Georgiou, S., Hadley, D. and Poe, G.L. (2004) On visible choice sets and scope sensitivity. Journal of Environmental Economics and Management 47:71-93.

Bateman, I., Cooper, P., Georgiou, S., Navrud, S., Poe, G., Ready, R., Riera, P., Ryan, M. and Vossler, C. (2005) Economic valuation of policies for managing acidity in remote mountain lakes: Examining validity through scope sensitivity testing. Aquatic Sciences 67:274-291.

Bateman, I. and Brouwer, R. (2006) Consistency and construction in stated WTP for health risk reductions: A novel scope-sensitivity test. Resource and Energy Economics 28:199-214

Bedate, A., Herrero, L. and Sanz, J. (2004) Economic valuation of the cultural heritage: application to four case studies in Spain. Journal of Cultural Heritage 5,1:101-111.

Biel, A. (2006) Emotions, morality and public goods: The WTA-WTP disparity revisited. Department of Economics, School of Business, Economics and Law, Goteborg University, Working Papers in Economics, no. 193.

Bille Hansen, T. (1997) The willingness to pay for the Royal Theatre in Copenhagen as a public good. Journal of Cultural Economics 21:1-28.

Bille, T. and Schulze, G. (2006) Culture in urban and regional development. Handbook of the Economics of Art and Culture. Ginsburgh, V. and Throsby, D. (Eds.) North Holland:Amsterdam.

Bohm, P. (1972) Estimating demand for public goods: An experiment. Scandinavian Journal of Economics 3:113-130.

Bohm, P. (1979) Estimating willingness-to-pay: Why and how? Scandinavian Journal of Economics 81:142-153.

Bohm, P. (1984) Revealing demand for an actual public good. Journal of Public Economics 24:135-151

Booysen, F. (2001) Non-payment of services: A problem of ability-to-pay. South African Journal of Economics 69,4:674-697.

Botelho, A. and Pinto, L. (2002) Hypothetical, real and predicted real willingness to pay in open-ended surveys: experimental results. *Applied Economics Letters* 9:993-996.

Boter, J., Rouwendal, J. and Wedel, M. (2005) Employing travel time to compare the value of competing cultural organizations. Journal of Cultural Economics 29,1:19-33.

Boyce, R. and Brown, T. (1992) An experimental examination of intrinsic values as a source of the WTA-WTP disparity. The American Economic Review 82,5:1366-1372.

Brown, T. (1994) Experiments on the difference between willingness to pay and willingness to accept: Comment. Land Economics 70,4:520-522.

Carson, R. and Mitchell, R. (1993) The issue of scope in contingent valuation studies. American Journal of Agricultural Economics 75,5:1263-1268.

Carson, R., Mitchell, R., Conway, M. and Navrud, S. (1997) Non-Moroccan Values for Rehabilitating the Fes Medina. World Bank Report: Washington.

Carson, R.T. (1997) Contingent valuation: Theoretical advances and empirical tests since the NOAA panel. American Journal of Agricultural Economics 79,5:1501-1507.

Carson, R., Flores, N. and Mitchell, R. (1999) Theory and measurement of passive use value in Bateman, I. and Willis, K. Valuing Environmental Preferences: Theory and Practice of the CV method in the US, EU and Developing Countries. Oxford University Press: New York.

Carson, R., Flores, N. and Meade, N. (2001) Contingent valuation: Controversies and evidence. Environmental and Resource Economics 19:173-210.

Carson, R., Mitchell, R., Hanemann, M., Kopp, R., Presser, S. and Ruud, P. (2003) Contingent valuation and lost passive use damages from the Exxon Valdez oil spill. Environmental and Resource Economics 25;257-286.

Chambers, C., Chambers P. and Whitehead, J. (1998) Contingent valuation of quasi-public goods: validity, reliability and application to valuing a historic site. Public Finance Review 26,2:137-155.

Champ, P. and Bishop, R. (2001) Donation payment mechanisms and contingent valuation: An empirical study of hypothetical bias. Environmental and Resource Economics 19:383-402.

Cuccia, T. and Signorello, G. (2002) Heritage Conservation in Sicily. Rizzo I. and R. Towse (eds.), Methods for Measuring the Demand for the Arts and Heritage: Theoretical Issues. Edward Elgar Publishing 2002

Cummings, R. and Taylor, L. (1999) Unbiased value estimates for environmental goods: A cheap talk design for the contingent valuation method. American Economic Review 89,3:649-666.

Del Saz Salazar, S. and Marques, M. (2005) Valuing cultural heritage: the social benefit of restoring an old Arab tower. Journal of Cultural Heritage 6:69-77

Del Saz Salazar, S. and Menendez, L. (2007) Estimating the non-market benefits of an urban park: Does proximity matter? Land Use Policy 24:296-305.

Desvousges, W., Johnson, F. Dunford, R. Boyle, K., Hudson, S. and Wilson, K. (1993) Measuring natural resource damages with contingent valuation: Tests of validity and reliability. In Hausman, J. (Ed.) Contingent Valuation: A critical assessment. Elsivier Science Publishers: Amsterdam.

Diamond, P. and Hausman, J. A. (1993) On contingent valuation measurement of nonuse values. In Hausman, J. (Ed.) Contingent Valuation: A critical assessment Elsivier Science Publishers: Amsterdam

Diamond, P. and Hausman, J.A. (1994) Contingent valuation: Is some number better than no number? Journal of Economic Perspectives 8,4:45-65.

Diamond, P. (1996) Testing the internal consistency of contingent valuation surveys. Journal of Environmental Economics and Management 30:337-347.

Dupont, D. P. (2003) CVM embedding effects when there are active, potentially active and passive users of environmental goods. Environmental and Resource Economics 25:319-341.

Dutta, M., Banerjee, S. and Husain, Z. (2007) Untapped demand for heritage: A contingent valuation study of Prisep Ghat, Calcutta. Tourism Management 28:83-95.

Eftec (2005) Valuation of the historic environment: Annotated bibliography of heritage valuation studies. Economics for the Environment Consultancy Ltd. London.

Epstein, R. (2003) The regrettable necessity of contingent valuation. Journal of Cultural Economics 27:259-274.

Glass, R., Clifford, N., Harris, B., Wollsey, C. and Krider, C. (1999) Economic scope, impact and marketing study of the Kansas Arts Commission. The University of Kansas, Institute for Public Policy and Business: Research report number 257.

Guzman, R. and Kolstad, C. (2006) Researching preference, valuation and hypothetical bias. Environmental and Resource Economics. Springer Online Publication.

Hanemann, M. (1991) Willingness to pay and willingness to accept: how much can they differ? The American Economic Review 81,3:635-647.

Hanemann, M. (1994) Valuing the environment through contingent valuation. Journal of Economic Perspectives 8,4:19-43.

Harless, D. and Allen, F. (1999) Using the contingent valuation method to measure patron benefits of reference desk services in an academic library. College and Research Libraries January:56-69

Hausman, J. (Ed.) (1993) Contingent Valuation: A critical assessment. North-Holland: Amsterdam.

Holt, G. and Elliott, D. (1999) Proving your library's worth: A test case. Library Journal November:42-44.

Inder, B. and O'Brien, T. (2003) The endowment effect and the role of uncertainty. Bulletin of Economic Research 55,3:289-301.

Johansson, P. (1993) Cost-Benefit Analysis of Environmental Change. Cambridge University Press: London.

Kahneman, D., Knetsch, J. and Thaler, R. (1990) Experimental tests of the endowment effect and the Coase theorem. *Journal* of Political Economy 98,6:1325-1348.

Kahneman, D and Knetsch, J. (1992) Valuing public goods: The purchase of moral satisfaction. Journal of Environmental Economics and Management 22:57-70

Kahneman, D., Ritov, I. and Schkade, D. (1999) Economic preferences or attitude expressions: an analysis of dollar responses to public issues. Journal of Risk and Uncertainty 19, 1-3:203-235.

Kim, S., Wong, K. and Cho, M. (2007) Assessing the economic value of a world heritage site and willingness to pay determinants: A case of Changdeok Palace. Tourism Management 28:317-322

Kling, R., Revier, C. and Sable, K. (2004) Estimating the public good value of preserving a local historical landmark: The role of non-substitutability and citizen information. Urban Studies 41,10:2025-2041.

List, J. and Shogren, J. (1998) Calibration of the difference between actual and hypothetical valuation in a field experiment. Journal of Economic Behavior and Organization 37:193-205.

List, J. (2001) Do explicit warnings eliminate the hypothetical bias in elicitation procedures? Evidence from field auctions for sportscards. The American Economic Review 91,5:1498-1507.

List, J. and Gallet, C. (2001) What experimental protocol influences disparities between actual and hypothetical stated values? Environmental and Resource Economics 20:241-254.

List, J. (2003) Does market experience eliminate market anomalies? The Quarterly Journal of Economics Feb: 41-71.

Lusk, J. (2003) Effects of cheap talk on consumer willingness to pay for golden rice. American Journal of Agricultural Economics 85,4:840-856.

Noonan, D. (2002) Contingent valuation studies in the arts and culture: An annotated bibliography. The Cultural Policy Center at the University of Chicago: Working Paper.

Maddison, D. and Mourato, S. (1999) Valuing different road options for Stonehenge. CSERGE Working Paper GEC 99-08

Maddison, D. and Foster, T. (2003) Valuing congestion costs in the British Museum. Oxford Economic Papers 55:173-190.

Mansfield, C. (1999) Despairing over disparities: Explaining the difference between willingness to pay and willingness to accept. Environmental and Resource Economics 13:219-234.

Mitchell, R. and Carson, R. (1993) Current Issues in the Design, Administration, and Analysis of Contingent Valuation Surveys, University of California at San Diego, Economics Working Paper Series 93-54, Department of Economics, UC San Diego

Morrison, W. and West, E. (1986) Subsidies for the performing arts: Evidence of voter preference. Journal of Behavioral Economics 15, Fall:57-72.

Morrison, G. (1997a) Willingness to pay and willingness to accept: some evidence of an endowment effect. Applied Economics 29:411-417.

Morrison, G. (1997b) Resolving differences in willingness to pay and willingness to accept: Comment. The American Economic Review 87,1:236-240.

Mourato, S., Kontoleon, A. and Danchev, A. (2002) Preserving cultural heritage in transition economies: A contingent valuation study of Bulgarian monasteries. Navrud, S. and Ready, R. (Eds.) Valuing Cultural Heritage. Edward Elgar Publishing.

Mourato, S., Ozdemiroglu, E., Hett, T. and Atkinson, G. (2004) Pricing cultural heritage: A new approach to managing ancient resources. World Economics 5, 3:1-19.

Mundy, B. and McLean, D. (1998) Using the contingent valuation approach for natural resource and environmental damage application. Appraisal Journal 66,3:290-298.

Murphy, J., Allen, G., Stevens, T. and Weatherhead, D. (2005a) A meta-analysis of hypothetical bias in stated preference valuation. Environmental and Resource Economics 30:313-325.

Murphy, J., Stevens, T. and Weatherhead, D. (2005b) Is cheap talk effective at eliminating hypothetical bias in a provision point mechanism? Environmental and Resource Economics 30:327-343.

Navrud, S. and Strand, J. (1992) The preservation value of Nidaros Cathedral, in Pricing the European Environment (Navrud, S. (ed.) Oxford University Press: New York.

Nestor, D. (1998) Policy evaluation with combined actual and contingent response data. American Journal of Agricultural Economics 80,2:264-277.

NOAA (1993) Arrow, K.J., Solow, R., Leamer, E., Radner, R. and Schuman, H. Report of the NOAA Panel on contingent valuation. National Oceanic and Atmospheric Administration Federal Register 58,10

Ozdemiroglu, E. and Mouraton, S. (2001) Valuing our recorded heritage. Paper presented at the Economic Valuation of Cultural Heritage conference, University College, London.

Papandrea, F. (1999) Willingness to pay for domestic television programming. Journal of Cultural Economics 23:149-166

Pollicino, M. and Maddison, D. (2001) Valuing the benefits of cleaning Lincoln Cathedral. Journal of Cultural Economics 25:131-148.

Poor, J. and Smith, J. (2004) Travel cost analysis of a cultural heritage site: The case of historic St. Mary's city of Maryland. Journal of Cultural Economics 28,3:217-229.

Ready, R., Berger, N. and Blomquist, G. (1997) Measuring amenity benefits from farmland: hedonic pricing versus contingent valuation. Journal of Urban and Regional Policy 28,4:438-458.

Ringanti, P. and Scarpa, R. (1998) Categorical nesting and information effects on WTP estimates for the conservation of cultural heritage in Campi Flegrei. Bishop, R. and Romano, D. (Eds.) Environmental and Resource Valuation. Kluwer: Boston.

Samuelson, P. (1954) The pure theory of public expenditure. Review of Economics and Statistics 36:378-389.

Sanz, J., Herrero, L. and Bedate, A. (2003) Contingent valuation and semi-parametic methods: A case study of the National Museum of Sculpture in Valladolid, Spain. Journal of Cultural Economics 27:241-257.

Scarpa, R., Sirchia, G. and Bravi, M. (1998) Kernel vs logit modelling of single bounded CV responses: Valuing access to architectural and visual arts in Italy. In Bishop, R. and Romano, D. (Eds.) Environmental Resource Valuation: Applications of the Contingent Valuation Method in Italy. Kluwer: Boston.

Seaman, B. (2003a) Contingent Valuation vs. Economic impact: substitutes or complements? Paper delivered at the Regional Science Association International Conference, North American Meetings: Philadelphia

Sen, A. (1985) Well-Being, agency and freedom: The Dewey lectures 1984. The Journal of Philosophy 82,4:169-221.

Shogren, J., Shin, A. Hayes, D. and Kleinbenstein, J. (1994) Resolving differences in willingness to pay and willingness to accept. The American Economic Review 84,1:255-270.

Shogren, J. and Hayes, D. (1997) Resolving differences in willingness to pay and willingness to accept: Reply in The American Economic Review 87,1:241-244.

Smith, K. and Osborne, L. (1996) Do contingent valuation methods pass a 'scope' test? A meta-analysis. Journal of Environmental Economics and Management 31:286-301.

Snowball, J. (2000) Towards more accurate measurement of the value of the arts to society: Economic impact and willingness to pay studies at the Standard Bank National Arts Festival. Unpublished Masters Thesis: Department of Economics, Rhodes University, Grahamstown, South Africa.

Snowball, J. and Antrobus, G. (2001) Measuring the value of the arts to society: the importance of the value of externalities to lower income and education groups in South Africa. South African Journal of Economics 69,4:752-766.

Snowball, J. and Antrobus, G. (2003) Results of the WTP household survey at the Klein Karoo Nationale Kunstefees. Unpublished research paper, Rhodes University: South Africa.

Snowball, J. (2005) Art for the masses? Justification for the public support of the arts in developing countries – two arts festivals in South Africa. Journal of Cultural Economics 29:107-125.

Sunstein, C., Kahneman, D., Schkade, D. and Ritov, I. (2001) Predictably Incoherent Judgments. Paper presented at the Cultural Policy Center at the University of Chicago workshop. [On line] Available: http://cutural policy. Uchicago.edu/workshop/sunstein.Html [Accessed: 19/02/03].

Sunstein, C. (2002) Coherent and incoherent valuation: a problem with contingent valuation of cultural amenities. The Cultural Policy Center at the University of Chicago: Working paper.

Thampapillai, D. (2000) Willingness to pay and willingness to accept: a simple conceptual exposition. Applied Economics Letters 7:509-511.

Thompson, B., Throsby, D. and Withers, G. (1983) Measuring community benefits from the arts. Research paper 261 School of Economic and Financial Studies: Macquarie University.

Thompson, E., Berger, M. and Allen, S. (1998) Arts and the Kentucky economy. Center for Business and Economic Research, University of Kentucky.

Thompson, E., Berger, M. and Blomquist, G. (2002) "Valuing the arts: A contingent valuation approach" *Journal of Cultural Economics* 26:87-113.

Throsby, D. (1984) The measurement of willingness-to-pay for mixed goods. Oxford Bulletin of Economics and Statistics 46,4 279-289

Throsby, D. and Withers, G. (1985) What price culture? Journal of Cultural Economics 9,2:1-33.

Throsby, D. and Withers, G. (1986) Strategic bias and demand for public goods: theory and application to the arts. Towse, R. (Ed.) Cultural economics: The arts, the heritage and the media industries. Vol 2 Edward Elgar: Cheltenham.

Throsby, D. (2003) Determining the value of cultural goods: How much (or how little) does contingent valuation tell us? *Journal* of Cultural Economics 27:275-285.

Vossler, C. and McKee, M. (2006) Induced-value tests of contingent valuation elicitation mechanisms. Environmental and Resource Economics 35:137-168.

Whitehead, J., Haab, T. and Huang, J. (2000) Measuring recreation benefits of quality improvements with revealed and stated behavior data. Resource and Energy Economics 22:339-254.

Whitehead, J. and Finney, S. (2003) Willingness to pay for submerged maritime cultural resources. Journal of Cultural Economics 27:231-240.

Willis, K. (1994) Paying for heritage: What price for Durham Cathedral? Journal of Environmental Planning and Management 37,3:267-278.

Willis, K. and Powe, N. (1998) Contingent valuation and real economic commitments: A private good experiment. Journal of Environmental Planning and Management 41,5:611-620.

5 Using Willingness to Pay Studies to Value Cultural Goods

Now that the theoretical basis for willingness to pay studies and some examples from cultural economics have been discussed, this chapter sets out to examine the more practical issues involved in designing such a study. In particular, how to design a questionnaire that will minimize the various forms of bias that willingness to pay studies are prone to, is explored, like the information bias and starting point bias. Validity tests and detection of problems like "protest zeros" and "warm glow" responses are also included. An example of a willingness to pay questionnaire from a study conducted at the South African National Arts Festival in Grahamstown is examined and can be found in the appendix to this chapter.

5.1 Data Collection and Sampling

There are a great number and variety of willingness to pay study designs in cultural economics and such decisions depend largely on the sort of good being valued and on the researcher's assumptions about who the affected population is. For example, Dutta et al. (2007) interviewed a sample of all Calcutta residents (stratified to reflect the demographics of the city) when valuing the Prinsep Ghat restoration. This included those who might have visited the site in the past or the future (use values), but also those who might never go, but still value heritage conservation (non-use values). Bille Hanson (1997) sampled the whole Danish population in valuing the Royal Theatre in Copenhagen because it was assumed that, although only a small percentage of the sample actually attended the theatre, it was so important that there were significant non-use values that accrued to the rest of the population.

In 2003, a study was conducted of the WTP of the local populations to support two South African arts festivals, The South African National Arts

Festival in Grahamstown and the *Klein Karoo Nationale Kunstefees* in Oudtshoorn (Snowball and Antrobus 2003, Snowball 2005). The total willingness to pay to avoid a 25% reduction in festival size was calculated using the mean willingness to pay figures for each area (high and low income) for the populations of the two smalls towns in which the festivals took place. For Grahamstown, willingness to pay was almost R3 million (about 300 000 where 1 is equal to about 10 South African Rands) and for Oudtshoorn R2.9 million (290 000) per year. Since these are both national arts festivals that attract visitors from the whole country and, to a small extent, from other countries, it could be argued that the use and especially non-use values could be extended to the whole South African population. However, for the purposes of a cost-benefit analysis, it was more significant to determine the non-market value to town residents, since it is the municipalities of these towns (and thus the citizens) who carry a significant share of the festivals' costs. Also, for a meaningful comparison with the economic impact study (discussed in chapter 3) it was useful to conduct the WTP study in the same area (town residents only). However, if the study was to be extended, a new sample, including non-residents would have to be used, since it is quite likely that the values of residents differ significantly from those who live in other towns.

Table 5.1. Total WTP at Two South African Arts Festivals

	Grahamstown Festival			**Oudtshoorn Festival**		
	High income	Low income	Total	High income	Low income	Total
Number of residents	27 548	97 219	124 767	14 400	65 600	80 000
Average number of people per household	3.2	5.2		2.8	4.5	
Total number of households	8 608	18 695	27 305	5 143	14 578	19 721
Average WTP per month per household	R14.80	R6.55		R17.42	R10.33	
WTP per year by all households	R1.53m	R1.49m	R3.02m	R1.07m	R1.8m	R2.87m

(Snowball 2005:123)

Some studies, like the one by Maddison and Mourato (1999), which valued different road options around Stonehenge, and the one by Thompson et al. (2002) of the arts in Kentucky, stratified their samples to give greater weight to those actually using or affected by the site (UK tourists on site and "arts patron" households respectively) as well as taking a general sample of the whole population. In valuing Armenian heritage sites, Alberini and Longo (2006) concentrated exclusively on visitors to the sites. The important question to answer at this stage of the research design is, "Who is assumed to gain use and non-use benefits from this cultural good?". Despite its apparent simplicity, once one starts to think about the non-use value in particular, it can be difficult to know when to stop. While most studies are limited to national boundaries, Carson et al. (1997) calculated the value of improvements to the Fes Medina in Morocco to visitors to the site, to Moroccan non-visitors and to the European population in general.

Table 5.2. Examples of WTP Study Designs in Cultural Economics

Source	Method used	Sample size	Sampling method	Population
Bille Hansen (1997) (Theatre)	Telephone and follow-up visits to those with no phone	1843	Random sample of those over 16 years old	Danish population
Maddison and Mourato (1999) (Archaeological site)	Face to face	500 households; 300 visitors	Random, with a focus on households in the area around Stonehenge	British households (off-site) and UK tourists (on site)
Thompson et al. (2002) (Arts)	Postal surveys (3 copies sent to non-respondents)	600 to each sub-sample	1. Random 2. "arts patron" households	Kentucky households
Snowball 2003 (Arts Festival)	Telephone	193	Random, but stratified to include high and low income area residents	Grahamstown population
Alberini and Longo (2006) (Armenian heritage sites)	Face to face	125 at each site (500 in all)	Random	Domestic visitors on site
Dutta et al. (2007) (Heritage in Calcutta)	Face-to-face interviews	181	Purposive to reflect socio-economic make-up of Calcutta	Calcutta residents

Similar considerations apply when deciding on data collection method and sample size. The best method, and the one recommended by the NOAA panel (1993), is face to face interviews. These are particularly important if there is a low literacy level in the sample population (for example the Dutta et al. 2007 study in Calcutta) or language barriers (Snowball and Antrobus 2003 study in South Africa). The great advantages of face to face interviews are that one can use visual material to illustrate a particular good, or a change in the hypothetical scenario, and that they facilitate communication, since interviewers are more likely to be able to determine whether respondents are understanding the questions and to clarify or repeat if need be. Of course, interviewers can also bias results and care needs to be taken in selection and training. For example, the Dutta et al. (2007) study found that female interviewers positively and statistically significantly affected WTP bids. Many large studies use companies who specialise in gathering survey data.

In cases where the cost of face to face interviews is prohibitive and literacy levels are low, some studies have successfully used telephone interviews to gather data. A common criticism of using telephone interviews is that this biases the average household income of respondents upwards, since only those households who can afford a telephone are surveyed – particularly an issue in developing country studies. However, in the case of the South African arts festival (Snowball and Antrobus 2003), the results show that households with very widely ranging incomes were included, perhaps as a result of telephone sharing between low income households. In addition, it was easier to cater for different language groups when conducting telephone interviews (questionnaires were available in English, Afrikaans and Xhosa). If respondents preferred to answer in a language in which the initial interviewer was not proficient, the interview could easily be continued with someone else. The Bille Hanson (1997) Danish theatre study used telephone interviews, with follow-up face to face interviews where sampled households did not have access to a telephone.

There are very few WTP studies that have successfully used postal surveys. The Thompson et al. (2002) study of the arts in Kentucky used this method with a random sample of 600 general Kentucky households and 600 "arts patron" households. Despite the advantage of a fairly homogenous, English speaking population with high literacy levels, and sending up to three questionnaires to non-responding households, their response rates were fairly low: 30% from the general household sample and 57% from the "arts patron" households.

Finally, the size of the samples used in WTP studies varies widely and depends on how homogenous the population being surveyed is and on the resources of the study. The number of observations needed will also depend on the format of the WTP question (discussed later in this chapter) and on the kind of statistical analysis and degree of reliability required. Some of the largest studies, like the Danish theatre valuation (Bille Hanson 1997), which had 1843 observations, are part of national surveys rather than stand-alone studies. Alberini and Longo (2006) interviewed 125 people at each heritage site (500 in all), Maddison and Mourato (1999) interviewed 300 visitors to Stonehenge as well as 500 UK households. However, there are also smaller studies, where single towns or cities are involved, like the Dutta et al. (2007) study with a sample size of 181 and the Snowball and Antrobus (2003) study which conducted 193 telephone interviews.

5.2 Questionnaire Structure in WTP Studies

Most WTP questionnaires can be divided into a few major sections: (i) a section on use values, gathering information on frequency of visits or attendance, purpose of visits and perceptions of the quality of the experience. This may also include information on spending at the site, and, if appropriate, earnings as a result of the cultural good or event; (ii) a section on non-use values, gathering data on the opinions and knowledge of respondents regarding cultural goods generally, other recreational activities, perceived benefits that the good provides and so on; (iii) the WTP question itself, including information on the good, the hypothetical scenario to be valued, the payment vehicle and payment amounts. This section can also include debriefing questions probing why the respondent was willing or unwilling to pay and a post-decision confidence measure; (iv) finally, socio-demographic information regarding the respondent's age, race, educational level, household income, occupation, religion, political affiliations and so on. Each of these sections will be discussed in detail below.

Examples of WTP Questionnaire Structure in Cultural Good Valuation

Alberini & Longo (2006) Armenian cultural heritage

1. Information about site visits (number of trips in past 12 months; travel mode, purpose of visit, use of shops and accommodation; time spent on site; rate of satisfaction with site visit)
2. WTP for 3 hypothetical scenarios
3. Other recreational activities, cultural interests and attitudes
4. Demographics.

Snowball (2005) South African National Arts Festival

1. Opinions regarding the public good values of the festival
2. Use values: attendance and spending at the festival
3. Earnings as a result of the festival
4. WTP questions
5. Demographic information

Maddison and Foster (2003) Congestion costs in the British Museum

1. Current use of and attitudes towards the British Museum
2. WTP questions
3. Socio-economic characteristics

Ozdemiroglu and Mourato (2001): Surrey History Centre

1. Use of the institution (number and purpose of visits, quality perceptions)
2. Perception and attitudes towards recorded heritage generally and perceived benefits from preservation
3. WTP questions
4. Socio-economic characteristics

5.3 Opinions and Externalities: Measuring Non-use Values

An effective way of gauging the opinions of respondents before giving any information about the specific good being valued, is to begin the interview with questions about their feelings towards the good, or cultural goods in general. In addition to being an ice-breaker, opinion questions can also provide a useful internal consistency check in that responses can be compared to later, open-ended reasons for being willing or not willing to pay for the good in question. Such general opinions can be important determinants of WTP responses and, if they are coded using a score or a dummy variable, useful in econometric analysis.

Opinions and knowledge of non-use values, like the benefits to the general population of having a museum or library in the city, or the value of an archival history centre or cultural heritage building, can be solicited in a number of ways, depending on the good being valued and the interview format. Open-ended questions can be revealing, especially if it is likely that the respondents will be familiar with the good in question. Respondents can also be asked to agree or disagree with statements about the good, or to indicate the strength of their feelings using a numerical scale, or categories, like “strongly agree”, “agree”, “neutral”, “disagree”, “strongly disagree” or “don’t know”.

The South African National Arts Festival study followed the questionnaire design of Thompson, Throsby and Withers (1983), who conducted a survey of 827 Sydney residents to determine their interest in the arts, including their attendance, participation, perception of benefits and cost and WTP to support them through public funding. A number of more specific questions from a study on the impact of the Mildura Arts Center (Throsby and O’Shea, 1980), a community centre consisting of a theatre, gallery and museum in Victoria, Australia were also used. Respondents were asked to respond to various opinion statements on the feelings of pride the festival evoked, its possible future use values, educational potential and its possible harmful effects on society by stating "agree", "disagree" or "don't know".

The town in which the South African National Arts Festival (NAF) takes place is a typical small South African town. As a result of the Apartheid era, wealth (and thus residential areas) is still largely divided along racial lines. The East part of the town consists largely of Xhosa speaking, African-origin households which generally have lower incomes compared to the largely European-origin, English speaking households in the West. One of the assumptions that the research wanted specifically to test was the generally held view that poorer households do not benefit as much as wealthier households and thus value the festival less. The 2003 study results were also compared to an earlier study conducted in 2000 as a test of temporal reliability. As a pilot test, a similar study was conducted in 2003 in another small festival town, Oudtshoorn, also divided along race/wealth lines. Table 5.3 compares the results of the opinion questions from these two festivals with those of the Sidney and Mildura studies.

Results show that, in general, high and low income communities in both South African towns felt that their arts festival provided them with positive, non-market externalities in the form of feelings of pride, improved community education and value to future generations (or future use options for themselves). The same is true of the Sydney and Mildura studies, although these showed a higher percentage of people agreeing with positive statements, perhaps as a result of a greater homogeneity in population. Overall, the results suggest that the inclusion of only the market benefits derived from the festivals in their valuation (in other words, economic impact studies) would underestimate festival value for the majority of both communities.

As a test of temporal reliability, that is, whether preferences are stable over time (discussed further in section 7 of this chapter), opinion responses to earlier studies can be compared with later ones. Looking at the 2000 and 2003 Grahamstown studies, the comparison of results does not show any startling reversal of opinion that cannot be explained by changing circumstances, suggesting that there is a reasonable degree of temporal reliability in opinions. In terms of future-use value and educational potential especially, opinion results seem to have remained fairly stable.

Table 5.3. A Comparison of Arts Opinion Surveys

	2000	**2003**	**2003**	**2003**	**2003**		
Statement	**Ghst Total**	**Ghst Total**	**Ghst. High Income**	**Ghst. Low Income**	**Oudtsh. Total**	**Sydney**	**Mildura**
The Festival gives all the people of [town name] a sense of pride (% agree)	78	86	79	92	87	95	94
The Festival only benefits those who actually pay to go to the ticketed shows (% disagree)	71	62	81	49	n/a	64	n/a
The arts at the Festival harm society because they are too critical of our way of life (% disagree)	81	71	69	73	83	81	93
The Festival should be kept going so that people or their children have the choice of attending it in the future (% agree)	93	94	100	91	94	n/a	96
The arts offered at the Festival are useful in educating the community of all ages (% agree)	86	84	70	93	78	97	96

(Snowball 2001, Snowball 2005; Throsby and O'Shea 1980 and Throsby and Withers 1985)

Such opinion questions can also serve as a useful way to determine whether there are significant differences in the values recognized by different communities within the sample population. Although not large in most cases, there are some interesting differences between high and low income communities in the case of the South African arts festivals. In both towns, more people from the low income areas agreed that the festival gave all the people in the community a sense of pride, despite the fact that people from these areas attended fewer shows and festival events than did those from the high income areas. Another interesting difference is that, in both cases, more low income area respondents valued the educational potential of the festivals than did high income respondents, probably because so little else is available to low income respondents in the way of extra mural and cultural activities. In both cases, however, high income groups were more responsive to the idea of future or option use value, perhaps as a result of the fairly transient and migratory nature of many low income residents as compared to those in the high income area.

Another important test is that of reliability, that is, whether study results can be replicated in a different context or at a different time. While the

Sydney and Mildura studies valued different goods (the arts in general and a community arts centre), a comparison with opinions about the arts in general is still interesting, especially given that Australia is a developed country context, while South Africa is still developing. In general, it is surprising how similar the results of the South African studies are to those done in Australia, except that more people in the Australian studies (97% and 96%) agreed that the arts had an important role to play in community education than in the South African studies (86%, 84% and 78%).

In the 2003 Grahamstown festival study, positive opinions were included as an explanatory variable in a Tobit model regression with WTP as the dependent variable. A positive opinion was assigned a score of 1 and negative or "don't know" responses a zero score. Results show that positive opinions about the festival are a significant determinant of whether or not a respondent is likely to be willing to pay in both the high and low income areas: an increase in the opinion score of one unit increases the probability of being WTP some amount nearly 26 times.

5.4 Attendance, Spending and Earnings: Measuring Use Values

As discussed in chapter 5, WTP studies are prone to a "mixed good" or "user" bias – that is, that although the method measures both use and non-use values, respondents who have use values are likely to be willing to pay more than those who have only non-use values. It is thus important to determine to what extent WTP is affected by use values, or the intention to use the good in the future (option use value), particularly in cases where the results are going to be generalized to a population which might have a significant proportion of non-users.

The South African National Arts Festival 2003 study found that 66% of Grahamstown high income area residents attended at least one ticketed show compared to only 16% of low income area residents. However, 88% of festival goers attended at least one free show, like art exhibitions, street theatre, craft market, and outdoor music performances, but the number of low income area residents attending free shows was greater than the high income area ones. The ratio of free to ticketed shows for the high income area was 1:1.24 and 1:0.16 for the low income area. Thus, while wealthier residents, who have a higher average disposable income, attend more of the ticketed events, poorer residents still benefit from the festival by attending the free shows. Attendance at both free and ticketed events was shown to be a statistically significant determinant of WTP to support the festival. However, free show attendance was more significant in the low income area, while ticketed show attendance was more significant in the high income area.

This section of the questionnaire can also contain questions about respondents' spending on the cultural good (number of tickets bought), and related activities (shopping, meals, accommodation, travel costs and so on). While usually highly correlated with income, such market data can be a useful indicator of the resources respondents allocate to the cultural good and of differences in taste between various groups of consumers. As in the Alberini and Longo (2006) study of the value of Armenian heritage, such spending information can also be used to apply a complementary valuation technique – in their case, the travel cost method. Studies which have combined WTP and economic impact valuation methods are the Throsby and O'Shea (1980) valuation of the Mildura Arts Centre in Australia, the Thomson et al. (1998 and 2002) studies of the arts in Kentucky and the Glass et al. (1999) study of the arts in Kansas.

If an economic impact study is also being conducted, one might include a question asking respondents if they spent more during the festival or event than usual and, if they did, what they might have spent the money on if there had been no arts event. These questions (as mentioned in the economic impact section) are designed to test the theory that additional local spending should be included in economic impact calculations of such events and to determine, as suggested by Crompton (1999), whether the additional spending would have taken place outside the impact area if no event had been held.

In an attempt to measure the elasticity of ticket prices, Grahamstown arts festival respondents who had done some ticket spending were asked whether they would have attended the same number of shows if ticket prices had been 10%, 20% or 50% higher. As pointed out by Noonan (personal correspondence 2003), this question is open to "lumpiness", since dropping a whole show as a result of a relatively small increase in price would result in a far greater percentage decrease in attendance. However, as an experiment to determine whether attenders of ticketed shows were aware of their consumer surplus (and to test whether the presence of acknowledged consumer surplus affects WTP) it provided interesting data and could also be used to test the idea put forward by Thompson et al. (2002) that, for attenders, WTP may be partly a donation of consumer surplus (linked to the mixed good bias discussed in chapter 4). Figure 5.1 below shows the results for both the Grahamstown and Oudtshoorn festival respondents.

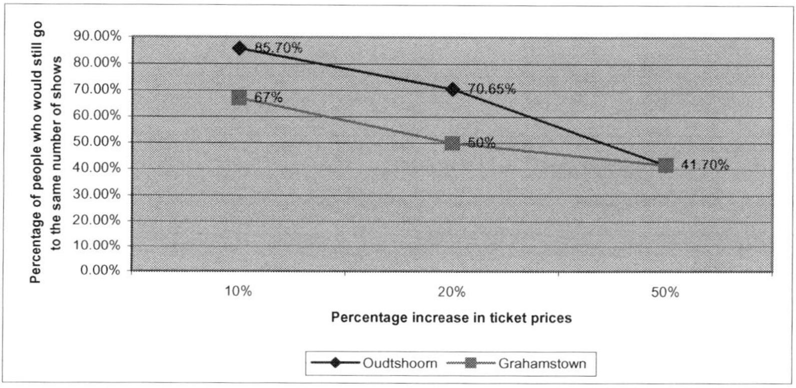

Fig. 5.1. Consumer Surplus at Two Arts Festivals in South Africa

All one can usefully say about these results is that they conform to expected economic theory (i.e. as price rises, demand falls), and that there does appear to be a fairly high level of consumer surplus at both festivals, although it is initially much higher at the Oudtshoorn festival than at the Grahamstown festival. However, consumer surplus was not shown to be a significant determinant of WTP in this case.

Finally, if appropriate, questions about the earnings of respondents as a result of the cultural event could be included here. Seaman (2003) suggests that part of what WTP may be capturing is the current or future expected financial benefits associated with the event and that this may be biasing WTP upwards. As discussed in the previous chapter, this did indeed turn out to be the case at the South African arts festivals (Snowball 2005).

5.5 The WTP Question

The central part of the questionnaire is the WTP scenario and question. In addition to the WTP question, information on the good being valued (and sometimes the status quo) needs to be provided in order to allow respondents to make an informed decision. There are also several possible formats that the WTP question can take, that is, open ended or closed ended (dichotomous choice), or a combination of the two. Follow-up questions and confidence measures after the WTP question can also be important in interpreting the results. The following section discusses these issues, using examples from the Grahamstown National Arts Festival study and other studies done on cultural goods.

5.5.1 The Provision of Information and Information Bias

One of the most problematic features of designing a WTP study is in deciding what level of information to provide to respondents. Bohm (1972; 1979; 1984) argued strongly that, in order for respondents to be able to express their WTP accurately, detailed information must be made available to them regarding the proposed project. Kenyon and Edwards-Jones (1998) summarize the two main schools of thought on this issue. The "not too much argument" points out that better information does not always mean more and that too much can lead to assimilation problems for the respondent. On the other hand, the "not too little" school holds that, for respondents to make reasonable decisions, some threshold of information about the good being valued is required. Ideally, some "adequate" level of information is needed; the problem is how to test for it.

Niewijk (2001) is highly critical of the whole WTP method, but focuses particularly on information bias. Not only does he argue that an attempt to provide as much information as possible is bound to cause some bias, he also points out that, even if all this information is provided, the respondent must assimilate it and accept it as true in order to give an accurate valuation. He also argues that contingent valuation measures are supposed to be measuring pre-existing values, but if respondents are not directly aware of the existence of a particular good before the survey, the information provided might in fact create the value it proposes to measure.

Kenyon and Edwards-Jones (1998) ran a field experiment in which four ecologically interesting sites were valued by (environmental) experts and the public (WTP study). Their hypothesis was that, if the ranking of the sites in ecological interest by the experts matched the public's ranking in terms of willingness to pay for a ticket to the site, then they would have arrived at the ideal level of information. When varying the amount of information supplied to the WTP study respondents, they found that small amounts of information were characterized by large numbers of protest bids (zero WTP responses not related to the value of the good, but in protest against some aspect of the survey) and a ranking of sites inconsistent with that of the experts. However, when much more information about the sites, including photographic, textual and ecological data, as well as a visit to the site, was provided, WTP study respondents were able to rank the sites in the same order as the experts. They conclude therefore, that, given enough of the right kinds of information, WTP studies could be used effectively to make land-use decisions. However, they acknowledge that the comparison of expert with public valuations may not always be appropriate, since WTP studies are meant to include precisely those public good characteristics which the experts may not value, for example, that it is "a nice place to walk" or that it provides "open space".

Krueger (2002) conducted an experiment on groups of university students on their WTP to convert livestock farms to game farms in the surrounding area. Three different levels of information were provided to three different groups of respondents, the first group receiving only a very brief statement, group 2 being provided with more details and background information and group 3 receiving the most comprehensive explanation of the proposed project. In agreement with Kenyon and Edwards-Jones (1998) he found that low levels of information correlated with a high number of non-responses and zero WTP bids. Mean WTP for those given the smallest amount of information was also significantly lower than for the other two groups. The biggest difference in mean WTP occurred between group 1 and 2, group 2 respondents being willing to pay 7.2% more than group 1. While mean WTP of group 3 respondents was still higher than for group 2, it was only 4.5% higher, suggesting that, as some "adequate" level of information is approached, providing more information does not significantly affect WTP bids and that attempting to provide "complete" information is not necessary.

Ajzen et al. (1996), using the Elaboration Likelihood Model of persuasion, argue that information given in WTP studies is often persuasive, even when it is judged by the researcher to be unbiased. They suggest that information bias will be affected by two things, the quality of the argument and the personal relevance of the good or situation to the respondent. Using an experiment conducted on university students for both a public good (campus movie theatre) and a private good (personal noise filter) they show that both these factors have a significant effect on WTP bid amounts.

As expected, argument quality was positively related to WTP amount, as was personal relevance. It appears that when the good is perceived as being personally important to the respondents, they are much more sensitive to the strength or weakness of the argument.

In addition, the experiment contained an interesting attempt to check whether "moral satisfaction" (warm glow) significantly affected WTP (Ajzen et al. 1996). Before the WTP scenario, the questionnaire, through a series of cognitive exercises, activated either individualistic or altruistic motives. They found that, for those respondents for whom the scenario had little personal relevance (therefore making them less sensitive to the strength of the argument), the "superficial motivational cues" provided by the individualistic or altruistic priming had a highly significant effect on WTP bids (Ajzen et al. 1996:56). In other words, while all WTP responses were shown to be correlated with primed attitudes, warm glow responses are likely to be much more of a problem when respondents do not perceive the way in which the good can be of personal relevance to them and/or the argument presented is weak.

Information Bias in Cultural Economics Studies

In a theoretical paper Throsby and Withers (1986) suggest that information bias may appear particularly in WTP studies for complex mixed goods (like cultural goods) when responses are given under conditions of incomplete information: "This problem is compounded by the fact that information itself may be sub-optimally supplied because of its own public good properties". A further source of information bias may be that consumers misunderstand or don't know their actual amount of liability for the good, particularly if it is funded by non-specific taxes (Throsby and Withers 1986:615).

In order to test and control for the postulated information bias, Throsby and Withers (1985:15) in their study of the arts in Australia, used the Bohm interval method twice - once when respondents were non-informed, and again once certain information about current tax liability for the support of the arts had been provided by the interviewer. (A card handed to the respondent showed alternative income levels and consequent current payments out of tax for arts support.) A huge range of answers resulted (averages between $15 and $200 a head were recorded). In almost every case, however, both liable and non-liable WTP responses were higher once interviewees had been informed of current arts support levels.

Morrison and West (1986:60) criticize the solution to the information bias problem of a 1983 study on the public finance of the arts in Ontario, Canada, commissioned by the Special Committee for the Arts. This study asked directly (with a list of various monetary amounts provided), how much of every 100 provincial tax dollars the respondent thought went towards support of the arts. The study found that a majority of people seemed misinformed about how much provincial tax support for the arts there was, suggesting either a number well in excess of the actual amount or being unable to express any opinion (18% of the sample). The Canadian study then provided the following information and asked for WTP information:

> "In fact, less that $1 of every 100 provincial tax dollars goes towards support of the arts. Would you be willing to pay ([interviewer] READ EACH AMOUNT) more in taxes per year if you knew the money would be used to support arts facilities or would you not be willing to do that?" (Morrison and West 1986:60).

Morrison and West (1986) identified several problems with the above survey method. They argued that asking for an estimate of spending per 100 tax dollars assumed an unrealistic knowledge of tax allocation. They also pointed out that most people in Canada perceive the level of arts funding as being made up of federal, provincial and municipal taxes together, and may be more aware and interested in the total support provided by the three together. They thus suggested caution when deciding on the manner in which the information about current levels of finance is given, particularly the use of phraseology. The Canadian study found that, once respondents had been informed (as quoted above), 77% of them indicated their willingness to accept a tax increase. "If the question had been phrased (as it could have been), 'In fact, more than ten million dollars in provincial tax dollars goes towards support of the arts...' we might expect a completely different result from that reported in the survey" (Morrison and West 1986:61).

In their own study, Morrison and West (1986) informed respondents of their total tax liability (not just provincial tax) and attempted to avoid the sort of bias, mentioned above, introduced by the phraseology of the questions. In addition they placed the performing arts in the context of a wide range of public expenditure, such as education, pollution control, housing, etc. Their results contradicted those of the 1983 Canadian study despite being conducted in the same country and only a few years later, in that they concluded that current levels of Canadian public finance for the arts were "equal to the social cost at the margin", that is, no further funding would be socially efficient (Morrison and West 1986:70).

Designing the informative section of the Grahamstown National Arts Festival study was made significantly easier by the fact that a high percentage of the local population actually attends the arts festival each year and could thus be expected, not only to have a reasonable level of knowledge about the good being discussed, but also to have some personal interest in it. The greatest difficulty in designing the scenarios was the lack of information on funding and costs. While it had been widely publicized that the festival was receiving R7.5 million over 3 years from the Eastern Cape Government, general figures on national per capita spending on the arts were not available. On the cost side, sponsors are often not willing to allow exact amounts to be disclosed and in the case of many of them (for example, cell phone operators, car hire firms, accommodation providers, etc) their contributions were in-kind and hard to quantify. Noonan (2003) found, in a meta-analysis of WTP studies, that information about current tax burdens decreased WTP amounts, while information about the costs of the project increased WTP. It is thus desirable to include both or neither of these measures in an attempt to avoid bias.

Providing this sort of information in an unbiased way, however, is far from simple. As in the Canadian study (cited in Morrison and West 1986), did one say that, for example, the festival cost about R10 million a year and that government sponsorship covered only about a quarter of this? Or that arts funding in South Africa overall was less than 1% of the national budget? All these figures are true, but it is debatable how they would be interpreted, especially by the poorer sections of the population who could have little idea of relative costs and government budgets. While more contextual and comparative information could have been provided, it is debatable how much of this would have been assimilated by respondents and since it would have made the telephone interview longer, might have reduced response rates.

As pointed out by Sunstein (2002), it is also important to give respondents a context in which to make the decision and a reminder that there are substitutes (for example, sporting events and environmental conservation) that could also provide cultural externalities. As such, it was pointed out that government funding was required in many areas, "like schools and hospitals" and that these might be regarded as "more important than arts festivals".

Two studies in cultural economics designed specifically to test for information bias are the Kling et al. (2004) study of the WTP to restore an important local historical landmark, the Northern Hotel in Fort Collins, and the Alberini et al. (2005) WTP study of the S. Erasmo island in the Venice lagoon. In the Kling et al. (2004) study the sample of local residents was divided so that some respondents were given a "high information" version, which included two pages of text about the Hotel and an additional photograph, and the others were given a "low information" version which consisted of only half a page of text. They find that the sub-sample provided with more information had a significantly higher average WTP than the low information group. In addition, they find that more information resulted in demand curves with a significantly lower price elasticity, (less responsive to changes in price), which, they argue, is a result of the lack of any close substitutes for such cultural heritage.

In the Alberini et al. (2005) study both sub-samples were given the same initial information, but one group was given the following additional summary or "caveat" of possible reasons for being willing or unwilling to pay:

> "To explain the uses more clearly, I will describe to you the main reasons why other people have answered 'yes" or 'no'. Other respondents who answered 'yes' believe that:
>
> 1. The island is an environmental resource that deserves protection in itself, whether or not one has visited it or knows of it.
> 2. You may be interested in visiting the island of S. Erasmo in the future.
> 3. As an environmental resource, the island of S. Erasmo should be protected for future generations.
> 4. The environmental problems that affect the island are serious and the public works are necessary.
>
> Other respondents who answered 'no' believe that:
>
> 1. There is no reason to finance the protection of an island that they do not know or visit
> 2. There are other public works that deserve more attention and priority in financing.
> 3. They will never visit the island.
> 4. The public works are not adequate and will not remedy environmental problems at S. Erasmo."

(Alberini et al. 2005:161-2)

They find that providing the summary did not have a statistically significant effect on WTP responses in general. However, when the "caveat" dummy variable is interacted with an "education" variable they find a positive, significant effect. They conclude that, for less highly educated people, the summary may have highlighted important aspects of the project that they may not have considered themselves, thus increasing WTP for this group.

In conclusion, providing the right amount of unbiased information will remain one of the challenges of WTP studies and testing for this sort of bias should be an important part of pre-study pilot tests of the questionnaire and/or focus group discussions. As Alberini et al. (2005) conclude, much research is still needed in this area.

5.5.2 WTP Question Elicitation Format

Initially, WTP studies for the same good were expected to produce similar results, even if the question format differed, and, when this was shown not to be the case, the method was criticized (Carson et al 2001). However, it is now generally accepted that different elicitation formats yield different strategies and that question format can have a significant effect on WTP bids (Carson 1997). There are two main ways of structuring WTP questions. The first is an open-ended (OE) format, which simply asks respondents what the maximum amount is that they are willing to pay for a particular good, with no suggested amount. The second method is the dichotomous choice (DC), closed-ended format, which asks respondents whether they are WTP *x* amount for a particular good, eliciting a yes/no answer. The DC question format can be followed up by another round of bidding (double-bounded) or by an OE question (Carson et al. 2001). The latter design is based on the iterative bidding (IB) method, not much used recently (Willis 2002). Much research and debate has surrounded question format, focused mainly on the differences between the DC and OE format and whether the NOAA (1993) recommendation that only the DC format be used is justified.

The NOAA (1993) recommendation that only the DC question format be used is based on the idea that, in order to obtain meaningful WTP bids, respondents need to take the hypothetical market as seriously as possible. In order to encourage this, a familiar and realistic pricing mechanism should be used. Since in most (western) countries, consumers are faced with purchasing decisions at set prices, the NOAA recommended the DC or referendum format as being more familiar to respondents and also because, since most respondents would not be familiar with pricing public goods, the DC format reduces the cognitive difficulty of the task. While these arguments certainly carry some weight, it has also been shown by many studies that the DC format WTP questions result in consistently higher WTP estimates than OE questions, and the NOAA recommendation is thus at odds with their call for "conservative" questionnaire design.

The problem seems to be exacerbated for public goods in hypothetical markets. For example, in a study done by Kealy and Turner (1993) it was found that, while there was no significant difference between open and closed-ended WTP questions for private goods, the closed-ended responses were 1.4 to 2.5 times as large as the open-ended questions for public goods. In a later study, Loomis et al. (1997) found that, in experiments where real payments were made, there was no significant difference between the two question formats, but in hypothetical markets, DC values were 2.54 times higher than OE question values. A series of experiments conducted by Balisteri et al. (2001) also concludes that, while both OE and DC format questions produce upwardly biased results, the effect was more pronounced for DC questions. Reaves et al. (1999), in comparing various question formats in a study to value an endangered species, actually find that the double bounded DC format has a lower response rate and a higher level of protest responses than OE or payment card options.

All studies suggested that it was premature to abandon the open-ended WTP format although, as Carson et al. (2001) point out, OE format questions are known to elicit many zeros, few small amounts and a few very large amounts, making mean values sensitive to outliers[1]. Bennett and Tranter (1998) also find that OE questions result in a particularly high number of non-responses where respondents are not familiar with the good being valued.

Dichotomous Choice Questions and Starting Point Bias

A problem with the DC format is the so-called "anchoring" bias, that is, the fact that final WTP amounts will depend on the initial starting point bid. As Boyle et al. (1997) and later Willis (2002) point out, people tend to use the starting point as a suggested norm and an indication of what is expected of them or, as in the case of a private good, use price (suggested by the initial bid) as a proxy for value. The problem is that bid amounts are

[1] Extremely high and low values, even if there are only a few of them, can change the mean or average value quite considerably. This is one reason that some WTP studies quote both the mean and median values.

usually chosen to maximize the efficiency of the research design, not to convey information about the good, and that the starting point bid may thus displace the prior WTP, which is what the researcher is interested in finding out (Herriges and Shogren 1996). An additional issue, particularly when only one yes/no question is asked (single-bounded DC) is the statistical interpretation of the results. Giraud et al. (2001) show that significant differences in referendum style WTP estimates can be obtained depending on which statistical technique is used to analyze the data and suggest caution until an industry standard can be developed.

One way in which the efficiency of DC format WTP studies could be increased is to have follow-up questions, bidding up or down depending on the response to the initial questions. However, several studies (cited in Herriges and Shogren 1996) have shown significant differences between the WTP distribution implied by initial and follow-up bids. Herriges and Shogren suggest that, as with the iterative bid design, this is because follow-up bids are also sensitive to starting point bias and that even if this is controlled for, the efficiency gains from using follow-up questions are reduced. Carson et al. (2001:191) suggest that follow-up questions are biased because they signal to respondents that, "the cost is uncertain, that the quality of the good has changed or that the government is willing to bargain over costs" and that any of these suggest that WTP distributions between the first and follow-up questions should be different.

Willis (2002) used an iterative bid (IB) design to determine the revenue maximizing ticket price for entry into an historical park in Naples. He argues that, where there is uncertainty about parameters and distribution, the IB design, where WTP amounts are increased in small, equal increments, will capture the highest price consumers are willing to pay and measure all of consumer surplus. Willis (2002) finds that leaving some bid levels out (as the DC format does) significantly affects the demand curve for the good, and the greater the number of bid levels, the more accurate the study is likely to be.

All DC format surveys are, however, expensive, since sample size has to be large in order to generate statistically significant results. Bille Hansen (1997), in one of the first WTP surveys on specific cultural goods, used an open-ended question to determine the maximum WTP to preserve the Danish Royal Theatre. She argued that, where the good is likely to be known to everybody and especially where respondents are used to the idea that they pay taxes to support it, the use of the open-ended format question is justified. The Australian arts study (Thompson et al. 1983) also used the

OE format, as did the Canadian study (Morrison and West 1986), although the question was only asked after respondents had been informed of and commented on current spending ("too little", "too much" or "just right").

The Mildura Arts Centre survey (Throsby and O'Shea 1980) used a form of payment card, that is, respondents were asked their maximum WTP, followed by suggested amounts. While this method appears to be promising, as reported in Reaves et al. (1999) it is, of course, only possible in face-to-face interviews and postal surveys, but has the additional benefit of revealing the whole choice set to respondents, which, as argued by Bateman et al. (2004), may be an important determinant of bid accuracy.

The DC format has, however, largely been accepted as the way to structure WTP questions in cultural economics. For example, the Kentucky arts WTP survey (Thompson et al. 2002) asked only one DC format question with varying, randomly assigned amounts. While this appears to be the only method not prone to starting point bias, a very large number of responses is required at each "price" level to make results statistically significant. A telephone survey in North Carolina, eliciting WTP for submerged maritime cultural resources (Whitehead and Finney 2003) attempted to use the double bounded DC format in order to increase the efficiency of results. However, significant starting point bias was detected in the second round of bids.

Another option is to combine DC and OE format questions. For example, a study done on WTP for domestic television programming in Australia (Papandrea 1999) used this method, first asking respondents whether they were WTP an additional $12 per household for a 10% increase in local programming and then following up with an open-ended question asking for the maximum WTP (for those who answered "yes") or whether they were WTP anything (for those who answered "no"). Santagata and Signorello (2000), in their study of the WTP for the "Napoli Musei Aperti" in Naples, used an even more advanced combination of DC and OE format questions: if respondents answered "yes" to the first DC question (random variations in starting point), then this was followed up by a further two DC bids and finally an open-ended question. They comment that, while this method results in richer data, it could be prone to starting point bias in the later phases and this is in fact what is found, although the OE response mean is lower than the DC format response, thus probably controlling for this form of bias.

Vossler and McKee (2006) tested four different question formats in a series of laboratory experiments: DC, DC with follow-up certainty questions, payment cards and multiple bound DC. They find the smallest difference between stated and actual payments in the DC format questions and recommend payment card and multiple-bounded DC format questions because they "force respondents to think more about the decision" (2006:165).

In the case of the South African arts festivals, the Oudtshoorn pilot study used first a DC question, with three randomly assigned starting points (10, 20 and 30 Rand), followed-up by an open ended question asking for maximum WTP. While the logit model based on the first DC format question and the log-linear model used to analyze the final WTP figures performed fairly well without showing significant starting point bias, a great many responses (nearly 21%) were greater than 1% of household income and were thus excluded on the grounds that they showed hypothetical bias (unrealistically high WTP responses). It was hypothesized that higher initial bids were also encouraging zero responses, since South Africans are not used to bidding and regarded the amount mentioned first as a "price" to which a final binary response was made. In an attempt to mitigate this, the later (2003) Grahamstown study used a format closer to the iterative bid design discussed by Willis (2002) in which a number of up and down bid amounts were included, all respondents starting from a level of R10 (the median in the pilot study), followed-up by an OE question for respondents who answered "yes" or "no" to all bid levels.

A "don't know" or "would not vote" (WNV) option was provided for all WTP questions. For bidding purposes, such responses were treated as "no" votes and interviewers proceeded to the lower bid or OE question. Although interviewers did not prompt respondents to use this option, as it was feared that many respondents would see it as an easy way out of a question requiring some thought, this response was accepted. (Krosnick et al. (2002) find that "no opinion" options discourage respondents from thinking carefully about results, particularly those with low levels of education.)

A study by Carson et al. (1995) suggests that, in dichotomous choice WTP questions, the "would not vote" responses can be treated as having voted "no" without altering the distribution of responses, the estimate of WTP or the construct validity of the results. They suggest that some respondents may not want to admit that they are not willing to pay for more of a socially desirable good, particularly if the interviewer somehow conveys (by manner or tone) that the "right" answer would be a positive WTP. Accepting a "would not vote" or "don't know" response may give respondents a more socially acceptable way to indicate that they do not support the program (Carson et al 1995).

In concluding their section on elicitation formats, Carson et al. (2001:193) state that, "At present, the choice a CV researcher typically faces is between using an elicitation format that is unbiased, but with a large confidence interval [single DC format] and using one that is potentially biased, but with a much tighter confidence interval". Willis (2002:320) also points out that, in deciding on WTP question format, there is the "usual trade-off between survey costs and model accuracy and reliability". The choice of question format ultimately depends on how large a sample one can afford, the interview format (face to face, postal or telephone, internet), the researchers' assumptions about bias, and how knowledgeable respondents are about the good being valued.

Finally, the payment vehicle needs to be carefully considered. It should be realistic and familiar to respondents, like a form of tax or a ticket price, and not a once-off donation, which some research has found to produce unreliable results. In order to reduce protest responses, try not to choose a payment vehicle which respondents may associate with a particular ideological standpoint, like a payment to a politically biased organisation.

5.5.3 Detecting Biased Responses: Follow-up Questions and Sureness Measures

The NOAA Panel report on contingent valuation suggested that probing reasons for willingness or unwillingness to pay is vital to the study, not only because it adds to its explanatory power, but because it can be used to detect biased responses. The simplest way to find out why respondents are willing or unwilling to pay is to ask an open-ended question after the WTP question. For positive responses, this can work fairly well and be a good way to spot unsure, inconsistent or otherwise biased results. However, for those not willing to pay, it might be more difficult, since respondents may be reluctant to give truthful answers, especially if the interviewer or questionnaire text has somehow given the impression that a positive WTP response is the "correct" answer. In such cases, it may be better to provide a number of reasons for not being willing to pay (as in the Alberini et al. (2005) study discussed above) and ask respondents to agree or disagree.

As with the opinion questions, reasons for WTP can also be useful in highlighting the different values various sections of the population get from the cultural good. At the Grahamstown National Arts Festival for example, a dominant reason for being willing to pay in the lower income area to prevent the event from getting smaller was the perceived economic benefits that it provides: "Creates employment", "Brings jobs", "Jobs for the children", "Helps the unemployed" and so on. Future or potential earnings, either by the respondent or by a member of their family or the community as a whole, were also cited, one respondent stating clearly that, "Others get jobs, maybe next year I will be lucky". Reasons for not being willing to pay to support the festival amongst the low-income group, were quite often related to their perceived lack of financial benefit from the event. However, there was also a high level of awareness amongst low income area respondents of the non-financial benefits that the festival provides. The most commonly cited reasons were that the festival provides entertainment and contact with the outside world, educational benefits, especially for the youth, community pride and bringing "life to the town" and the showcasing of artistic talent, particularly that of local residents.

Reasons for positive WTP in the high-income area were much more focused on the non-financial benefits offered by the festival, although a significant number still cited employment creation, tourism and personal and/or community financial gain. Many respondents mentioned the entertainment value of the festival, the benefit to local schools and their pupils, the importance of fostering the arts, community pride and general community education. Reasons for not being willing to pay in the high-income area were mostly related to the perceived deterioration in the quality or organization of the festival.

In addition to such valuable qualitative information, the debriefing section can also be useful in spotting biased responses, for example, respondents who do not accept the contingent market, are free riders or who are protesting against some aspect of the survey rather than valuing the good. The following section discusses ways in which biased responses can be detected and how they can be dealt with in order to achieve reliable results.

Protest Zeros, Warm Glow and Inconsistent Responses

Some respondents may give a zero willingness to pay response not because the good genuinely is of no worth to them, but because they do not accept the contingent market (those who do not think that the money will be spent on the good or that the proposed change is likely to be carried out) or are protesting against some aspect of the survey, like the payment vehicle (Chambers et al.1998). These respondents may introduce bias through the use of "protest zeros" since they are not expressing a value for the good in question.

Some commentators, like Lindsey (1994) and Chambers et al. (1998), suggest that some protest responses should be excluded from results on the grounds that they do not represent a valuation of the good in question. Zero bids may also be an indication of free rider behavior, if associated with positive opinions about the good. Even if such zero responses reflect a genuine budget constraint, they do not provide an estimate of the value of the good to the respondent. Bille Hansen (1997) comments that protest zeros are most likely to occur when respondents regard the study as illegitimate in some way, but that, especially amongst non-users, a reasonable percentage of zero responses may be reflecting true willingness to pay. Some biased responses can be detected in the debriefing section, but, as Boyle and Bergstrom (2001:198) point out, "Why would someone who is behaving strategically reveal this motive to an interviewer?"

In opposition to the view that zero bids should be excluded is that of Jorgensen and Syme (1994) who argue that second guessing respondents is a dangerous game and that the only defensible reason for excluding zeros is if they can be shown to be arbitrary. Stazzera et al. (2003:462) also comment that excluding selected data may affect the validity of the results, since "the remaining sub-sample of non-protestors would be biased". At the moment, decisions on the inclusion or exclusion of such responses appear to be *ad hoc* and context and study specific.

One way to test whether zero WTP responses are arbitrary or "real" valuations is to determine whether the explanatory variables in the model explain WTP better or worse when zero responses are included. In order to test whether zero responses were protest zeros or could be explained by willingness to pay determinants, log-linear regressions of results from the South African arts festivals were run, first including and then excluding zero responses[2]. Results showed that the number of significant variables and the goodness of fit of all models improved when zero responses were included. The "opinion" variable (recorded as a score where a positive opinion about the festival counted as one and a negative opinion, zero) became less significant when zero bids were excluded. These results suggest that, on average, zero WTP bids were related to negative opinions regarding the "good" being valued and were not random or protest responses and should thus be included. Even Lindsey (1994), who makes a strong case for the exclusion of all zero responses, agreed in a later note (1995) that the inclusion of zero responses is appealing and that, at the very least, contingent valuation reports should indicate whether they have done so or not.

While a defense can be made for excluding very high and some zero responses on the grounds that one is following the conservative design suggested by the NOAA Panel (1993), Bille Hansen (1997) points out that such truncation comes at a price, which is that the mean WTP is considerably altered, especially in quite small sample sizes. This is what Throsby and Withers (1986) referred to as the "social choice bias". They show that using the median rather than the mean measurement of explanatory variables in the valuation of local arts assistance projects in Australia yields better WTP estimates. Median measures of WTP were considerably smaller than mean values (the mean values are more than three times those of the median), indicating the presence of quite a large social choice bias. "This result suggests a wide disparity between economically efficient (mean-based) levels of provision of public good and democratically determined (median based) levels of provision" (Throsby and Withers 1986:321). Morrison and West (1986) agree that the median value is particularly useful in eliminating bias from extremely high or low responses and that the median voter theorem predicts that it is the median value which will dominate political outcomes.

McFadden (1994:694) concurs that when some respondents use the survey as an opportunity to express protest for or against the proposed project by stating unrealistically high or low WTP values, "Even a tiny fraction of consumers giving responses more extreme than their true WTP could lead to estimates of resource value that are in error by orders of magnitude". However, he also points out that, when distribution is skewed, median values may themselves be biased. In his meta-analysis, Noonan (2003) compares mean and median WTP estimates from 48 studies. On average, he

[2] In order to include zero responses in the log-linear regression, a constant was added to the willingness to pay amounts. Since the log of a constant is zero, this would not affect the coefficients obtained.

finds that the mean is 1.5 times higher than the median value. However, for goods involving primarily use values, public payment vehicles (like tax) and large-scale goods, lower ratios are obtained.

As discussed in chapter 4, some respondents may not be valuing the specific good in question, but simply gaining moral satisfaction by donating to a good cause. In this case, responses may be biased because respondents are not making a market decision, taking into account such considerations as their budget and available substitutes, but simply gaining a "warm glow" by contributing to a good cause. Chambers et al. (1998) suggest that those respondents who reported that they supported a "good cause" or words to that effect, could be responding to a warm glow and should be omitted from the sample. The debriefing section can also act as an internal consistency check, since responses to this question could be compared to opinions expressed earlier in the interview. For example, those who agree that the cultural good in question is important to community education, but later on in the interview state that they are not willing to pay for it because it does not benefit the community, are showing inconsistency.

In both the South African arts festival surveys those respondents whose reasons for positive willingness to pay were vague ("I don't know") or whose stated willingness to pay was some positive amount (usually small), but who expressed strong negative feelings ("The festival is useless", "The money is spent on unimportant things", etc) were excluded. Such excluded responses made up 9% of the Oudtshoorn and 3% of the Grahamstown sample.

Hypothetical Bias and Very High WTP Amounts

As discussed in chapter 4, willingness to pay estimates may be prone to hypothetical bias – that is, hypothetical responses are higher than responses when real payment must be made. Sometimes, questionnaire design can help to control such bias or test for it directly (like the Bohm interval). However, it may still result in unrealistically large WTP responses (in relation to the size or importance of the good and/or their income) from some people in the sample. Such large responses are generally regarded as indicating a positive response to supporting the good, but an unrealistic numerical indication of willingness to pay. Jorgensen and Syme (1995:400) note that the exclusion of biased responses in WTP surveys "seems to be largely ad hoc" and requires a judgment call on the part of the researcher. This is very much the case in excluding unrealistically high

WTP responses, since one's definition of "unrealistic" is dependent on the good being valued and on the socio-economic position of the particular population. Exclusion of such responses is also very seldom discussed in the WTP literature and a "rule of thumb" is thus even more difficult to determine.

In the South African arts festivals study, it was decided that a positive monthly WTP of more than 1% of household income would be judged as representing an unrealistically large amount for a 10 day festival held once a year, especially given the poverty of respondents from the low income areas. However, nearly a quarter of respondents fell into this group, by far the majority of these cases occurring in the low income areas. Two approaches were adopted to deal with the problem: firstly, an upper bound of 1% of household income was set (for those who did not state household income, average income for their area in each town was used); secondly those whose willingness to pay was greater than 1% of household income were excluded from the sample. Both results are reported in table 5.4.

Table 5.4. Average WTP at Two South African Arts Festivals

	Grahamstown festival		**Oudtshoorn festival**	
	High income	Low income	High income	Low income
% of the sample willing to pay some amount > 0	77.5	79.6	65.5	64.7
Average WTP amount (WTP > 1% household income excluded)	R10.42 ($1.60)[3]	R8.09 ($1.24)	R17.50 ($2.69)	R8.96 ($1.38)
Average WTP (Upper bound of 1% of household income)	R14.80 ($2.28)	R6.55 ($1)	R17.42 ($2.68)	R10.33 ($1.59)

(Snowball 2005:114)

An important result is that, despite a much lower attendance at ticketed events and lower earnings from the festival, a similar percentage of respondents from low income groups were willing to pay something to support the festival as were those from high income groups at both festivals. As would be expected though, the average WTP for those from high income areas was more than for low income areas. The difference between the two becomes more marked when willingness to pay responses greater than 1% of household income are recoded to a maximum of 1% of house-

[3] Dollar amounts were calculated using the current exchange rate of R6.50 to the dollar.

hold income, rather than being excluded entirely (especially the case in the Grahamstown high income area, where average WTP increases by about 40%), but the general pattern remains the same.

The Post Decision Confidence Measure

A "post decision confidence measure" (Bennett and Tranter 1998:255) can be used to determine the extent to which respondents regard their responses as accurate. As discussed in chapter 5, the exclusion of unsure respondents could play an important role in controlling for hypothetical bias (Champ and Bishop 2001). Thompson et al. (2002) use such a measure in their study of WTP for the arts in Kentucky: after the closed ended (yes/no) WTP question, respondents were asked how certain their stated donation was on a scale from 1 to 10, where 10 was certain. Respondents who chose 9 or 10 on the certainty scale were considered willing to pay, but any response from 8 down was not considered really willing to pay and was excluded from the mean WTP calculation. Thomson et al. (2002) argue that this is an effective way of controlling for hypothetical bias.

However, Vossler and McKee (2006) caution that stated uncertainty may be as a result of the question format of the WTP question, rather than any real preference uncertainty. In their induced value experiments, they find that certainty questions capture both "value" uncertainty and uncertainty regarding the decision task. Thus, when multiple-bounded DC format questions are used (a number of up and down bids) the certainty of respondents tends to decrease.

> "This suggests that by increasing the action space we are sending a signal to respondents that they should exercise their additional options. This suggests that stated response uncertainty in field studies should be interpreted with care as not all stated uncertainty appears to be genuine" (Vossler and McKee 2006:165).

Initially, the South African arts festival studies used a certainty question with the 1 to 10 scale suggested by Thompson et al. (2002), asking respondents to rate their sureness that they had accurately shown their WTP to support the festival. However, many respondents chose the extremes (1 or 10), refused to answer the question or responded with "don't know", or a percentage amount ("100% sure"). Interviewers suggested that it was the numeric scale that was the problem, particularly amongst those respondents with low levels of formal education. Another reason for the problems could have been that the South African studies were conducted via telephone with no visual cues, whereas the Thompson et al. (2002) study used a postal survey. As a compromise, a qualitative scale, ("not at all sure", "fairly sure", and "very sure") which is not as precise, but performed better, was used.

5.6 Socio-demographics

The final section of most WTP studies collects general socio-demographic information on respondents and their households. Given that some of the information required, like household income, political affiliation, race and religion, might be regarded as sensitive, it may be prudent to remind respondents that the survey is anonymous, especially if it is being conducted via telephone or in the respondent's home.

Table 5.5. Socio-demographic Variables in WTP Studies of Cultural Goods

Variable	Format
Income: Household income gross/net of tax or income per household member.	Usually in categories, using cell mean for regression
Household size	Number of people resident in HH
Occupation	In categories or binary, for example: 1 if professional, 0 otherwise
Education	In years or as a binary variable, for example: 1 if completed high school, 0 otherwise.
Religion	In groups
Age	In years or categories or as a binary variable, for example: 1 if younger than 50, 0 otherwise
Race	In groups
Sex	Binary
Home language or Mother-tongue	In categories
Marital status	Binary
Residence : area of residence in town/city; period of residence	Binary (high income/ low income); number of years or binary, e.g. 1 if more than 10 years, 0 otherwise.
Political affiliation	By party

Socio-demographic information can be used for a number of purposes. Firstly, such characteristics are often significant determinants of WTP, since cultural taste tends to be highly correlated with personal characteristics and background. Secondly, it is important to show that the socio-demographic profile of the sample is representative of the population (by, for example, comparing the sample profile to that of the census data for the region) if the WTP results are to be generalized. Finally, income can be used as a useful validity check, since it is expected that, in most cases,

WTP will be positively and significantly correlated with income if respondents are taking the hypothetical "purchase" of the good (assumed to be a normal good) seriously. Such data can also provide useful information for the suppliers of the cultural good on target markets. Below is a list of some of the socio-demographic variables included in WTP studies for cultural goods. It is by no means complete, since the kind of information collected will depend very much on the population and the good being valued, but it gives examples of some of the most common categories used.

As expected in South African arts festival studies, the demographics of the high and low income area samples differed dramatically, but in most cases, proved to be a representative sample of the population when compared to statistical data on the town. In both areas, however, a much higher percentage of women (71%) were interviewed than was representative of the population as a whole (56% women according to Stats SA 1996 Census data). As shown in table 5.6, the high income areas consist largely of European-origin people, who speak mainly English or Afrikaans at home, and have higher levels of income and education. The low income areas consist of African-origin people who speak mainly Xhosa and Afrikaans and have much lower levels of income and education.

Table 5.6. Comparison between the Demographics of Arts Festival Samples

	Grahamstown		**Oudtshoorn**	
	High income	Low income	High income	Low income
Race group	86% European-origin	100% African-origin	95% European-origin	92% mixed-origin
Language	85% English	100% Xhosa	92% Afrikaans	95% Afrikaans
Sex (% female)	62%	77%	56%	66%
Average age (yrs)	49.4	39.5	49.5	41.2
Average years of education	14.6	10.3	13.7	10.8
% Completed high school	91%	43%	92%	47%
Average monthly per capita income	R3632	R251	R4 525	R731

(Snowball 2005:121)

Since race, income and residential area were shown to be highly correlated, an "area" variable (1 if from a low income area, 0 otherwise) was used as a proxy for household income. Regression results showed that this variable was negative and statistically significant, indicating that the probability of being WTP some positive amount to support the festivals was greatly increased if the respondent was from the high income area. When the sample for the National Arts Festival in Grahamstown is divided into high and low income areas and a household income amount used in the regression, it is shown to be a positive and significant determinant of WTP in the low income area.

There is mixed evidence regarding the significance of income in determining WTP to support culture. Brooks (2004) finds that income is positively related to private donations to the arts (as one would expect), but not with direct government support. Rather, it is the ideological position of the person that influences their support for government aid to the arts most strongly. For example, in his study, liberal, Christian, European-origin people are most likely to be in favor of government support. Rushton (2005), in his study of a referendum to increase property taxes in metropolitan Detroit to fund cultural institutions, also finds that per capita income is not a significant factor in determining whether the respondent will vote in favor of the tax increase (although there is a positive correlation), but that his/her political party is a significant determinant.

Years of formal education were not significant in any of the South African festival WTP models. Findings in many other studies on the characteristics of people who support increased arts funding, however, do show education as an important determinant of willingness to pay. Brooks (2001 and 2004) and Rushton (2005) find that higher levels of education are associated with both support for increased government spending on the arts and with private donations to arts organizations in the United States. This supports the idea, discussed in chapter one, that cultural capital, often obtained via formal education, is needed to make meaning of or promote an appreciation of the arts.

The insignificance of education in explaining willingness to pay in the South African case could have a number of possible explanations. Firstly, one could argue that the wide variety of shows offered at the festivals allows for a range of levels of engagement, so that shows that require a large amount of cultural capital to be understood can be avoided by people without it in favour of more easily accessible entertainment. This, however, does not take into account the many different sorts of cultural capital present in South Africa – some of which may not be directly related to years of formal education, but rather to traditional upbringing and informal education. This might be the case especially where strong oral traditions are still operating. A much more complex measure of cultural capital, including informal and traditional education, would thus need to be used in order to gauge accurately the relationship between education and willingness to pay to support the arts.

Age was a significant determinant of WTP in the low income areas, a one year increase in age being associated with a decrease in the probability of being willing to pay. The sex variable was only significant in the high income area, showing that women from this area were more likely to be willing to pay than men. This may be related to women having a greater use value for the festival, since a number of previous studies have shown that the event attracts more women than men.

The demographic variables included in WTP studies depend to a large extent on the good being valued and on the nature of the population being sampled. For example, if a heritage site based in a particular city or town is being valued, it may be important to determine how long respondents have lived in the area, since this may be associated with more use values or knowledge of non-use values. If a population is fairly homogenous, it may not be important to find out their race or home language, since this will be known. Since answering socio-demographic questions is potentially sensitive and not particularly interesting, it usually concludes the WTP interview.

5.7 Validity and Reliability Tests

Once the WTP study is complete there are a number of tests that one can conduct to determine how valid and reliable the results are. Carson and Mitchell (1993:1267) concluded that it is the quality of the response to a WTP question that will determine the accuracy of the study. This is determined, in their view, by the survey design and administration or content validity:

> "Respondents must (i) clearly understand the characteristics of the good they are being asked to value; (ii) find the CV scenario elements related to the good's provision plausible; and (iii) answer the CV questions in a deliberate and meaningful manner" (Mitchell and Carson 1993:1267).

In a later work, Carson et al. (2001) suggested three other ways in which WTP estimates can be judged for accuracy in addition to content validity: convergent validity, construct validity and reliability. "Validity" in this context refers to the success of the study in measuring what it actually set out to measure.

The construct validity test measures the extent to which the WTP findings are consistent with theoretical expectations. As discussed above, these *a priori* expectations, based on economic theory, could include sensitivity to scope (WTP more for a larger good), that users would be WTP more than non-users and that WTP would be related to the income of respondents. The convergent validity test requires that the WTP estimates be compared to actual market (or simulated market) values. This could take the form of a comparison between a WTP study and a travel cost study, or as discussed in chapter 4, a comparison between a hypothetical and a real market situation. Reliability refers to whether the study can be replicated, either in a different context, or at a different time (temporal reliability).

The NOAA panel report (1993) calls for such "temporal averaging", particularly in the case of the valuation of environmental goods which change over time.

> "Time dependent measurement noise should be reduced by averaging across independently drawn samples taken at different points in time. A clear and substantial time trend in responses would cast doubt on the 'reliability' of the finding" (NOAA 1993:19).

One of the largest tests of temporal reliability was conducted by Carson et al. (1995), who compared the original Exxon oil spill study conducted in 1991 with a similar survey, which had a comparable sample, conducted two years later. Temporal reliability was tested for in three ways: the distribution of "for" and "against" votes at various bid levels, the parameters of the models and the mean WTP amounts. They find no significant differences or trends over time and conclude that "the [NOAA] Panel's concerns are unsubstantiated and not as important as its recommendation could be interpreted to imply" (Carson et al. 1995:19).

Reliability and Validity Tests in Cultural Economics Studies

One of the earliest WTP studies in cultural economics designed to test specifically for validity and reliability is the Chambers et al. (1998) study of the value of Ste. Genevieve historical academy in Missouri. Tests for construct validity showed that WTP increased as income increased, indicating that respondents who could realistically afford to pay would be most likely to do so, as one would find in a real market situation. Education is also found to be a positive determinant of WTP. As a test for internal reliability, they show that stated concern about the academy is positively related to WTP, which is an indication that the WTP figure is measuring the value of the good in question.

A study that combines hypothetical and real (travel cost) behaviour is that of Alberini and Longo (2006) who measure the welfare benefit of improving four heritage sites in Armenia. By using both real behaviour (actual number of trips and spending) as well as hypothetical scenarios (WTP for improvements in the sites) they can provide "reasonable and conservative estimates of the benefits of conservation of monuments in Armenia" (2006:300). They test for construct validity of both real and hypothetical goods by showing that spending and WTP are well predicted by the model variables like the negative and significant relationship between the good and its price.

The Alberini et al. (2005) study of the WTP to preserve the island of S. Erasmo in the Venice Lagoon also showed internal consistency, "in that WTP increases with knowledge of the island, current use of the lagoon and expected use of S. Erasmo after the works have been completed. WTP depends in predictable ways on income [positive], education [positive] and age [negative]" (2005:170).

The results of the contingent valuation study at the South African National Arts Festival in Grahamstown were tested for validity in three ways. Firstly, the results were compared with those of a similar festival study in Oudtshoorn (the pilot study) conducted in the same year and using a very similar survey instrument. Secondly, internal, construct validity tests were conducted to determine whether results were consistent with what economic theory would predict: as the "price" of the good increases, the quantity demanded should fall; and the results should show sensitivity to scope. WTP amounts also need to show some evidence of being constrained by the budget of the respondent – WTP figures and per capita or household income should have a significant negative relationship. Finally a test for temporal reliability was conducted by comparing the 2003 study findings to an earlier, similar study conducted in 2000 to determine whether the results could be replicated over time and show stable preferences.

The first internal test regards the price of the good, that is, as bid amounts increase, fewer respondents should be willing to pay the amount and the probability of a "yes" response should decrease. As the following data for the festival shows, as bid amounts increased, the percentage of respondents willing to pay the amount did indeed fall.

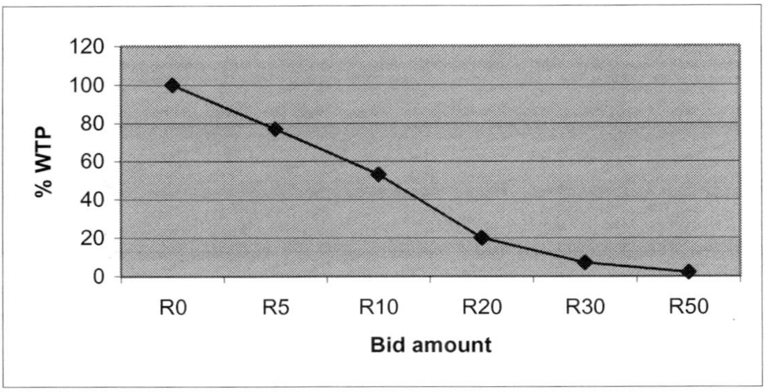

Fig 5.2. Percentage of Festival Respondents WTP at Each Bid Amount

The study also included a split-sample scope test, referring to a 25% or 50% decrease in festival size – simply defined as fewer shows and fewer visitors. The scope variable, coded as zero for a 25% decrease and one for a 50% decrease in festival size, was not significant in any of the regression models applied. However, the scope variable was positive in the Tobit model and approaching significance (at the 20% level). The coefficient interpretation shows that if respondents were given the 50% scenario, they were 1.17 times more likely to be willing to pay and that the probability of being willing to pay (holding all else constant) for the 50% scenario was 0.54.

Arrow et al. (1994), in their comments on the NOAA proposed rule on natural resource damage assessment, require WTP responses to be "adequately" responsive to scope, but also point out that the definition of "adequate" is dependent on the context of the research and ultimately a 'judgment call". Factors which would reduce the sensitivity of WTP bids to the scope of the good include such things as risk, that is, whether respondents believe the proposals would be effective (Carson et al. 1997), and the fact that the saved resource might not be considered a perfect substitute for the original resource (Smith and Osborne 1996). Foster and Mourato (2003) also cite Poe et al. (1994) as showing that non-overlapping confidence intervals could lead to an "understatement" of the confidence interval in scope tests. In the case of the South African festival, a positive scope coefficient, approaching statistical significance, is judged to show a reasonable sensitivity of the data to scope.

The final construct validity test requires that WTP had a positive and significant relationship with income. Statistical results showed a negative relationship between area (used as a proxy for income, where 1 was the low income area and 0 was the high income area) and willingness to pay. The relationship was statistically significant in the Tobit model. Also, household income was shown to be a statistically significant positive determinant of willingness to pay in the low income areas.

In addition to the internal validity tests, National Arts Festival results were compared to an earlier study (test for temporal reliability) and the KKNK study conducted in the same year, but at a different, comparable festival. While the 2000 study results are not directly comparable because of the use of a different hypothetical scenario and question format, the percentage of respondents from each area (high and low income) who were WTP some amount was similar, with a higher percentage WTP to preserve the larger good (2000 study scenario). The same is true of the pilot study (Oudtshoorn festival) results discussed above. Opinions, discussed in section 3, also showed a high degree of stability both over time and between similar events. The study thus appears to pass all validity tests, suggesting that results are relatively unbiased.

The number and sort of validity and reliability tests conducted on WTP study results depends on the nature of the study and its resources, but at least some comment should be made on how reliable and valid the researcher considers the results to be. This is especially important if results are (or may be) the basis for policy decisions and/or funding changes, or if they are going to be generalized to other cultural goods.

5.8 Conclusions

This chapter has described the ways in which WTP studies can be designed in order to minimize the amount of bias and to result in valid and reliable estimates of value. Although some issues, like the information and starting point biases, have no clear-cut solutions, they can be decreased through careful questionnaire design and pre-testing. In interpreting the results, validity and reliability tests can indicate the presence of significant bias.

Despite the difficulty of conducting WTP studies, they can be a very useful way of placing a value on the non-market part of cultural resources. In the case of the South African National Arts Festival, the WTP study was able to demonstrate that respondents from the low income areas of the town hosting the festival did receive, and were aware of, significant non-market benefits from the festival. In most countries, but especially developing ones, where the income-race divide still exists, such evidence can provide a powerful argument for the public funding of culture that purely market-based valuation studies cannot. Using such data, the argument that arts and culture funding benefits only the wealthy minority of society can be questioned, particularly with regard to the positive externalities that such cultural goods generate.

A problem with WTP scenarios however, is that, unless the good in question is described in some detail, or a large number of different studies are run, the results are not very informative about exactly which attributes of the composite good the respondents value most. Organizers wanting to increase the participation of a particular group of people would need to know what attribute/s of the good they should change or enhance. First used in transport economics, conjoint analysis (or the choice experiment method) is being used with increasing frequency in cultural economics and it holds great promise, not only in providing a more detailed valuation of the various attributes of a good, but also in controlling for some of the forms of bias detected in WTP studies. Chapter 6 discusses this method and case studies of cultural goods.

Appendix 5.1

WTP telephone survey for the South African National Arts Festival

Good evening. My name is __________ from Rhodes. We are doing a survey to find out what Grahamstown people think of the festival. Would you be prepared to spend about 10 minutes answering some questions?

1. Opinion

Firstly, I'd like to know what you think of the Festival as a whole. Please tell me if you agree or disagree with the following statements:

1.1 The festival gives **all** the people of Grahamstown a sense of pride
1 agree 0 disagree 2 don't know

1.2 The arts offered at the festival harm society and cause trouble because they are too critical of our way of life.
0 agree 1 disagree 2 don't know

1.3 The festival should be kept going so that people or their children have the choice of attending it in the future.
1 agree 0 disagree 2 don't know

1.4 The shows and events at the festival are useful in educating the community.
1 agree 0 disagree 2 don't know

1.5 The festival only benefits people who go to the shows you have to buy tickets for.
1 agree 0 disagree 2 don't know

2. Attendance & Spending

.

2.1 Did you go to the festival this year? 1 Yes → Q2.3 0 No

IF NO

2.2 Did you go to the festival last year? 1 Yes → Q 2.3 0 No →Q4

How many shows did you go to at this year's (last year's) festival that you had to buy tickets for?

____

FOR THOSE WHO ATTENDED AT LEAST ONE:

2.3 About how much did you spend on these tickets? ________________

FOR THOSE WITH TICKET SPENDING > ZERO

2.5 If the ticket prices had been 10% higher, so a R30 ticket would have cost R33, would you still have gone to the same number of shows?
1 Yes → 2.6 0 No → 2.7

2.6 If the ticket prices had been 20% / 50% higher, so a R30 ticket would have cost R36 / R45, would you still have gone to the same number of shows? 1 Yes 0 No

2.7 How many free shows, including art exhibitions, street theatre and Sundowner concerts, did you go to? ____________________

2.8 At this last festival, (or the 2002 festival) about how many times did you visit the craft markets? ____

2.9 About how much did you spend on shopping at the craft market? R_______

2.10 About how much did you spend on eating out at festival/local restaurants during the festival including drinks? R__________

2.11 Would you say that you spent more during festival time than you normally do?
1 Yes 0 No 2 don't know

2.12 IF YES
If there was no festival, do you think that you would have spent the money outside the Grahamstown area (for example on a beach holiday) or would you probably have stayed at home and spent it here anyway?

1 Spent here 0 Spent outside Grahamstown
2 Don't know 3 Not spent (saved)

3. Earnings

3.1 Did you earn any money because of the festival? For example, by providing accommodation, running a stall, or working overtime at your normal job 1 Yes
0 No → Q 5

IF YES
3.2 What sort of work was it?
1 accommodation 2 food stall 3 arts & crafts 4 overtime
5 other:______________________________
3.3 How much did you earn from this? R________________________
ONLY ASK THOSE WHO HAVE SOME EARNINGS FROM FEST.
3.4 What does your household mainly spend your festival earnings on?
1 food, transport and other monthly expenses 2 festival events

4 WTP

Thanks very much. The next section is about measuring the value of the festival to you through your willingness to pay to support it. As you might know, arts festivals, like schools and hospitals, don't make enough profit to survive on their own and rely quite heavily on sponsorship from private companies and the government. Government funding comes from the taxes that we pay – income tax and indirect taxes, like VAT.

In developing countries, like South Africa, there are many things that government funds need to be spent on and some of them are regarded as more important than arts festivals. Some private sponsors also feel that their money is better spent on, for example, sports or wildlife conservation. This means that there would be less money available for the festival in the future and that there would be fewer shows and fewer visitors.

I am now going to ask you if you would be willing to pay some amount per month to support the festival. The amount I mention may sound ridiculously low or high to you. It isn't a price, but just a starting point and you can choose a higher or lower amount. OK?

4.1 Would you be willing to pay an extra R10 out of your monthly income to stop the festival from getting 25%/50% smaller? That means you wouldn't have the R10 each month to spend on other things that you normally buy, like food, transport or entertainment.
1 Yes 0 No 3 don't know

IF YES: Bid up to maximum amount

4.2 Would you be willing to pay R20 a month? 1 Yes 0 No
4.3 Would you be willing to pay R30 a month to stop the festival from getting 25%/ 50% smaller? 1 Yes 0 No
4.4 Would you be willing to pay R50 a month? 1 Yes 0 No
4.5 What is the maximum amount that you would be willing to pay per month to prevent the festival from getting 25%/50% smaller? R________________

IF NO: Bid down
4.6 Would you be willing to pay R5 a month? 1 Yes 0 No
4.7 Would you be willing to pay any amount of money per month to prevent the festival from getting 25%/50% smaller? R________________

For all:

4.8 How sure are you that your answers have shown your accurate willingness to pay to support the festival?
PROMPT: 0 not at all sure 2 fairly sure 1 very sure

FOR THOSE WITH POSITIVE WTP

4.9 Why are you willing to pay to support the festival?

___

If more than one reason in 4.8:

4.10 Which of the reasons you have mentioned is the most important?

___

FOR THOSE WITH NO/DON'T KNOW WTP

4.11 Why are you not willing to pay to support the festival?

___

5. Demographics

Finally, I'd just like to know some details about you. Please remember that your name isn't attached to any of this information. Your phone number was selected at random from the phone book and none of the information you provide will be used for anything other than this research.

5.1 How old are you? ___

5.2 What is your home language?

1 Xhosa 2 Afrikaans 0 English3 other: ___

5.3 and 5.4 only to be asked if not obvious from language **[Ask if ANY doubt]**

5.3 What is your race group?

1 black 2 Coloured 0 white 3 Indian 4 other:___

5.4 Are you male or female? 1 male 0 female

5.5 How many years of education have you had? [MAY PROMPT] ___

Primary school up to grade 7 (std 5) = 7 years

Standard 6 (grade 8) = 8 years

Standard 8 (grade 10) = 10 years

Matric (grade 12) = 12 years

1 university degree = 15 years

2 degrees = 16 years

Diploma = school (12) + diploma duration

5.6 What is your job at the moment? [MAY PROMPT]

[INTERVIEWER: Write actual job, then classify:___]

1 professional (doctor, business person, lecturer, teacher)

2 white collar worker (secretary, clerk, shop assistant, agent)

3 service person (police, army, navy, air force, nurse)

4 blue collar worker (builder, cook, cleaner, security guard, labourer)

5 student

6 housewife

7 retired

8 unemployed

5.7 What is the normal monthly income for your whole household, after tax?

___

5.8 How many people are in your household? ___

6 Thanks very much for your time and help. Before we finish, is there anything else about the Festival that you would like to tell us?

References

Adjzen, I., Brown, T. and Rosenthal, L. (1996) Information bias in contingent valuation: Effects of personal relevance, quality of information, and motivational orientation. Journal of Environmental Economics and Management 30:43-57.

Alberini, A., Rosato, P., Longo, A. and Zanatta, V. (2005) Information and willingness to pay in a contingent valuation study: The value of S. Erasmo in the Lagoon of Venice. Journal of Environmental Planning and Management 48,2:155-175.

Alberini, A. and Longo, A. (2006) Combining the travel cost and contingent behaviour methods to value cultural heritage sites: Evidence from Armenia. Journal of Cultural Economics 30:287-304.

Arrow, K., Learner, E., Schuman, H. and Solow, R. (1994) Comments on NOAA proposed rule of damage assessment 69.

Balistreri, E., McClelland, G., Poe, G. and Schulze, W. (2001) Can hypothetical questions reveal true values? A laboratory comparison of dichotomous choice and open-ended contingent valuation with auction values. Environmental and Resource Economics 18:275-292.

Bennett, R. and Tranter, R. (1998) The dilemma concerning choice of contingent valuation willingness to pay elicitation format. Journal of Environmental Planning and Management 41,2:253-258.

Bille Hansen, T. (1997) The willingness to pay for the Royal Theatre in Copenhagen as a public good. Journal of Cultural Economics 21:1-28.

Bohm, P. (1972) Estimating demand for public goods: An experiment. Scandinavian Journal of Economics 3:113-130.

Bohm, P. (1979) Estimating willingness-to-pay: Why and how? Scandinavian Journal of Economics 81:142-153.

Bohm, P. (1984) Revealing demand for an actual public good. Journal of Public Economics 24:135-151

Boyle, L., Johnson, F. and McCollum, D. (1997) Anchoring and adjustment in single-bounded, contingent valuation questions. American Journal of Agricultural Economics 79,5:1495-1501.

Boyle, K. and Bergstom, J. (2001) Doubt, doubts and doubters in Bateman, I and Willis, K. (Eds.) Valuing Environmental Preferences. Oxford University Press: Oxford.

Brooks, A. (2001) Who opposes government arts funding? Public Choice 108:355-367.

Brooks, A. (2004) In search of true public arts support. Public Budgeting and Finance 24,2:88-100.

Carson, R. and Mitchell, R. (1993) The issue of scope in contingent valuation studies. American Journal of Agricultural Economics 75,5:1263-1268.

Carson, R.T., Hanemann, W.M., Kopp, R.J., Krosnick, J.A., Mitchell, R.C., Presser, S., Ruud, P.A. and Smith, V.K. with Conaway, M. and Martin, K. (1995) Referendum design and contingent valuation: The NOAA Panel's No-Vote recommendation. Resources for the Future Discussion Paper 96-03.

Carson, R., Mitchell, R., Conway, M. and Navrud, S. (1997) Non-Moroccan Values for Rehabilitating the Fes Medina. World Bank Report: Washington.

Carson, R., Flores, N. and Meade, N. (2001) Contingent valuation: Controversies and evidence. Environmental and Resource Economics 19:173-210.

Chambers, C., Chambers P. and Whitehead, J. (1998) Contingent valuation of quasi-public goods: validity, reliability and application to valuing a historic site. Public Finance Review 26,2:137-155.

Crompton, J. (1995) Economic impact analysis of sports facilities and events: Eleven sources of misapplication. Journal of Sports Management 9:14-35

Dutta, M., Banerjee, S. and Husain, Z. (2007) Untapped demand for heritage: A contingent valuation study of Prisep Ghat, Calcutta. Tourism Management 28:83-95

Foster, V. and Mourato, S. (2003) Elicitation format and sensitivity to scope. Environmental and Resource Economics 34:141-160.

Giraud, K., Loomis, J. and Cooper, J. (2001) A comparison of willingness to pay estimation techniques from referendum questions. Environmental and resource Economics 20:331-346.

Glass, R., Clifford, N., Harris, B., Woolsey, C. and Krider, C. (1999) Economic scope, impact and marketing study of the Kansas Arts Commission. The University of Kansas, Institute for Public Policy and Business: Research report number 257.

Herriges, J. and Shogren, J. (1996) Starting point bias in dichotomous choice valuation with follow-up questioning. Journal of Environmental Economics and Management 30:112-131.

Jorgensen, B. and Syme, G. (1995) Market models, protest bids and outliers in contingent valuation: Discussion. Journal of Water Resources Planning and Management Sept/Oct: 400-401.

Kealy, M. and Turner, R. (1993) A test of the equality of closed-ended and open-ended contingent valuations. American Journal of Agricultural Economics 75,2:321-323.

Kenyon, W. and Edwards-Jones, G. (1998) What level of information enables the public to act like experts when evaluating ecological goods? Journal of Environmental Planning and Management 41:463-476.

Kling, R., Revier, C. and Sable, K. (2004) Estimating the public good value of preserving a local historical landmark: The role of non-substitutability and citizen information. Urban Studies 41,10:2025-2041.

Krosnick, J., Holbrook, A., Berent, M., Carson, R., Hanemann, W., Kopp, R., Mitchell, R., Presser, S., Ruud, P., Smith, V., Moody, W., Green, M. and Conaway, M. (2002) The impact of 'no opinion' response options on data quality. Public Opinion Quarterly 66:371-403.

Krueger, S. (2002) Assessment of contingent valuation studies with specific reference to the role of information. Unpublished honours research thesis, Department of Economics, Rhodes University, Grahamstown.

Lindsey, G. (1994) Market models, protest bids and outliers in contingent valuation. Journal of Water Resources Planning and Management Jan/Feb: 121-129.

Maddison, D. and Mourato, S. (1999) Valuing different road options for Stonehenge. CSERGE Working Paper GEC 99-08

Maddison, D. and Foster, T. (2003) Valuing congestion costs in the British Museum. Oxford Economic Papers 55:173-190.

McFadden, D. (1994) Contingent valuation and social choice. American Journal of Agricultural Economics 76,4:689-709.

Morrison, W. and West, E. (1986) Subsidies for the performing arts: Evidence of voter preference. Journal of Behavioral Economics 15, Fall:57-72.

Niewijk, R. (2001) Misleading quantification: the contingent valuation of environmental quality. The Cato Review of Business and Government [On line] Available: http://www.cato.org/pubs/regulation/reg17n1-niewijk.html [Accessed 22/01/06].

NOAA (1993) Arrow, K.J., Solow, R., Leamer, E., Radner, R., Schuman, H. Report of the NOAA Panel on contingent valuation. National Oceanic and Atmospheric Administration Federal Register 58,10

Noonan, D. (2003) Contingent valuation and cultural resources: A meta-analysis. Journal of Cultural Economics 27:159-176.

Ozdemiroglu, E. and Mouraton, S. (2001) Valuing our recorded heritage. Paper presented at The Economic Valuation of Cultural Heritage conference, University College, London.

Papandrea, F. (1999) Willingness to pay for domestic television programming. Journal of Cultural Economics 23:149-166.

Reaves, D., Kramer, R. and Holmes, T. (1999) Does question format matter? Valuing an endangered species. Environmental and Resource Economics 14:365-383

Rushton, M. (2005) Support for earmarked public spending on culture: Evidence from a referendum in Metropolitan Detroit. Public Budgeting and Finance 25,4:72-85.

Santagata, W. and Signorello, G. (2000) Contingent valuation of a cultural public good and policy design: The case of Napoli Musei Aperti. Journal of Cultural Economics 24:181-204.

Seaman, A. (2003) Contingent Valuation vs. Economic impact: substitutes of complements? Paper delivered at the Regional Science Association International Conference, North American Meetings: Philadelphia

Smith, K. and Osborne, L. (1996) Do contingent valuation methods pass a 'scope' test? A meta-analysis. Journal of Environmental Economics and Management 31:286-301.

Snowball, J. (2000) Towards more accurate measurement of the value of the arts to society: Economic impact and willingness to pay studies at the Standard Bank National Arts Festival. Unpublished Masters Thesis: Department of Economics, Rhodes University, Grahamstown, South Africa.

Snowball, J. and Antrobus, G. (2001) Measuring the value of the arts to society: The importance of the value of externalities to lower income and education groups in South Africa. South African Journal of Economics 69,4:752-766.

Snowball, J. and Antrobus, G. (2003) Economic valuation of the 2003 Grahamstown National Arts Festival: economic impact, business and household surveys. Department of Economics, Rhodes University: Grahamstown.

Snowball, J. (2005) Art for the masses? Justification for the public support of the arts in developing countries – two arts festivals in South Africa. Journal of Cultural Economics 29:107-125.

Stazzera, E., Genius, M., Scarpa, R. and Hutchinson, G. (2003) The effect of protest votes on the estimates of WTP for use values of recreational sites. Environmental and Resource Economics 25:461-476.

Sunstein, C. (2002) Coherent and incoherent valuation: a problem with contingent valuation of cultural amenities. The Cultural Policy Center at the University of Chicago: Working paper.

Thompson, B., Throsby, D. and Withers, G. (1983) Measuring community benefits from the arts. Research paper 261, School of Economic and Financial Studies: Macquarie University.

Thompson, E., Berger, M. and Allen, S. (1998) Arts and the Kentucky economy. Center for Business and Economic Research, University of Kentucky.

Thompson, E., Berger, M. and Blomquist, G. (2002) Valuing the arts: A contingent valuation approach. Journal of Cultural Economics 26:87-113.

Throsby, D. and O'Shea, M. (1980) The regional economic impact of the Mildura Arts Centre. School of Economic and Financial Studies: Macquarie University Research paper number 210.

Throsby, D. and Withers, G. (1985) What price culture? Journal of Cultural Economics 9,2:1-33.

Throsby, D. and Withers, G. (1986) Strategic bias and demand for public goods: theory and application to the arts. Towse, R. (Ed.) Cultural economics: The arts, the heritage and the media industries. Vol. 2, Edward Elgar: Cheltenham

Vossler, C. and McKee, M. (2006) Induced-value tests of contingent valuation elicitation mechanisms. Environmental and Resource Economics 35:137-168

Whitehead, J. and Finney, S. (2003) Willingness to pay for submerged maritime cultural resources. Journal of Cultural Economics 27:231-240.

Willis, K. (2002) Iterative bid design in contingent valuation and the estimation of the revenue maximizing price for a cultural good. Journal of Cultural Economics 26:307-324.

6 The Choice Experiment Method and Use

Chapters 4 and 5 demonstrated that willingness to pay (WTP) techniques can be used to show that cultural resources do generate significant positive externalities or non-market benefits. However, there is great need for a more detailed analysis of the valuation of such goods, both in terms of the specific attributes that make up the good and their value to different population groups. The relatively new choice experiment (CE) or conjoint analysis method is also a type of contingent valuation stated preference technique, but with significant advantages over willingness to pay studies. While conjoint analysis has been used for some time in other branches of economics, it has only recently made its appearance in the cultural economics field. Rather than being asked their willingness to pay for one scenario, respondents in this method are asked to choose between bundles of attributes at different levels that make up the cultural good. Price is usually one of the attributes, which enables the calculation of marginal willingness to pay for each attribute, as compared to the composite value for the whole good obtained with WTP studies.

For example, the attributes of a study to value an archaeological site might include the degree of preservation of the artifacts, the infrastructure around the site, other facilities (like restaurants and child care centres) and information provision (audiovisual presentations, printed material etc.). Levels could be defined in qualitative terms (high, medium, low) or quantitatively (hectares preserved, kilometres of road, number of restaurants, etc.). The price attribute could refer to ticket price for visitors or tax increases for a wider population. Using statistical design procedures, choice sets showing different levels for each attribute are constructed. Respondents are then asked to choose between pairs of sets, sometimes including a *status quo* or "no change" option.

While comparatively few choice experiments have been used to value cultural goods, they have been used successfully in quite a wide variety of cases. These have included cultural events (Louviere and Hensher 1983; Snowball and Willis 2006), cultural heritage, like the Yorkshire Dales

(Garrod and Willis 1999), St Anne's Square (Alberini et al. 2003) and the Washington monuments (Morey et al. 2002), archaeological sites, like Greek heritage in Crete (Apostolakis and Jaffry 2005) and stone age remains in Denmark (Bille et al. 2006) and cultural institutions, like museums (Mazzanti 2003). Most of the studies have been fairly successful and positive about the use of choice experiments in cultural economics.

The following chapter discusses the methodology of the choice experiment technique and its uses in cultural economics and compares it to the willingness to pay method. It should be noted at the outset that there is still significant debate about best practice in the model design and analysis of choice experiment data (see for example, Hensher 2006 and Louviere 2006 in a recent special edition of *Environmental and Resource Economics*, 34). The aim of this chapter is not to enter into this debate, but to discuss the use of the method with regards to cultural good valuation and to illustrate what sorts of results can be obtained.

6.1 Examples of Choice Experiments in Cultural Economics

Whilst contingent valuation techniques have been widely used to value environmental goods (see Navrud and Ready 2002), there are relatively few published applications of choice experiments to the analysis of the conservation and provision of cultural goods. As the method gains in popularity, the quantity is sure to increase and, as appendix table 6.1 shows, is already starting to do so. The following section reviews some of the published papers in this area.

Cultural Events

One of the earliest (and seminal) choice experiments was conducted by Louviere and Hensher (1983) who examined the effect of attributes and ticket price on attendance at a proposed bicentennial international exposition in Australia. Attributes included cultural exhibits, technological displays, food and drinks from different nationalities, shows and amusements (rides and games) and location. Respondents were asked which exposition they would prefer to attend, given various attribute levels, including variation in ticket price. The study was able to predict what the attendance figures would be, given various changes in attribute levels. Socio-demographic information was used to predict what sort of people would attend any particular exposition. For example, larger households and males were less likely to attend than smaller households and women. Younger people were more likely to attend if more shows, amusements and foods and drinks were offered, while older people preferred cultural exhibits. Although the exposition was never held (hence the results could not be verified) Louviere and Hensher (1983) concluded that choice experiments are a useful way to predict consumer demand for multi-attribute cultural events, particularly in cases where the event is unique and no market data exists.

Two choice experiments have been conducted at the National Arts Festival in South Africa (Snowball and Willis, 2006a, 2006b). The first study, conducted in 2003, used various sections of the festival programme as attributes, namely, shows on the Main programme, shows on the Fringe, free shows and street theatre, art exhibitions and craft markets. Ticket cost was used as the price attribute, and levels were presented as percentage changes in the number of shows or exhibitions and craft market stalls. When the sample was split into different socio-economic groups, results showed significant differences in the utility these groups derived from the various festival attributes. Results were also used to conduct a financial cost-benefit analysis. The study concludes that such data could be useful to festival organizers both in terms of deciding in which areas to spend more or less, but also in attracting previously excluded groups by offering more shows that provide a higher utility level to them (Snowball and Willis 2006a).

The second National Arts Festival study in 2004 (Snowball and Willis 2006b) used a larger sample than the first study (230 interviews as compared to 78 in the previous study). While using the same attributes (except ticket price, which was excluded), the 2004 study used changes in actual numbers of shows, exhibitions and stalls, rather than percentage changes, as the levels. A quadratic multinomial logit model with interaction terms to take into account socioeconomic differences (like income, education and sex) was used to analyze the data. Results were also used to analyze the effects of welfare changes by examining attribute trade-offs for various groups of festival-goers and the market acceptability of changes to the festival.

Heritage and Urban Sites

Santos (1997) conducted one of the early cultural heritage choice experiments on the Yorkshire Dales (reported in Garrod and Willis 1999). More intensive modern farming is putting the picturesque Yorkshire countryside under pressure and the Dales were designated Environmentally Sensitive Areas in 1987. Traditional farming practices, while less efficient, do not have such a detrimental effect on the land, which is characterized by a number of features of historical and cultural importance, like stone walls, field barns, rich hay meadows and broad-leaved woodland.

The Dales study was conducted in two phases. Firstly, a contingent ranking experiment, followed by an open-ended willingness to pay question was used, in which respondents were shown paintings of different land use alternatives and asked to rank their top three alternatives. The majority of respondents chose the *status quo* as their most preferred option, indicating some bias. However, the benefit-cost ratio for "today's landscape" was four times higher than the cost to the public of maintaining it. In a continuation of this research Santos (1997) used a contingent ranking choice experiment to value the attributes of the Dales separately. The major findings were that stone walls and barns are the most important attributes of the Dales landscape.

A choice experiment used to value cultural heritage goods was conducted on an urban cultural site, St Anne's Square in Belfast, by Alberini, Riganti and Longo (2003). The study focused on the value of regenerating this culturally and historically significant square, using building height, amount of open space and distribution between residential and retail usage as the variable attributes. Pictures of the square, digitally remastered to show various different attribute levels and an associated once-off cost, as well as a verbal description were shown to respondents (not including a *status quo* option), who were then asked to choose an option (presented in pairs).

The results of the St Anne's Square study showed that the chosen attributes did explain the choices respondents made – generally, people preferred more open space and lower building heights. However, contrary to economic theory, the sign on the price coefficient was positive and significant. The authors suggest various reasons for this anomaly, including that the price may have been interpreted as an indication of the quality of the proposed regeneration.

Boxall et al. (2003) used a choice experiment combined with a revealed preference approach (travel cost method) to examine the factors determining the choice of wilderness canoe routes in the Precambrian Shield region in Canada. In particular, they investigated whether the discovery of Aboriginal pictographs (rock paintings) in either pristine or vandalized and weathered condition would affect the choice of route. The stated preference data were combined with the actual travel cost data of respondents to examine potential dependence between the two. Attributes of the stated preference choice experiment were travel cost to the route, hectares of recently burnt area, area of black spruce, area of white spruce, pristine pictographs and defaced pictographs. Results showed that 42% of respondents would change their route to see pristine pictographs, but only 10% would change to see defaced ones. They estimate that pristine pictographs increase the value of the trip by an average of between $61.31 and $77.26 per trip, depending on the route. However, this drops to between $3.96 and $8.39 if the pictographs are vandalized. Boxall et al. (2003) argue that the results indicate that resources should be spent on the protection of pictographs and that stated and revealed preference techniques can be successfully combined in such valuation studies.

In a recent study, Tuan and Navrud (2006) investigated the value of the My Son World Heritage Site in Vietnam using both willingness to pay and choice experiment methods. The site is threatened by natural environmental degradation as well as human activities and neglect. Using a choice experiment, they calculated the value to foreign visitors and local residents of site restoration using four attributes: price (entrance fee for foreign visitors and tax increase for locals), a proposed preservation plan, infrastructure upgrading, and additional services. They found that the price variable was significant and had a negative effect on choice, that restoration and infrastructure were both positive and significant and additional services were an insignificant determinant of choice. They also included socioeconomic variables by using interaction terms. When the CE and WTP data were pooled, they found that both methods produced very similar results.

Archaeological Sites

Recently, choice experiments have also been used successfully to value archaeological sites. Apostolakis and Jaffry (2005) used the method to value Knossos Palace and the Heraklion museum on the Greek island of Crete. The study was particularly interested in determining the value of various site attributes to different groups of tourists and potential tourists. Respondents were asked to choose between two options, with attributes of promotion methods (hotel exhibits and advertising), number of people on the site, promotional incentives (like reduced prices for students and late entry), "wine and dine" facilities and "other facilities" (like audiovisual material and child care facilities) and a "would not visit" option. They included socioeconomic characteristics, like age and country of origin, using interaction terms, and also examined the welfare effects of changing the site characteristics. Findings show that respondents would be prepared to pay an additional 3.6 to see museum replicas of site artifacts in their hotel and would be willing to pay to reduce congestion on the sites.

In a related paper using the same data set, Apostolakis and Jaffry (2006) investigated the effect of cultural capital (using socio-demographic variables like age, education and income as a proxy) on the probability of visiting cultural heritage sites on Crete. They found that, for all tourists, price was the least important determinant of a visit, with site characteristics (such as congestion, information facilities and "wine and dine" facilities) being much more important. Advertisement of the site, or information provided beforehand also had a significant positive influence on "frequent" heritage tourists and tourists with an "average" level of income. Senior tourists were more likely to visit if "wine and dine" facilities were provided on site and younger tourists were put off by increases in congestion.

Bille et al (2006) presented a paper at the 14th Conference of the Association of Cultural Economics International on the valuation of Stone Age artifacts in Denmark. The interesting thing about the study is that preservation of the artifacts entails submerging them by re-establishing the wetland on which they are found. This means that their value is entirely non-use, that is, it refers only to existence and bequest values, since one would not be able to see the artifacts once they are submerged. Attributes of the wetland restoration project were: improvement in biodiversity, level of protection of the archaeological artifacts, degree of public access and recreational possibilities. The price attribute was an extra payment in annual tax. A "*status quo*" option was also included. Another interesting aspect of the study was that it was conducted via the internet, which proved more cost effective and faster than a postal survey. They found that the Danish population had a significant positive WTP for the protection of the artifacts: an average of DKK800 per person per year for reducing their destruction and DKK1200 for permanent protection. However, Bille et al. (2006) consider their figures to be an overestimate and suggest reasons for this, such as the "warm glow" phenomenon and lack of understanding of project scope and problems with the payment vehicle – forms of bias which also occur in the WTP studies discussed in chapter 4.

Willis and Kinghorn (2007) investigated the value of the Roman fort at Vindolanda on Hadrian's Wall in the UK. A unique feature of the site is that it has ongoing archaeological excavations and also a very good on-site museum, with displays of finds and audiovisual material about the texts discovered on the site and their preservation. The study interviewed visitors to the site using the following attributes: excavation and research, interpretation provided within the site, display of artifacts in the museum, reconstructions and visitor facilities. Results showed that visitors gained most utility from ongoing excavation and also from being able to see the finds displayed in the on-site museum. Price and the introduction of a children's play area would decrease utility. The latter is a similar finding to Apostolakis and Jaffry (2005), who also found that providing kindergarten facilities would not increase visitor utility. Similar reasons for these findings are also suggested by Bille et al. (2006), that is, that visitors are more interested in maintaining the integrity of the site than including more recreation or amusement facilities. Also, similar to the Cretan study, when socioeconomic interaction terms are included in the Vindolanda study, the price attribute becomes insignificant. It is also found that interaction between substitute sites nearby and the Vindolanda entry fee (price) is negative and significant, suggesting that the WTP for Vindolanda entry is much reduced by the intention of visiting other sites.

Museums and Monuments

Mazzanti (2003) used a choice experiment to value the various attributes of the *Galleria Borghese Museum* in Rome. He argues that phases of increasing public funding for cultural heritage in Italy "should be rooted in evaluation and appraisal efforts aimed at assessing what the most valuable options for the development for the cultural sector are" (2003:600). Attributes chosen were admission charge (three levels), conservation activity (two levels), access policy (two levels) and additional services, including multimedia and audiovisual services and temporary exhibitions (three levels).

The results showed that a change in conservation activities and the price coefficient was significant across all models. Older, high-income foreign visitors and those with university degrees were willing to pay most for conservation, while less educated people were more interested in additional services. Access policy was least important. Age and income were positively related to WTP and foreigners were willing to pay more than Italians. Total economic surplus figures were calculated by multiplying mean WTP with the number of paying visitors per year. Mazzanti (2003:600) concluded that choice experiments "look encouraging" as a way to value cultural heritage resources and to guide policy makers in appropriate expenditure. However, this particular study is rather weak in that the attributes had so few levels that it could be argued that a CV study could have provided the same information. Also, goodness-of-fit was poor, with adjusted R-squared values being very low for all models (0.067, 0.0076 and 0.074).

Morey et al. (2002) used a choice experiment to value the preservation of 100 historical marble statues in Washington DC. The damage to the statues is being caused by sulphur dioxide in the air (commonly known as acid rain). Using verbal descriptions, photographs of two of the statues showing their current average state and computer generated images of their possible decay (including the *status quo*), the survey asked respondents to choose between various levels of treatment, and associated prices, to delay the decay of the statues by various amounts of time. Results showed that there was significant positive WTP for all the treatment options and that passive-use or bequest values are a very important part of the value of the monuments.

A problem with the study was that it did not allow for the possibility that some population groups, in this case young non-Caucasians, would not wish to preserve the statues at all, in other words, had a negative WTP to preserve them because of the culture and heritage they celebrate. Using a "mixture" model combining multinomial logit (MNL) and random parameters logit (RPL) models, Morey and Rossmann (2003) further analyzed the results in terms of sub-populations within the sample to highlight such differences in preference.

Broadcast and Broadband

Finn et al. (2003) conducted a study of the value of the programming provided by the Canadian Broadcasting Corporation (CBC) to English and French speaking Canadians. Using both open-ended willingness to pay questions and a choice experiment, distributed via the mail, they were able to draw conclusions about the total value of the CBC, the relative value of various programming types and the presence or absence of externalities to the two population groups. They found that Canadian drama and sports were the most popular programming types and that significant differences in preference exist between French and English language speaking households. Finn et al. (2003) conclude that choice experiments, in conjunction with WTP studies, provide a greatly improved way of obtaining input from citizens as to the value of a public broadcaster compared to activist participation in various hearings.

A later study (Finn et al. 2006) valued the Alberta SuperNet, built by the Alberta Government to enable affordable Internet connectivity to public institutions, like schools, hospitals and libraries in the province, but also available to households. In particular, they wanted to investigate the public versus private good values of the service, having found in the earlier CBC study that public good values measured using the CE approach were insignificant. In addition to using all sorts of Internet services (like e-Mail, online news, e-Learning, e-Government, e-Shopping and entertainment) as attributes, two versions of the choice question were asked – one emphasizing "own use only" while the other payment covered "benefits to your household of all other Albertans having high-speed access". They found no evidence of non-use values and that private goods like e-Mail, e-Transactions and e-Files were the most significant in determining choice. Improved local and provincial government services (as a result of the SuperNet) were valued at less than $15 per household per month, casting doubt on the benefits of building the network, which cost $193 million.

6.2 The Underlying Theory of Choice Experiments

Having examined some examples of how the choice experiments method can be used in cultural economics, we now examine the theoretical underpinnings of the method. Choice experiments were first used in marketing and transportation literature and arose out of stated preference methods in these fields, but were different from the usual analysis because respondents were asked to choose between "bundles" of options, not to rate or rank them (Adamowicz *et. al.* 1998:64). In choice experiments customers are presented with sets of alternative combinations of attributes (or characteristics) of a "good" and are asked to choose their most preferred alternative.

Choices by customers from sets of alternatives reveal the trade-offs they are willing to make between good attributes.

Choice modelling is based on Lancaster's (1966) characteristics theory of value which stated that the utility derived from a good is the sum of the utility of the good's attributes or characteristics. "Utility or preference orderings are assumed to rank collections of characteristics and only to rank collections of goods indirectly through the characteristics they possess" (Lancaster 1966:133). Since each individual is asked to choose one alternative from the choice set (made up of various levels of the good's characteristics), Random Utility Theory (RUT) is used to model the choice as a function of the attribute levels. According to Hanley et al. (2001:438) choice modelling has four main alternatives; choice experiments (that provide the most information about attributes and welfare consistent estimates, if they include a *status quo* option), contingent ranking, contingent rating and paired comparisons.

The CE approach was originally developed by Louviere and Hensher (1983) and has a common theoretical framework with dichotomous choice contingent valuation in RUT, which assumes that individuals will make choices based on the attributes and attribute levels (an objective component observable to the researcher) along with some degree of randomness (a random, unobservable component). This random component arises either because of randomness in the preferences of the individual or because some attributes of the good have been left out of the research design. Referring to equation (1), the utility that person i gets from choice set j is equal to V_{ij}, which is the systematic, observable component and ε_{ij}, which is the random, unobservable component (see Train 2003).

$$U_{ij} = V_{ij} + \varepsilon_{ij} \qquad (1)$$

If it is assumed that V_{ij} is a linear utility function, then the utility of person i for good j is equal to some base level of utility β_0 plus the sum of the attributes of good j, plus the random component. The βj coefficients show the contribution of each attribute to total utility of good j.

$$U_{ij} = \beta_0 + \sum \beta_j X_{ij} + \varepsilon_{ij} \qquad (2)$$

Assuming that each respondent maximizes their utility and gains some utility from each attribute, the choice of one option over another indicates that the utility gained from the chosen option is greater than that from the alternative. That is, the individual (i) will choose good j over alternative good k if $U_{ij} > U_{ik}$. The probability that any individual will choose good j over good k can thus be expressed as the probability that good j's utility (given by the observable attributes plus the unobservable random component), is greater than the observable and random utility of good *k*. Selecting an alternative is expressed as

$$U_{ij} > \mathbf{max}_{k \quad Ci\,,\, k \neq j}\; U_{ik} \qquad (3)$$

In order to calculate the trade-offs made between attributes, leading to the choice of the preferred option, a conditional multinomial logit model (CLM) is used (Willis 2002b). The CLM is derived by placing restrictive assumptions on the random component of the utility: error disturbances are assumed to have a Type 1 extreme value (Weibull) distribution with the distribution function

$$\exp(-\exp(-\varepsilon_{ij})) \qquad (4)$$

From the Type 1 extreme value distribution, the probability of choosing an alternative j among n_i choices of individual i

$$P_i(j) = P[\mathbf{x'}_{ij}\beta + \varepsilon_{ij} \geq \mathbf{max}_{k \quad Ci}(\mathbf{x'}_{k}\beta + \varepsilon_k)$$

$$= \exp(\mathbf{x'}_{ij}\beta) \,/\, \Sigma_{k \quad Ci} \exp(\mathbf{x'}_{ik}\beta) \qquad (5)$$

(Willis and Garrod 1999)

An assumption of the CLM is the independence of irrelevant alternatives (IIA) property, which states that "the relative probabilities of two opinions being selected are unaffected by the introduction or removal of other alternatives" (Hanley et al. 2001:439). IIA assumes all cross-effects are equal, so that if one attribute of the good gains in utility it draws shares from other attributes in proportion to the current market share of these sections. Different assumptions about the error term lead to different multinomial logit models. A distribution of ε_{ij} that is independent and non-identical leads to a heteroskedastic extreme value (HEV) model; whilst a mixed logit (MXL) permits parameter heterogeneity by allowing the random error components to have different distributions.

6.3 A Comparison between Choice Experiments and WTP Studies

Choice experiments (CEs) have a number of advantages over willingness to pay methods (also referred to as contingent valuation (CV) methods). Firstly, they can describe the good's attributes and the trade-offs between them more accurately than contingent valuation methods (CVM) and one can then value these attributes separately and in combination, thus "they allow the researcher to 'value' attributes as well as situational changes" (Adamowicz *et. al.* 1998:65). Hanley *et. al.* (2001:447-8) agree, adding that, while the same results could be obtained by including a number of CV scenarios with differing attributes in a questionnaire, this is a more "costly and cumbersome" alternative to the CE approach. For example, the WTP for changes in the levels of various attributes of a good could be valued using WTP, but only by including a number of different scenarios in each questionnaire or by having many different questionnaires. CE is thus better for measuring the marginal values of changes in a particular scenario and may thus be more useful in multidimensional policy design and in setting taxes (Hanley *et. al.* 2001:452).

Secondly, choice experiments, with attributes both higher and lower than the current value, allow one to work out willingness to accept compensation for loss (WTA) without all the endowment effect problems of CV (Adamowicz *et. al.* 1998:66). As discussed in chapter 4, the NOAA panel (1993) recommended that WTA measures should not be used, since such figures are not constrained by the respondent's budget and may be limitless. However, a willingness to accept measure, for example a drop in taxes in exchange for a decline in the provision of some public good, may be very useful in making budgetary allocation decisions.

Hanley et al. (2001:448) and Adamowicz et al. (1996) also point out that, since respondents are focused more on the trade-offs between choices rather than on willingness to pay, CEs may limit some of the problems, like warm glow, protest bids, strategic behaviour and "yeah saying", found with the CVM, "but this has yet to be demonstrated". Willis and Garrod (1999:75) found that strategic bias and free riding were reduced when using choice experiments to value the low flow alleviation programs of certain UK rivers to recreational users, as compared to using CV. Morey et al. (2002) also argue that CEs encourage respondents to focus on the good attributes rather than on more emotive issues, like environmental policy, which may reduce warm glow responses.

However, a marketing experiment done by Ding et al. (2005) suggests that choice experiments may still be prone to hypothetical bias. The authors compare choice experiment results for hypothetical and "incentive aligned" techniques used to value Chinese dinner specials and snacks. The incentive alignment takes the form of respondents being in a realistic setting for the good and in them having to actually purchase it (price being deducted from their participation fee), if their stated value is less than or equal to a random draw price. They find that there are significant differences in the preference structures revealed by the incentive aligned and hypothetical choices, with those in the "real" situation "having higher price sensitivity, exhibiting lower risk seeking and willingness to try new things, and are less prone to socially desirable behaviours" (Ding et al. 2005:76). This is a worrying result for CE practitioners in a cultural economics setting because public goods with non-use values can seldom, if ever, be valued in such a realistic incentive aligned setting. The Ding et al. results suggest that choice experiments, like WTP studies, may still be susceptible to hypothetical bias as a result of the lack of a budget constraint and have some "warm glow" responses.

The well-known hypothetical bias in CV studies (discussed in chapter 4) is probably also present in CE studies, but since CEs are a form of dichotomous choice CV, it is possible that one of the advantages of CEs is that they have a "natural internal scope test". While the internal test is weaker than the external one, a study by Foster and Mourato (1999 cited in Hanley *et. al.* 2001:451) found that CEs showed much stronger sensitivity to scope than did a similar CV study.

Willis and Garrod (1999: 75) suggest that, since CEs provide a much more detailed description of the good than CV and present it in a format similar to the price-quantity trade-offs that consumers have to make each day, it could provide a more accurate valuation of the good than the willingness to pay format.

There have been a few cultural economics studies that used both CE and CV methods to value a good with the intention of determining whether the two methods provide similar results. One of the earliest was the Morey et al. (2002) study of the preservation of marble monuments in Washington DC from degradation by acid rain. In a group setting, respondents were given information on the project and asked to make choices between various preservation options and price. Some of the respondents were also asked their maximum WTP for the most comprehensive treatment program using the CV format with a payment card. It was found that the choice experiment mean and median WTP values lay between the two payment card estimates. Morey et al. (2002) concluded that choice experiments are a useful valuation technique for goods with use and especially non-use values.

However, the Finn et al. (2002) study, on the value of programming provided by the Canadian Broadcasting Corporation (CBC), found that while CV and CE results were similar for use values, respondents indicated a much higher non-use value in the CV format than they did in the choice experiment. (They used both an open ended willingness to pay question (CV format) and a choice experiment.) When valued separately, the CV study showed a monthly household value of $5.03, 26% of which was non-use value. The CE study showed values of $5.76 for English and $5.46 for French households. However, the CE found no evidence of non-use values.

Tuan and Navrud (2006), in their valuation of the My Son heritage site in Vietnam, used a split sample to test variation in CV and CE methods as a test of convergence validity. The CV respondents were asked whether they would be willing to pay a set price for the proposed preservation plan or not. The CE respondents were asked to choose between various preservation plan attributes at a given price. Results show that there is no great difference between CE and CV responses, but that CV (willingness to pay) estimates are higher than CE estimates in most cases. In examining statistically significant differences between the two methods however, they found that, except in one case (residents with a non-parametric estimate) they cannot reject the null hypothesis that there is no difference between CE and CV willingness to pay estimates.

6.4 Choosing Attributes and Levels

Since much of the methodology of choice experiments is the same as for willingness to pay studies, which have been discussed in chapters 4 and 5, only areas of significant difference in study design will be discussed here. One of the most important differences is that choice experiments describe the good in terms of attributes and levels and that these need to be carefully chosen and tested.

Hanley et al. (2001) provide a useful guide to the stages of conducting a choice experiment (see table 6.1). Attributes should be realistic and easily understandable, as should their levels. Pre-testing and/or the use of focus groups can be an important stage in this process. While researchers may be tempted to increase the number of attributes and levels in order to describe the good and changes in it more fully, this can quickly lead to a huge number of choice options and problems with complexity, although some studies have been successful in including a greater number of attributes. For example, Willis et al. (2005) assess customer preferences and WTP for domestic water supply using 14 attributes. However, it was suggested by Hanley et al. (2001) that having more than seven attributes in a standard study design makes ranking difficult and increases inconsistency and inaccuracy.

Table 6.1. Stages of a Choice Modelling Exercise

Stage	Description
Selection of attributes	Identification of relevant attributes of the good to be valued. Literature reviews and focus groups are used to select attributes that are relevant to people while expert consultants help to identify the attributes that will be impacted upon by the policy. A monetary cost is typically one of the attributes to allow the estimation of WTP.
Assignment of levels	The attribute levels should be feasible, realistic, non-linearly spaced, and span the range of respondent's preference maps. Focus groups, pilot surveys, literature reviews and consultations with experts are instrumental in selecting appropriate attribute levels. A baseline '*status quo*' level is usually included.
Choice of experimental design	Statistical design theory is used to combine the levels of the attributes into a number of alternative scenarios or profiles to be presented to respondents. *Complete factorial designs* allow the estimation of the full effects of the attributes upon choices: that includes the effects of each of the *individual* attributes presented (main effects) and the extent to which behavior is connected with variation in the *combination* of different attributes offered (interactions). These designs often include an impractically large number of combinations to be evaluated: for example, 27 options would be generated by a full factorial design of 3 attributes with 3 levels each. *Fractional factorial designs* are able to reduce the number of scenario combinations presented with a concomitant loss in estimation power (i.e. some or all of the interactions will not be detected). For example, the 27 options can be reduced to 9 using a fractional factorial. These designs are available through specialized software.
Construction of choice sets	The profiles identified by the experimental design are then grouped into choice sets to be presented to respondents. Profiles can be presented individually, in pairs or in groups. For example, the 9 options identified by the fractional factorial design can be grouped into 3 sets of four-way comparisons.
Measurement of preferences	Choice of a survey procedure to measure individual preferences: ratings, rankings or choices.
Estimation procedure	OLS regression or maximum likelihood estimation procedures (logit, probit, ordered logit, conditional logit, nested logit, panel data models etc.). Variables that do not vary across alternatives have to be interacted with choice-specific attributes.

(Source: Hanley et al. 2001:437)

Using a fractional factorial design, rather than a full or complete factorial design can be a partial solution to the number of choice options generated. In the Tuan and Navrud (2006) study of the value of the My Son world heritage site in Vietnam, there were only four attributes, with between two and four levels each (table 6.2). A full factorial design thus gave 32 choice sets, four of which were removed because of a dominant alternative (one option which clearly offered more at a lower price). The remaining 28 choice sets were grouped into 4 versions of the questionnaire containing 7 choice sets each – that is, respondents were asked to make 7 choices between pairs of options.

Table 6.2: Attributes and Levels Used in the My Son Heritage Study

Attributes	Description	Levels
Price	Entrance fee for the foreign visitor if the alternative is selected. The current entrance fee is US$4 (the *status quo* – SQ) and four alternative levels.	$4 (the SQ), $5, $9, $14, $19
Preservation plan	From the current condition of preservation (the SQ) to the proposed preservation plan for My Son	The SQ, the proposed plan
Upgrading of infrastructure	From the current condition of infrastructures (the SQ) to the proposed level of upgrading infrastructures: upgrading of 30km of road to link My Son with the highway, building a new bridge and upgrading the drainage system at My Son.	The SQ, Upgrading infrastructures
Additional services	The existing basic services (the SQ), and multimedia audio-visual interactive services plus temporary exhibition in addition to the existing exhibition.	The SQ, Additional services

(Tuan and Navrud 2006)

Fractional factorial designs can be used when a greater number of attributes and levels are present, but they will not detect all the interactions, only the main effects or utility of each attribute regardless of changes in attribute levels. For example, the Willis and Kinghorn study of Vindolanda (2007) had six attributes, five of which had two levels, and one (price) had three levels. A full factorial design would have produced 96 combinations. They thus chose to use a fractional factorial design including interactions between two attributes. This produced 48 options which generated 14 randomly chosen choice pairs and a *status quo* option.

Sometimes choosing attributes can be fairly straightforward. For example, the South African National Arts Festival studies (Snowball and Willis 2006a, b) simply used the different sections of the festival as attributes. These were: shows on the heavily sponsored "Main" program, more experimental "Fringe" shows, street theatre, art exhibitions and the craft markets. Although the latter three attributes are free, ticket price was used as the payment vehicle for two reasons: most visitors are not from the area, so a local tax was not feasible and the many entry points to the town made a gate price unrealistic; secondly the vast majority of festival visitors had bought at least one ticket. Respondents could choose whether they would be WTP higher ticket prices for more shows (including subsidizing the free shows) or minimize ticket price and have fewer shows.

Changes	Option 1	Option 2
"Main" shows 	50% more	25% less
"Fringe" shows 	25% more	25% less
Free shows & street theatre 	25% less	25% more
Art exhibitions 	50% more	25% less
Craft markets 	50% more	50% more
Ticket price 	100% more	25% more

(Snowball and Willis 2006a:50)

Fig. 6.1. An Example of the Choice Cards Used at the South African National Arts Festival

In the first National Arts Festival study (Snowball and Willis 2006a) attribute levels were given by a percentage change in the number of shows, exhibitions and stalls. An orthogonal (balanced) main effects design generated 26 choices which were paired and presented with icons in 13 cards

(Figure 6.1 shows an example). Each respondent was given 3 randomly selected cards and asked to choose their most preferred option.

In the second National Arts Festival study (Snowball and Willis 2006b), quantitative attribute levels were used, showing changes in the actual number of shows, exhibitions and craft market stalls (as shown in table 6.3). However, despite a larger sample size, the model attributes did not explain choices as well as the smaller earlier study and the coefficient of free shows was negative and significant. A possible reason for this is that a relatively small number of free shows is offered at the festival (compared to the other attribute categories) and changes in absolute numbers therefore look insignificant and were disregarded by respondents when making their choice. In any event, it appears that the use of percentage changes (although less precise) was actually a more effective way of describing the attribute levels than using the number of shows or events.

Table 6.3. Attributes and Levels Used in the 2nd South African Arts Festival Study

Attributes	**Level -1 (10% decrease)**	***Status quo***	**Level +1 (10% increase)**	**Level +2 (25% decrease)**
Main	180	200	220	250
Fringe	225	250	275	313
Free	9	10	11	13
Art	31	35	39	44
Craft	240	267	294	334

(Snowball and Willis 2006b)

Bille et al. (2006) discuss the use of qualitative attribute levels in their study of the Stone Age site of Great Aamose in Denmark. While they admit that quantitative attribute levels can have some advantages, as they can be connected to "dose-response functions" for the wetland restoration, such information can be difficult, if not impossible, to come by. This is particularly the case in cultural economics studies, where improvements in the quality and provision of the good are often not directly quantifiable. In the Great Aamose study, attributes like the size of the protected area (hectares) and the extra tax payment (DKK) had quantitative levels, while others, like the level of biodiversity (low, some, high), the artifact preservation (continued devastation, reduced devastation, protection now and in the future) and access (restricted, extended) were qualitative.

A major problem with WTP studies, discussed in chapters 4 and 5, is the starting point, anchoring or framing bias that results from the questionnaire suggesting an initial value for the good. Hanley et al. (2005) set out to test whether the levels (amounts) of the price attribute affect valuation or welfare estimates in choice experiments, using a study of the benefits of river water quality improvement in northern England. Reassuringly, they found that, while higher prices resulted in fewer people choosing the option (more remaining with the *status quo*), it had no statistically significant effect on either preferences or willingness to pay, although they note the problems of preference heterogeneity as well. The selection of levels for the price attribute, then, is unlikely to cause major bias.

Finally, the number of times a respondent has to make a choice between options in an interview may also be important. Sattler et al. (2003) conducted an analysis of 22 choice experiments to determine whether the number of choice tasks affects the validity of results. They found that there is some evidence that preferences change as the interview progresses – in particular, respondents become more sensitive to price and less sensitive to other attribute levels. A greater number of tasks also increases the number of "none" options chosen as respondents become bored or tired and try to finish the interview quickly. In a test of predictive validity, they find that preferences are stable (predictive validity does not increase) after six choices (for a good with four attributes), and suggest that this is the optimal level. However, it should be noted that the Sattler et al. (2003) study was of choice experiments for marketing, focusing only on goods with use values. Being asked to value unfamiliar non-use goods may prove to be more cognitively difficult and few choice experiments in cultural economics use as many as six choice tasks per interview.

6.5 Potential Forms of Bias in Choice Experiments

While choice experiments improve on willingness to pay studies in a number of ways, they are still prone to forms of bias, some shared with WTP studies and others peculiar to the choice experiment method. The following discussion focuses on three major forms of bias: the *status quo* and endowment effect; complexity and choice consistency; and individual valuation and summation issues.

6.5.1 *Status Quo* and Endowment Effects

Adamowicz et al. (1998: 73) found that "the utility associated with moving away from the current situation [the good as it exists at present] is negative and significant" and that this shows either *status quo* or endowment effect bias. Similarly, Willis and Garrod (1999:76), using choice experiments, amongst other methods, to determine the value to the general public of increased flow of certain rivers in the UK, found that over 40% of respondents selected the *status quo* option. The coefficients on the other options were negative and statistically significant, indicating that "there is a negative utility associated with changing from the current situation to one of the other alternatives – this is regardless of any utility respondents may have for the attributes of these choices."

The effect is also found in many cultural economics studies, where it can be easily seen when the model includes an "alternative specific constant" (ASC) – a dummy variable describing preferences for the *status quo*. For example, in the Bille et al. (2006) archaeological valuation study, the ASC representing the *status quo* was -0.73852 and statistically significant, suggesting some negative utility in moving away from the current scenario. Willis and Kinghorn (2007), in their study of the Roman site at Vindolanda, also found that "*ceteris paribus,* visitors prefer the *status quo*". However, this is not found in all studies: the second South African National Arts Festival study (Snowball and Willis 2006b) found that positive utility was associated with moving away from the current situation. It was hypothesized that, in the South African context of dramatic political and social change, a move away from the *status quo* towards a broader, more inclusive festival could be regarded as a positive change.

An explanation for the negative utility sometimes associated with moving away from the *status quo* (also found in contingent valuation responses) is that people do not trust the administration to use the money for the stated purpose or believe that they have the resources to carry it out. It could also be that when the choice is too complicated, or the respondent is tired, they choose the current situation because they are "unsure about the value of the trade-offs they would be willing to make" or as a form of protest (as with "protest zeros" in CVM) (Adamowicz et al.1998: 73). Willis and Garrod (1999:78) suggest that respondents might simply have a psychological preference for things as they are, rather than some uncertain future state and that careful pilot testing can detect cases where the current situation is chosen because of confusion over the choice experiment.

Adamowicz et al. (1998:74) note that this form of bias could be avoided simply by not including a *status quo* option (as in the Alberini et al. (2003) urban sites case study). However, this would make welfare analysis difficult, since there would be no "base" to compare changes with. In general, commentators seem to agree that, while a *status quo* option will probably provide some bias, it is a necessary one if one is to have a starting point from which to calculate changes in welfare.

6.5.2 Complexity and Choice Consistency

Another important potential problem with CEs is that there is significant evidence that if too many choice options or too many attributes are used, respondents will get tired of undertaking the complex mental task of calculating marginal utilities based on trade-offs and will begin to use heuristics or rules-of-thumb to answer the questions. This can lead to some seemingly irrational choices and an increase in random errors. It is thus important to include some consistency checks in CEs and to limit the number and level of attributes included (Hanley et al. 2001:448 – 50).

The issue of how increases in the complexity of choices facing respondents affects the consistency of their decisions is further explored by DeShazo and Fermo (2001). They found that both the number of attributes and the variation in attribute levels could have a significant effect on "complexity-induced choice inconsistency" that could over- or under-estimate welfare measured by as much as 30%. In other words, as choice experiments become more elaborate, as they are quickly wont to do, the reliability of the results decreases beyond a certain threshold level.

Abley (2000) suggests that if "simplifying rules of thumb" are used by respondents to make complex choices (for example, choosing the choice set with the highest value for their most important attribute without considering other attribute levels), this has implications for the level of information being used by respondents. That is, although the researcher may have provided what she regards as an optimal level of information for making an informed choice, the respondent may be disregarding large parts of that information, leading to apparently irrational or inconsistent choices. Abley (2000) also cites other cases in which respondents add to or "embellish" the information provided (particularly if it is textual or verbal information) using past experiences and their own knowledge. This links to David Hensher's ongoing research into the effects of design on choice experiment results. Although not the focus here, he has also investigated the implications of respondents ignoring certain attributes (Hensher 2005, 2006) which could lead to significantly different WTP results.

DeShazo and Fermo (2001) suggest two ways of controlling for such bias. Firstly, extensive pilot testing, to determine the optimal number of attributes and levels, is required. Secondly, when the results are analysed, they recommend that such problems be identified and controlled for using a heteroskedastic logit model. A more alarming suggestion, however, is that preferences change over the sequence of responses. That is, preferences expressed at the beginning of the survey are not consistent with those made in the last choices. DeSarbo et al. (2004) suggest a model for determining such "change points" but acknowledge that it is unclear which observations reflect true preference.

> "It may be that experts and highly involved respondents give their most accurate responses early (before fatigue sets in) and novices and less involved respondents their most useful responses late in the sequence … after they develop a defined preference structure" (De Sarbo et al. 2004:204).

Adamowicz et al. (1994), however, found evidence that the underlying preferences used to make choices in a hypothetical choice experiment were very similar to those used to make actual decisions. The results of their study on the determinants of choice of recreation site which used both stated and revealed preference data, "lends support to the use of this stated preference technique, at least in the measurement of use values" (Adamowicz et al. 1994:289).

Some initially encouraging results are also reported by Hensher (2006) who investigates the effects of varying the number of choice sets presented, the number of attributes per alternative, the number of levels per attribute and the range of attribute levels. He finds that aggregated mean estimates of willingness to pay (for travel time savings amongst Sydney residents) cover a range appropriate for reporting a global mean and provides meaningful values for demand prediction. When other design dimensions are controlled for, he does not find that any particular design features affect WTP valuation significantly, which is reassuring. However, when the other design dimensions are not controlled for, he does find that the number of attributes and the number of alternatives in a choice set systematically affect mean WTP estimates.

Discussions about the levels and use of information and choice strategies have been a feature of contingent valuation research for some time. For example, in the List and Shogren (1998) and List and Gallet (2001) studies mentioned in chapter 4, it was found that the more that respondents knew about the good (experts, or those provided with more information) the less would be the so-called hypothetical bias. The repeated choices that respondents are asked to make in CEs have simply refocused attention on exactly how these hypothetical choices are made and whether they are likely to be consistent or not. CEs have provided a new opportunity to study consumer choices and all commentators agree that much more research is needed in this area.

6.5.3 Independent Valuation and Summation

In order to calculate overall WTP for a good, one has to assume that the value of the good is equal to the sum of its parts, that is, that there are no substitution effects and that no major utility-providing attributes have been left out. This may however, be unrealistic, as in the Yorkshire Dales study, where significant substitution between attributes was detected. Hoehn and Randall (1989) investigated the over-valuation of public goods as a result of using independent valuation and summation (IVS) in CV studies – that is, valuing independent public goods separately and then simply adding their values together. They use an effective intuitive example to explain their theory – that of the valuation of endangered species. Separately valued, each species might show a positive cost/benefit ratio, but, given that there are thousands of endangered species, the collective WTP to protect all of them, obtained by IVS, might leave even the most ardent wildlife supporter feeling fleeced.

Hoehn and Randall (1989:550) conclude that the error occurs at a very basic level – simply that there are limited resources and unlimited wants and that, given our limited productive capacity, this imposes substitution effects on us. They suggest, without much enthusiasm, that sequenced valuations might provide a better alternative, but as Willis (2002b:639) points out, sequencing introduces other problems, as goods which are valued first tend to be given higher values than those further down the list.

Perhaps this is one area in which choice experiments, which focus on a number of different attributes at the same time, can usefully solve one of the problems associated with CV. However, as a check, Hanley et al. (2001:449) suggest that a CV study of the whole good should also be included and compared with the additive CE value obtained. This was in fact done in the Morey et al. (2002) Washington monuments study, and results showed that the choice experiment results for the whole good (preservation of monuments) fell between normal and log-normal expected mean WTP values using a payment card. However, the Yorkshire Dales study (reported in Garrod and Willis 1999) found that there were significant substitution effects between attributes, so that summing the independent valuation of each attribute using a traditional CV study would overvalue the landscape.

While the above arguments address the issue of substitute values within a particular experiment, they still do not answer the broader Hoehn and Randall (1989) question of other substitute goods. One might expect that, with cultural goods, each one is unique and that no substitutes exist, but this may not be how consumers view them. For example, Willis and Kinghorn (2007) in their study of the Roman archaeological site of Vindolanda show that visits or the intention to visit other Roman forts along Hadrian's Wall in close proximity to Vindolanda, made respondents much more sensitive to Vindolanda entry price. They conclude that "the value of the Vindolanda site is determined by the availability and characteristics of the similar four neighbouring Roman forts open to visitors". The Bille et al. (2006) study of the preservation of Stone Age remains in Denmark produced what the researchers felt to be exaggerated WTP figures. One of the reasons they suggest for this is that respondents were not considering other alternative Danish national park projects in the country and may have "emptied their accounts" with regard to the preservation of ancient artifacts in general.

Thus, while the CE method appears to have a number of benefits compared to CV and to solve some of the bias problems, it also raises other issues to keep in mind when designing such a study. However, the type of results that CEs can provide are significantly more detailed and informative than those of CV, as the following section will show, and provide a strong incentive for the continued use of the method in cultural good and event valuation.

6.6 Interpreting Results

The analysis and interpretation of CE data is significantly more complex than that of WTP studies. In general, conditional logit models (CLM) are used, but heteroskedastic extreme value models (HEV) and mixed logit models (MXL) are also common. While not the focus of this chapter, it should be noted that there is still considerable debate about the design and analysis of choice experiments, including measures that can be used to control for various forms of bias. The special edition of the journal of *Environmental and Resource Economics* (volume 34, 2006) is a good place to start from for those interested in following this debate. The focus of this section is the interpretation of results and their uses in cultural economics, rather than the econometrics.

6.6.1 Odds Interpretation and Willingness to Pay

The coefficients of the attributes provide a direct way of ranking the utility that consumers receive from each attribute. For example, looking at the results from the Willis and Kinghorn (2007) study in table 6.4, one can immediately see that the greatest utility is from continued excavation and research of site, followed by the display of museum artifacts and reconstructions. The negative sign on the price coefficient indicates that higher prices decreased the probability of choosing that particular option.

Table 6.4 Results of the HEV model used in the Vindolanda Study

Attribute	**Coefficient**
ASC	0.4827***
Excavation & research	2.7042***
Interpretation	0.2328**
Museum artifacts	1.8560***
Reconstructions	0.6131***
Amenities	-0.2928**
Price	-0.0995*
Scale 3	22.9529***

*** significant at the 1% level
** significant at the 5% level
* significant at the 10 % level
(Willis and Kinghorn 2007)

Coefficients can also be used to calculate the odds of a respondent choosing a particular option when attribute levels change. For example, looking at the results from the first South African National Arts Festival shown in table 6.5 a 1% increase in the number of shows on the Main programme would increase the probability of respondents choosing this option by 1.01%.

Table 6.5. Odds Interpretation of the Attribute Coefficients at the South African National Arts Festival

Main attribute coefficient	0.0114***
Main attribute odds interpretation	An increase of 1% increases the probability of respondents choosing this option by 1.01147%
Fringe attribute coefficient	0.007358
Fringe attribute odds interpretation	An increase of 1% increases the probability of respondents choosing this option by 1.0074%
Free attribute coefficient	0.005132
Free attribute odds interpretation	An increase of 1% increases the probability of respondents choosing this option by 1.005145%
Art attribute coefficient	0.008223*
Art attribute odds interpretation	An increase of 1% increases the probability of respondents choosing this option by 1.00825%
Craft attribute coefficient	0.0102***
Craft attribute odds interpretation	An increase of 1% increases the probability of respondents choosing this option by 1.0252%
Price attribute coefficient	-0.0110***
Price attribute odds interpretation	An increase of 1% decreases the probability of respondents choosing this option by 1.01106%

Estimates of WTP for a change in each attribute can be calculated by estimating the marginal rate of substitution between the particular attribute and the price attribute. This is the rate at which the respondent is willing to trade off money for an increase in any particular attribute being examined. The estimate is obtained by dividing the coefficient of the attribute by the price attribute coefficient (Eftec 2002). That is, the marginal WTP for a change in any one of the attributes is the ratio $-\beta\kappa/\beta\eta$, where $\beta\kappa$ is the coefficient of the attribute and $\beta\eta$ is the coefficient of the price attribute (Tuan and Navrud 2006).

For example, in the Bille et al. (2007) study of WTP to protect the stone age site of Great Aamose, results showed that respondents were willing to pay 1192 DKK (7.3 EUR) per person per year in increased taxes to protect the artifacts permanently ("now and in the future") . This is calculated by dividing the negative of the coefficient of the artifacts attribute (-1.13179) by the price coefficient (-0.00095). Total willingness to pay for three different protection scenarios by the whole population was then calculated by multiplying the sum of the WTP for each attribute by the number of people in the Danish population. Since the values were very large, some sensitivity analysis was conducted by including only those over 18 years of age, then regarding WTP as being per household rather than per person and then comparing this to the WTP of individuals who live in the area of the site. For example, WTP for protection scenario one per person was about DKK 800, which aggregated to DKK 3.4 billion for all Danish people over 18 (4,184,858 people), but reduced to DKK 2 billion if it was assumed that this figure was per household (2,498,621 households) rather than per person. People living near the site (28 000) were willing to pay DKK 31 million for protection scenario one. Higher levels of protection (scenarios two and three) resulted in higher average willingness to pay amounts (DKK 3.7 billion and DKK 4.6 billion respectively for household results).

Once WTP for changes in various attributes of a good has been calculated, this data can be used very effectively for cost-benefit analysis. For example, in valuing the attributes of the Alberta SuperNet, Finn et al. (2006) find that high speed access to all forms of service (like e-mail, e-transactions and e-files) is $39.85 per household per month, while Dial-up access is only worth $2.43. However, because they find no evidence of non-use values, there is some doubt as to whether the SuperNet should be publicly funded. The case for government expenditure could be justified by the improved provincial and local government services as a result of the SuperNet, but these are worth less than $15 per household per month. Since the Government of Alberta paid $193 million to build the SuperNet, there is some doubt that the benefits outweigh the costs, although Finn et al. (2006) do not specifically calculate the ratio.

In the first South African National Arts Festival study (Snowball and Willis 2006a), a cost-benefit analysis was conducted for each attribute, since the cost of the attributes varied considerably. For example, looking at table 6.6, even though WTP for an increase in the number of shows on the Main programme was much higher than for any of the other attributes (shows on the Fringe, art exhibitions, free shows and street theatre, number of stalls at the craft markets), the cost of providing one more Main show was estimated to be R167 000. While ticket sales would generate revenue of about R11 700 per show, the costs of increasing Main shows by 10% (18 more shows and 50 more performances) would far outweigh the WTP for this increase (costs of R3 million and WTP of about R580 000). However, a 10% increase in Fringe shows would only cost around R90 000, but would generate benefits of about R440 000. An increase in the number of free shows would also be justified, but any increase in art exhibitions would not.

Table 6.6: Estimated Costs and Benefits of a 10% Increase in the Provision of Different Events at the South African National Arts Festival in 2003 prices.

Marginal (10%) change in	Number of Shows	Number of Performances	Cost in Rands	WTP in Rands
Main shows	18	50	3,000,000	579,536
Fringe	17	129	90,000	441,347
Free	1		80,000	159,791
Art	3		360,000	251,100
Craft		26 stalls	[a]Very high	311,190

[a.] It is difficult to estimate the marginal cost of the additional craft market stalls, since the Village Green is currently at capacity. Expanding it further would thus involve huge fixed costs in terms of additional marquees, electricity and water points, toilet facilities and so on. Conversely the marginal cost saving in reducing the number of stalls would be very small for this event.

(Snowball and Willis 2006a:53)

6.6.2 Including Socio-demographic Variables

An important aspect of the demand for cultural goods is the heterogeneity of preferences that arises because of different tastes, often included in such models by using some socio-economic variables. The multinomial logit (MNL) model can show differences in taste related to such variables which can be included, but (since they remain the same for all choices) only as interaction terms (dummy variables). As discussed in the previous section estimates of WTP for each attribute can be made and the individual's utility for each attribute (called part-worths) can be estimated as well as the value of the programme as a whole - simply the sum of all the values of the various attributes (Willis 2002b:643). However, given different tastes, these values may differ significantly between various groups of respondents.

One of the reasons that reliability in contingent valuation studies is so important is that results from one study are sometimes transferred to another case study or population in order to make policy decisions without repeating an expensive survey. This process is referred to as "benefit transfer". An interesting study done by Jiang et al. (2005) conducted two choice experiments on coastal land use options for Rhode Island and for Massachusetts. They used the Rhode Island survey to predict the Massachusetts results and compared these to the actual Massachusetts results as a test of the validity of such benefit transfer. Findings show that the transfer predictions ranked the attributes (in terms of preference) in a statistically significantly similar manner and that they were reasonably good at predicting Massachusetts choices. There was also significant correlation between the predicted and actual WTP estimates. However, an important way of improving the transfer model was to make provision for preference heterogeneity by including the socio-demographic variables of respondents as well as their (environmental) attitudes to the good. This suggests that for successful benefits transfer of equally complex cultural goods, it is important to take into account not only differences in the good, but also differences in the population characteristics and contexts. This point is also made by Tuan and Navrud (2006) in their study of a World Heritage site in Vietnam – one of the few conducted in a developing country context.

A way to explore possible differences in values across respondent groups is to split the sample. For example, in the first South African National Arts Festival study, it was hypothesized that there would be significant differences in attribute values between African-origin and European-origin festival goers and between men and women. As the four models for the various groups in the table below show, the split sample did reveal some interesting differences in preference between groups.

For example, the highly sponsored shows on the Main programme were more appealing to females and African-origin people, while art exhibitions were favoured by females and European-origin festival-goers. The Main show result is fairly surprising, given the rather Eurocentric nature of many of the offerings (including ballet, opera, a symphony orchestra, drama and so on). However, the festival director (Marais 2004) suggested that the preference for Main shows by African-origin race groups could be explained by the relatively recent participation of this section of the population in the festival. When faced with such a wide variety of mostly unknown artists, newcomers would probably naturally choose Main shows, because they are selected by the organizers (thus controlled for quality), are in larger, easier to find venues and heavily sponsored (sure to provide good value for money). In contrast, Fringe shows offer a bewildering number and quality of events and may be of a very poor quality. Since it is only in the last 10 years that South Africa has been a democratically ruled country and that an African-origin middle class has emerged, most people in this group are still fairly new to the festival experience. Marais (2004) speculates that it may take a whole generation (another 10 to 15 years) for African-origin people to feel as confident and comfortable as their European origin counterparts. African-origin people were also willing to pay most for a 10% increase in all attributes (57% increase in ticket prices), followed by males (47%).

Table 6.7. Results for the South African National Arts Festival Split by Sample Groups.

	Model 1: Females	**Model 2: Males**	**Model 3: European-origin**	**Model 4: African-origin**
McFadden R-squared	0.2583	0.1166	0.2668	0.1210
"Main" attribute coefficient	0.0155*	0.008073	0.007086	0.0173*
Rise in ticket price (WTP) for a 10% increase in "Main" attribute	10.62%	10.2%	4.72%	21.33%
"Fringe" attribute coefficient	0.003877	0.0102	0.0151	0.001145
Rise in ticket price (WTP) for 10% increase in Fringe shows	2.66%	12.89%	10.07%	1.41%
"Free" attribute coefficient	0.002992	0.006436	0.004313	0.0118**
Rise in ticket price (WTP) for 10% increase in Free shows	2.05%	8.13%	2.88%	14.55%
"Art" attribute coefficient	0.0111*	0.005206	0.0101*	0.04973
Rise in ticket price (WTP) for 10% increase in Art exhibitions	7.60%	6.58%	6.73%	6.13%
"Craft" attribute coefficient	0.0140*	0.007459	0.0107	0.0112
Rise in ticket price (WTP) for 10% increase in craft market size	9.59%	9.42%	7.13%	13.81%
"Price" attribute coefficient	-0.0146***	-0.0079**	-0.0150***	-0.00811**
Total WTP for an increase of 10% in all attributes.	32.52%	47.22%	31.08%	57.23%

*** significant at the 1% level
** significant at the 5% level
* significant at the 10 % level

Another way to examine the effect of socio-economic variables on choice is to include interaction terms in the model. The Tuan and Navrud (2006) study of the My Son World Heritage Site in Vietnam included the attributes (price, preservation plan, upgrading infrastructures) as well as variables like sex, age and income. In a third model, they added 'taste' variables, like knowledge of site and the visitor's satisfaction with their visit. While goodness of fit did not change much across models, it did reveal some interesting differences (younger people are more likely than older ones to support the preservation plan) and, in particular, could be used to check for validity. For example, the higher a respondent's income is and the more knowledge they have about the site, the more likely they are to support preservation.

Willis and Kinghorn (2007), in their study of the value of the Vindolanda Roman archaeological site in the UK, also show how important it is to include preference heterogeneity and interaction terms. Including interactions between the attributes and age, visitor attitudes and whether they had visited other, similar sites nearby dramatically improved the goodness of fit of the HEV model, as did exploring interactions between attributes. For example, they found that utility of on-site reconstruction increases with the age of the respondent and that there is a positive and significant interaction between the on-site museum and reconstructions, suggesting that these two factors mutually enhance each other. On the other hand, there are negative interactions between improved amenities (like a children's play area) and excavation and the museum.

These methods are useful, but taste can vary amongst people with the same socio-economic variables, and the mixed logit model (MXL) is able to capture this "heterogeneity in taste" (Eggert and Olsson 2004:6). The Washington DC marble monuments study (Morey et al. 2002; Morey and Rossmann 2003) used such a MXL model. This study explored the value of preserving about 100 historic outdoor monuments in Washington DC from damage by acid rain. They found that WTP results depend to a large extent on socio-demographic variables like gender, age and ethnicity.

Table 6.8. Expected WTP and Percentage of Individuals with Negative Values for Washington Monument Preservation

Increase in preservation timeline	**Models** 20-year old, low-income non-Caucasian males			
		Classic	**RPL**	**Mixture**
25%	E[CV]	$9	$38	$14
	% CVs negative	0%	13%	32%
50%	E[CV]	$10	$53	$16
	% CVs negative	0%	14%	36%
100%	E[CV]	$11	$88	$16
	% CVs negative	0%	16%	42%

(Morey and Rossmann 2003:226)

The "mixture" model (discussed in Morey and Rossmann 2003) combines multinomial logit (MNL) and random parameters logit (RPL) models. "Put simply, the preference parameters are assumed random variables that are a function of observable characteristics of the individual. The resulting model is a *mixture* model: the population consists of a mixture of sub-populations" (2003:220). They show that allowing for heterogeneity within sub-samples can produce interesting differences in valuation. For example, in the traditional MNL model, more preservation is associated with higher value for all groups. Using an RPL model, more preservation is shown to be associated with negative values for young non-Caucasians. In the MXL model, differences within groups are allowed for and it can be shown that not all 20 year old, male, low-income, non-Caucasians have negative WTP and that negative CV values increase as the level of preservation rises (seen in the table 6.8).

6.6.3 Welfare Changes and Market Acceptability

The parameter estimates of the choice experiment models represent the marginal rate of substitution between attributes. If one of the attributes is price, then the willingness to pay (the rate at which respondents trade-off money and the additional attribute provision) can be calculated. However, one can also calculate the marginal rate of substitution between attributes, to investigate the welfare effects of changes in the provision of the good.

In the second South African National Arts Festival study (Snowball and Willis 2006b) no price attribute was included, since three (free and street shows, art exhibitions and craft markets) of the festival attributes had no admission price (the remaining two being ticketed shows on the Main and Fringe programmes). However, the marginal rates of substitution between attributes could be calculated for different economic groups (socio-economic variables such as education, sex and income were included as interaction terms and the sample was split into African- and European-origin sub-samples). This information proved very useful to festival organizers who are interested in making the festival attractive particularly to African-origin people who had been excluded under the past Apartheid policies.

For example, table 6.9 shows the attribute trade-offs for African-origin festival goers with an average household income of R15 000 per month and tertiary education. Reading across horizontally, it can be seen that a 1% fall in the number of Fringe shows can be traded off against much smaller increases in the other festival attributes, but that a 1% fall in art exhibitions would require much bigger rises in the other attributes to make up for it. African-origin visitors with lower income and education levels were more interested in the craft markets, while higher income and education level European-origin visitors have a strong preference for the more experimental shows on the Fringe (Snowball and Willis 2006b).

Table 6.9. Attribute Trade-offs for African-origin Festival-goers with an average Household Income of R15 000 and Tertiary Education at the South African National Arts Festival

	Main	Fringe	Art	Craft
Main	1	1.94	0.13	0.55
Fringe	0.51	1	0.07	0.28
Art	7.32	14.23	1	4.02
Craft	1.82	3.53	0.25	1

(Snowball and Willis 2006b:30)

The market acceptability of changes in the composition of the cultural good can be estimated by calculating the probability that people from certain groups would choose a particular option rather than maintaining the *status quo*.

> "The dependent variable in a CL model is the log of the odds ratio. If alternative k is the *status-quo* and the new attribute level is alternative j, then $\exp(\Sigma_i b_i \Delta_{ij}^{*} x_i)$ shows the odds ratio of the probability of choosing alternative j set of attributes over the *status quo* set k when an attribute is changed from x_{ik} to x_{ij}^{*}. The change in the odds ratio, or the odds of choosing one alternative over another, is a feature of festival-goers preferences for changing the composition of the festival" (Snowball and Willis 2006b:31).

Table 6.10. Odds Interpretation for a 10% increase in attributes for African-origin, European-origin and all Festival-goers at the South African National Arts Festival

Attribute	Change (10% ↑)	African-origin Respondents	European-origin Respondents	All Respondents
Main shows	↑ 20 shows	19.02	1.93	2.26
Fringe shows	↑ 25 shows	4.18	18.36	8.60
Art exhibitions	↑ 4 exhibitions	59.48	2.59	6.90
Craft market stalls	↑ 27 stalls	14.78	1.46	3.10

Average household income of R15000; Tertiary education; Sex=men

(Snowball and Willis 2006b:31)

For example, as seen in table 6.10 above, increasing the number of art exhibitions and Main shows by 10% would increase quite considerably the probability of male, African-origin festival goers with an average household income of R15 000 a month and a tertiary education of choosing this option. European-origin visitors in the same category (men, income R15 000, tertiary education) would be more likely to choose an option in which Fringe shows were increased.

6.7 Combining Methods

The advantage of using revealed preference methods, like travel cost and hedonic pricing, is that values are determined in the market (price) and are thus not prone to the many forms of bias found in stated preference methods. However, revealed preference methods only work for goods that already exist, not for something proposed for the future and they are, of course, unable to measure non-use values.

An innovative study by Boxall et al. (2003) combined the benefits of revealed and stated preference methods (using a choice experiment) to determine what effect the possible future discovery of aboriginal rock paintings would have on respondents' choice of wilderness canoe routes in Manitoba, Canada. Since only those who had travelled to a canoeing site were included in the study, however, only use values were measured. Revealed preference data were collected using the travel cost method to establish the current value of the canoe routes. This was then augmented with choice experiment (i.e. stated preference) data on how preferences would change, should rock paintings be found along the route in the future. This was done by adding the rock paintings (in various states of degradation) as an attribute of the canoe trip. After accounting for dependence between revealed and stated preference data, the models were combined and the data could be used to value the welfare effects of the discovery of aboriginal pictographs and their protection level.

While not directly useful in valuing non-use values, such combinations are another way to use stated preference results that incorporate the benefits of both revealed and stated preference methods and are likely to be used more frequently in the future.

6.8 Conclusions

While choice experiments (also called conjoint analysis) are relatively new to cultural economics, they have been shown to be successful in valuing a wide variety of cultural goods including cultural events, heritage, museums, archaeological sites and others. Their big advantage over contingent valuation (i.e. the traditional WTP studies discussed in chapters 4 and 5) is that they can provide valuations for the attributes of the good, not just for the whole good. These attribute valuations (also called part-worths) can be very useful to policy makers and for benefit transfers because they can be used to evaluate several scenarios without having to repeat the research. The data is also useful for calculating changes in welfare and market acceptability and can be adapted to include preference heterogeneity.

The choice experiment approach seems to be able to address some of the forms of bias found in contingent valuations by providing, for example, a built-in scope test. Since respondents are focused on the attributes of the good, the method may reduce warm glow or other emotive responses. However, the design of these experiments is considerably more complex than that of contingent valuation studies and has its own difficulties, like choosing the best attributes and levels to describe a good and deciding on the number of choices. The choice of econometric models has also been shown to have a significant effect on the results and research in this area is ongoing.

Appendix Table 6.1

Examples of Choice Experiments in Cultural Economics

YEAR	AUTHOR	AREA	GOOD	SOURCE
1983	Louviere and Hensher	Exposition	Bicentennial exposition, Australia	*Journal of Consumer Research* 10,3:348-361
1997	Santos	Heritage	Yorkshire Dales	Book: *Economic Valuation of the Environment* (1999) Garrod and Willis (Eds.)
2001	Mazzanti	Museums	Services in Galleria Borghese, Rome	*Journal of Economic Studies* 30,6:584-604 (This case study also discussed in *Journal of Socio-Economics* (2003) 32:549-569.)
2002	Morey et al.	Historical site	Reducing damage to DC monuments	Book: *Valuing Cultural Heritage* (Navrud, Ready Eds.) *Journal of Cultural Economics* (2003) 27,3-4:215-229
2002	Boxall et al.	Heritage	Aboriginal rock painting, Nopiming Provincial Park, Manitoba, Canada	Book: *Valuing cultural heritage* Navrud, Ready (Eds) (This case study also discussed in *Journal of Environmental Economics and Management* (2003) 45:213-230
2003	Alberini et al	Urban sites	St Anne's Cathedral Square, Belfast	*Journal of Cultural Economics* 27, 3-4:193-213
2003	Finn et al.	Broadcast	Canadian television programme language	*Journal of Cultural Economics* 27:259-274
2005	Apostolakis and Jaffry	Archaeology	Knossos Palace and the Heraklion museum, Crete	*Journal of Travel Research* 43,3:309-318
2006	Finn et al.	Internet	Canadian broadband, the Alberta SuperNet	*14th Association of Cultural Economics International* Conference, Vienna
2006	Bille et al.	Archaeology	Stone-age village, Great Aamose, Denmark	*14th Association of Cultural Economics International* Conference, Vienna
2006	Apostolakis and Jaffry	Archaeology	Effects of cultural capital on visits to sites on Crete	*14th Association of Cultural Economics International* Conference, Vienna
2006	Tuan and Navrud	Heritage	My Son World Heritage Site, Vietnam.	*Environmental and Resource Economics,* 35 [Published online: Springerlink]
2006a	Snowball and Willis	Arts	Cost-benefit analysis at the South African National Arts Festival	*Leisure Studies*25,1:43-56
2006b	Snowball and Willis	Arts	Market acceptability and welfare changes at the SA National Arts festival	*South African Journal of Economics*
2007	Willis and Kinghorn	Archaeology	Vindolanda on Hadrian's Wall, UK	*Journal of Cultural Economics* (forthcoming)

References

Abley, J. (2000) Stated preference techniques and consumer decision making: New challenges and old assumptions. [On line] Available: https://dspace.lib.cranfield.ac.uk/bitstream /1826/664/2/SWP0200.pdf

Adamowicz, W., Louviere, J. and Williams, M. (1994) Combining revealed and stated preference methods for valuing environmental amenities. Journal of Environmental Economics and Management 26:271-292.

Adamowicz, W., Boxall, P., Williams, M. and Louviere, J. (1998) Stated Preference Approaches for Measuring Passive use Values: Choice Experiments and Contingent Valuation. American Journal of Agricultural Economics 80 (1): 64-75.

Alberini, A., Riganti, P. and Longo, A. (2003) Can People Value the Aesthetic and Use Services of Urban Sites? Evidence from a Survey of Belfast Residents. Journal of Cultural Economics 27: 193-213.

Apostolakis, A. and Jaffry, S. (2005) A choice modeling application for Greek heritage attractions. Journal of Travel Research 43:309-319

Apostolakis, A. and Jaffry, S. (2006) The effect of cultural capital on the probability to visit cultural heritage attractions. Paper presented at the 14th Association of Cultural Economics International Conference, Vienna 6-9 July.

Bille, T., Lundhede, T. and Hasler, B. (2006) Economic valuation of protected archaeological artifacts in Great Aamose, Denmark Paper presented at the 14th Association of Cultural Economics International Conference, Vienna 6-9 July.

Boxall, P., Englin, J. and Adamowicz, W. (2003) Valuing aboriginal artifacts: a combined reveal-stated preference approach. Journal of Environmental Economics and Management 45:213-230

DeSarbo, W., Lehmann, D. and Hollman, F. (2004) Modeling dynamic effects in repeated-measures experiments involving preference/choice: an illustration involving stated preference analysis. Applied Psychological Measurement 28,3:186-209.

DeShazo, J. R. and Fermo, G. (2002) Designing Choice Sets for Stated Preference Methods: The Effects of Complexity on Choice Consistency. Journal of Environmental Economics and Management 44: 123-143.

Ding, M., Grewal, R. and Liechty, J. (2005) Incentive-aligned conjoint analysis. Journal of Marketing Research 62:67-82.

Eftec (2002) Valuation of benefits to England and Wales of a revised bathing water quality directive and other beach characteristics using the choice experiment methodology. [On line] Available: www.defra.gov.uk/environment/ water/quality/bathing/bw_study4.htm [Accessed 8/07/04].

Eggert, H. and Olsson, B. (2004) Heterogeneous preferences for marine resources. [On line] Available: www.handels.gu.se/epc/archive/00003393/ [Accessed 6/07/04].

Finn, A., McFadyen, S. and Hoskins, C. (2003) Valuing the Canadian Broadcasting Corporation. Journal of Cultural Economics 27:177-192.

Finn, A., McFadyen, S. and Thomas, D. (2006) Use and non-use values of SuperNet enabled broadband content and services. Paper presented at the 14th Association of Cultural Economics International Conference, Vienna 6-9 July.

Garrod, G. and Willis, K. (1999). Economic Valuation of the Environment. Edward Elgar, Cheltenham

Hanley, N., Mourato, S. and Wright, R. (2001) Choice Modeling Approaches: A Superior Alternative for Environmental Valuation? Journal of Economic Surveys 15 (3): 435-462.

Hanley, N., Adamowicz, W. and Wright, R. (2005) Price vector effects in choice experiments: an empirical test. Resource and Energy Economics 27,3:227-234.

Hensher, D. (2005) The implication of willingness to pay of respondents ignoring specific attributes. Transportation 32,3:203-222.

Hensher, D. (2006) Revealing difference in willingness to pay due to the dimensionality of stated choice designs: an initial assessment. Environmental and Resource Economics 34,1:7-44.

Hoehn, J.P. and Randall, A. (1989) Too many proposals pass the benefit cost test. American Economic Review 79,3:544-551.

Jiang, Y., Swallow, S. and McGonagle, P. (2005) Contest-specific benefit transfer using stated choice models: specification and convergent validity for policy analysis Environmental and Resource Economics 31:477-499.

Lancaster, K. (1966) A new approach to consumer theory. Journal of Political Economy, 74, 134-57.

List, J. and Shogren, J. (1998) Calibration of the difference between actual and hypothetical valuation in a field experiment. Journal of Economic Behavior and Organization 37:193-205.

List, J. and Gallet, C. (2001) What experimental protocol influences disparities between actual and hypothetical stated values? Environmental and Resource Economics 20:241-254.

Louviere, J. and Hensher, D. (1983) Using discrete choice models with experimental design data to forecast consumer demand for a unique cultural event. Journal of Consumer Research 10, 3:348-361.

Louviere, J. (2006) What you don't know might hurt you: some unresolved issues in the design and analysis of discrete choice experiments. Environmental and Resource Economics 34:173-188.

Mazzanti, M. (2003) Valuing cultural heritage in a multi-attribute framework – microeconomic perspectives and policy implications. Journal of Socio-Economics 32:549-569

Mazzanti, M. (2003) Discrete choice models and valuation experiments. Journal of Economic Studies 30,6:584-604.

Morey, E., Rossmann, K., Chestnut, L. and Ragland, S. (2002) Modeling and Estimating WTP for Reducing Acid Deposition Injuries to Cultural Resources: Using Choice Experiments in a Group Setting to Estimate Passive-Use Values. Valuing Cultural Resources in Navrud, S. and Ready, R. (Eds.) Edward Elgar Publishing.

Marais, L. (2004) Personal communication (Interview) 10/04: Grahamstown.

Morey, E. and Rossmann, K. (2003) Using Stated-Preference Questions to Investigate Variations in Willingness to Pay for Preserving Marble Monuments: Classic Heterogeneity, Random Parameters and Mixture Models. Journal of Cultural Economics 27: 215-229.

NOAA (1993) Arrow, K.J., Solow, R., Leamer, E., Radner, R. and Schuman, H. Report of the NOAA Panel on contingent valuation. National Oceanic and Atmospheric Administration Federal Register 58,10

Sattler, H., Hartmann, A. and Kroger, S. (2003) Number of tasks in choice-based conjoint analysis. Research paper 013 on Marketing and Retailing, University of Hamburg.

Snowball, J. and Willis, K. (2006a) Estimating the marginal utility of different sections of an arts festival: the case of visitors to the South African National Arts Festival. Leisure Studies 25,1:43-56

Snowball, J. and Willis, K. (2006b) Building cultural capital: transforming the South African National Arts Festival. South African Journal of Economics 74,1:1-14.

Tuan, T. and Navrud, S. (2006) Valuing cultural heritage in developing countries: Comparing and pooling contingent valuation and choice modelling estimates. Environmental and Resource Economics 35: Dec 7 online publication.

Willis, K. and Garrod, G. (1999) Angling and Recreation Values of Low-Flow Alleviation in Rivers. Journal of Environmental Management 57: 71-83.

Willis, K. G. (2002) Stated Preference and the Estimation of Environmental Values. International Journal of Environmental Studies 59: 635-646.

Willis, K and Kinghorn, N. (2007) Managing an archaeological site: site characteristics, preference heterogeneity, two-factor interactions, and substitute site effects. Mimeo: School of Architecture, Planning and Landscape, University of Newcastle upon Tyne'.

7 Conclusions

> "Beauty is rarely soft or consolatory. Quite the contrary. Genuine beauty is always quite alarming".
> I looked at Camilla, her face bright in the sun, and thought of that line from the *Iliad* I love so much, about Pallas Athene and the terrible eyes shining.
> (*The Secret History* by Donna Tart 1992:44)

This book set out to explore ways in which culture, as represented by cultural goods, like arts festivals, theatre, museums, libraries, heritage and so on, can be valued. Originally grounded in the field of economics and, more specifically, cultural economics, the subject matter quickly spilled over into all sorts of other fields, like philosophy, cultural studies, sociology, history and even theology. And this is not a bad thing. Rather, it represents a gradual, but definite move in economic theory towards a far more pluralistic and interdisciplinary approach.

Anderson (1993:xiii) argues that to limit ourselves to the one measure of value provided by the market (that is, price) is an ultimately impoverishing choice.

> "We don't respond to what we value merely with desire or pleasure, but with love, admiration, honor, respect, affection and awe as well. This allows us to see how goods can be plural, how they can differ in kind or quality: they differ not only in *how much* we should value them, but in *how* we should value them."

She agrees with Klamer (2004b) and Throsby (2001) that values are socially constructed and determined through conversation and social interaction – talking about the reasons for our value judgments helps others to see and appreciate them too. The idea of utility or want satisfaction as being the ultimate measure of such values is simply not pluralistic enough to describe how we respond to things we value.

Economics makes free and frequent use of the word "good" to mean a desirable object – something that provides utility. The ancient Greek word, *kalos,* means good, but also beautiful – an unalterable link in the ancient Greek mind, so that it was at first inconceivable that a good person would be ugly or vice versa. This link has persisted in modern times, but like the students in *The Secret History*, we may find ourselves trembling before beauty or "good", not enjoying or wanting it all, but nevertheless valuing it.

What makes valuing culture or cultural expressions even more problematic is that our value judgments are largely based on the understanding of what good and bad is, opinions which are generated by the culture itself. If one understands culture and art as a way of making meaning, of understanding and interpreting reality, then it must be of ultimate value to us. But how to measure it? In some ways, it is rather like trying to open a box with the crowbar that is inside it.

It is acknowledged early on in this book that the market, while providing some useful guidance for policy makers, is not sufficient in the case of cultural goods with large externalities. It is also stressed that, out of a particular context, even non-market valuations are not much good. G. K. Chesterton, writing in 1901, also acknowledges this in his essay entitled, "A defense of nonsense". He argues that, while art does not have to have a direct relationship or reference to its context, it nevertheless draws inspiration from it. "The principle of *art for art's sake* is a very good principle if it means that there is a vital distinction between the earth and the tree that has its roots in the earth; but it is a very bad principle if it means that the tree could grow just as well with its roots in the air" (1935:126).

The best way of valuing complex cultural goods would thus seem to consist of a combination of valuation techniques that can give as holistic a picture as possible. Table 7.1 summarizes the four measurement techniques discussed, what they are supposed to measure and their strengths and weaknesses. The choice of the "correct" method for any particular cultural good will depend largely on what sort of values one is trying to measure.

Table 7.1. Methods of Valuing Cultural Goods

Method	What it measures	Advantages	Disadvantages
Qualitative/historical	Historical, social and political importance	Provides a context and long-term view. Does not rely on one monetary measure, but allows for a greater variety of indicators. Addresses the importance of art and culture specifically.	No generally agreed-upon indicators yet available. Is a subjective measure that may be contested more than other methods. Does not result in one, easily comparable figure.
Economic impact	Incremental monetary effects on real GDP of the region, tax revenues, jobs and personal income.	Provides one monetary figure easy to communicate and use in public funding advocacy. Is useful in comparing the return on investment of taxpayers and making comparisons between projects. The cultural institution or event does not need to be qualitatively valued, avoiding reference to what may be politically sensitive issues.	Method is not as "scientific" and objective as it seems and is open to many forms of methodological bias. The figures themselves are open to misrepresentation. Financial impact by itself is not a very effective argument for public funding. Does not take into account the aims of the cultural workers or their products.
Willingness to pay	The monetary value of use and non-use values generated by the event, specifically those values external to the market	Method takes into account non-market values that are usually more closely related to the goals of cultural workers. Can confirm/deny the existence of externalities to various groups. Only way to measure non-use values. Results in one monetary figure that can easily be communicated and combined with economic impact figures.	Numerous methodological problems as a result of the hypothetical nature of the questions. May be double-counting the financial benefits recorded in economic impact. Values the good as a whole, not the part-worth attributes.
Choice experiments	The monetary value of use and non-use values generated by the event (as above)	Has the same advantages as the WTP method as well as possible methodological improvements (e.g. built in scope test and possible reduction of hypothetical bias). Each attribute of the good valued separately. Willingness to accept as well as WTP can be measured.	Still plagued by some methodological problems. Can result in extremely complex choice tasks and associated problems. Respondents have to have quite detailed information about each attribute (some evidence that CE is better at measuring use than non-use values).

McCarthy et al. (2004) provide a very useful framework for thinking about the benefits that the arts may provide. The divide potential benefits up into "intrinsic" benefits associated directly with the particular artistic product, and "instrumental" benefits, not so closely related to the particular product and, at least to some extent, also provided by substitute goods. Intrinsic benefits can include private values, like captivation or our emotional absorption in an artistic work, pleasure or satisfaction, and cognitive growth. Some intrinsic benefits have a more public good nature, like creating social links, and expressing community views and dissent. Likewise, instrumental benefits can include private benefits, like improving learning ability, attitudes and health; and more public benefits, like improved social networks and the economic benefits of direct and indirect spending on the good (McCarthy et al. 2004).

The sort of study one would undertake would depend on which of these benefits one is trying to quantify. As McCarthy et al. (2004) demonstrate, both intrinsic and instrumental benefits occupy a continuum from the private to the public good sphere. The value of some of these can be effectively measured using market (economic impact) or contingent market (willingness to pay and choice experiment) methods, while others may only be captured in more historical, qualitative studies.

7.1 A Case Study of the South African National Arts Festival

As a brief case study of how these methods can be combined, consider the value of the South African National Arts Festival (NAF), to which all the methods discussed in this book have been applied. The NAF has been in existence since about 1974 and thus makes an interesting case study because it covers the politically turbulent period in South African history from apartheid to democracy. Modeled on the Edinburgh Festivals, it consists of a highly sponsored Main programme, selected by the festival committee, and a more experimental Fringe, not selected and run on a for-profit basis. Craft markets, art exhibitions and street theatre are also part of the 10 day event, which takes place annually in the small city of Grahamstown. Originally started as a celebration of English cultural heritage, the festival soon claimed to be inclusive of all South African art and culture.

From a political economy and an historical point of view, the NAF can be said to have played quite an important role in providing a pressure valve for political resistance, particularly during the height of the apartheid era in the 1980s. Despite doubt by some commentators (for example, Grundy 1993) on depth of the festival committee's commitment to including diverse art and artists (particularly African-origin and mixed-origin South Africans), by 1985 festival programs were including performances from many diverse cultural groups. This has continued to be the case in the New South Africa although market considerations and lack of funding are a constraining factor. Festival audiences have also become steadily more racially diverse and building new cultural capital may be one of the most important roles for the festival in the absence of the large, state funded arts councils (Snowball and Webb, forthcoming).

Other cultural indicators by which to judge the value of the NAF are: its role in maintaining South Africa's diverse cultural capital, its value as an outlet for political and social comment and its role in the valuation or "valorization" (Klamer 2002) of new works by artists, agents and audiences. Using such cultural indicators to place qualitative values on culture and heritage can show their historical progression and the changes that may have occurred over time. This may be especially important when considering the value of cultural events or products in developing countries that have undergone some important social and/or political change. However, until more consensus is reached on which cultural indicators to use and how to measure them, this sort of analysis will remain highly qualitative and will thus need to be supplemented by quantitative data if it is to be used in making policy decisions (Snowball and Webb, forthcoming).

Throsby (2001) points out that public policy has come to be dominated by economic policy and its major goal of efficiency. Within this framework, the economic (meaning financial) impact of the NAF is a very important consideration when lobbying for public funds, particularly in the context of a developing country where so many demands are made on the public purse. Despite some vehement criticism of the method, both from methodological and conceptual points of view, there is some evidence (in the case of the NAF and others) that economic impact figures can be used to great effect in motivating for public funds for the arts.

The economic impact of the NAF to the Grahamstown economy was shown to be R38.5 million (about 3.85 million at current exchange rates) for 2006 and about R35.5 million for 2004. In real terms (2000 prices) this shows a slight decline in Festival impact over these two years. Being a seasonal event of short duration, the festival does not generate many additional jobs and a number of these are taken up by students from outside the region, or by people who are already employed. Nevertheless, there is no doubt that there is some trickle-down effect and that the region would be considerably financially worse-off without the Festival.

A problem is that, when one examines who is benefiting financially from the event, it quickly becomes clear that the wealthier, European-origin residents are gaining far more in terms of money than the poorer African-origin residents who need it most. From an equity point of view, therefore, using economic impact figures to argue for public support is rather problematic. Another big problem is that, by using such valuation methods, arts proponents are not focusing on the attributes of the good that they themselves value – the purpose of the arts – usually not related to generating financial profits. These values, often external to the market, could be argued to be much more central to arts valuation and, as argued by a number of commentators, they cannot be valued by using only market data.

This is especially the case since, as Klamer and others point out, market values for art works tend to be unstable over time. Schneider and Pommerehne (1983) and also Baumol (1986) showed this early on in the development of cultural economics. Examining data from arts markets over several centuries, they both came to the conclusion that, while the price of art works is partly determined by the forces of supply and demand, there is no equilibrium price level and "their prices can float more or less aimlessly" (Baumol 1986:10), especially as the study time period lengthens. While this criticism applies to all short-term studies, including stated preference techniques, contingent valuation has gone some way towards solving the problems of using purely market data to value the arts.

Contingent valuation techniques, where the valuation is contingent upon the scenario presented, includes willingness to pay and choice experiment (or conjoint analysis) studies. Their great benefit, compared to revealed preference techniques, is that they can also measure non-use values. As with economic impact analysis, however, there are major methodological and conceptual problems with such hypothetical measurement techniques, although the huge proliferation of especially willingness to pay (WTP) studies in cultural economics indicates a general acceptance of the method, at least at a functional level.

While the WTP studies conducted at the NAF produced values far below those of the economic impact surveys (R2.8 million or 280 000 to avoid a

25% reduction in festival size), they have been very successful in examining the non-market benefits to various sectors of the population of Grahamstown. Unlike the financial benefits, which accrue mostly to the wealthier residents, the WTP study showed that significant positive non-market benefits do flow from the festival and that they accrue to both low and high income area residents.

Until recently, WTP and economic impact figures were simply added together to produce an overall value of the good (that is, market + non-market value = total value). However, as Seaman (2003a) points out, there are two problems with this. Firstly, the WTP measure is often (as in the NAF case) a partial measure, for example the willingness to pay to avoid a percentage reduction (25% in the NAF case) or increase in the size of the event. Because of substitution effects, simply multiplying WTP by four to estimate the total non-market value of a 100% reduction in the Festival is not feasible. It is thus fairly meaningless to add the WTP for a partial reduction in festival size to the total financial impact figure.

The second problem, suggested by Seaman (2003a) and found in the NAF case study (Snowball 2005), is that the WTP figure may also be capturing some of the current or future expected financial benefits that the cultural event provides. Simply adding the two figures would thus represent double counting of the value of the cultural good or event. The problem is particularly evident amongst low-income residents in the Grahamstown study, and any combination of WTP and economic impact data would need to discount the WTP figure to take this into account.

The two choice experiments conducted on the NAF (Snowball and Willis 2006a; 2006b) addressed the question of how various social and ethnic groups value the differing attributes of the festival. While having some of the same methodological problems as the WTP studies, choice experiments do seem to offer additional useful information on how different parts of a cultural good are valued, rather than the overall valuation resulting from one WTP question. It is also possible that they can improve on the methodology of WTP studies in terms of providing an internal scope test and greater insight into how respondents make decisions.

Festival choice experiments were used to conduct a cost-benefit analysis of the various attributes of the South African National Arts Festival. Taking into account revenue from ticket sales and marginal social benefit (willingness to pay) the study concluded that increasing the number of Fringe and Free shows would increase welfare, while increasing shows on the

Main programme and art exhibitions would not (Snowball and Willis 2006a). However, since African origin festival visitors are most interested in Main shows, there are equity grounds for continuing to fund them at their previous level.

Choice experiment results can also be used to calculate market acceptability, that is, the attribute trade-offs that specific groups of festival visitors are willing to make. For example, African-origin festival visitors (with a household income of R15 000 per month and tertiary education) would be willing to trade off a 1% reduction in Fringe shows for much smaller increases in other attributes (Main shows, art exhibitions and the craft market), but a 1% fall in Main shows could also be traded off against much bigger increases in other attributes (Snowball and Willis 2003b). Such information can be very useful to providers of cultural goods, especially when broadening participation from previously excluded groups of attenders is a goal.

It thus appears that the NAF has considerable value in terms of its historical and ongoing contribution in maintaining and building cultural capital in South Africa. It has a positive economic impact on the Grahamstown economy and provides considerable non-market benefits to all residents, including previously excluded African-origin people. While not measured in this research, it is also likely that non-use benefits are enjoyed by a wider group of South African residents, particularly given the extensive media coverage of the event and its development into a truly "national" festival, including a variety of art forms from various ethnic groups. As far as the make-up of attributes of the festival are concerned, the choice experiment indicates that all the attributes are valued positively by festival goers. Increasing the number of Fringe and free shows on offer would increase the utility of visitors. The festival also seems to have had some success in diversifying its audience to include a greater number of African-origin visitors.

7.2 Conclusions

Throsby (2001:67) argues that, "The re-conceptualizing of development in human terms brings culture from the periphery of development thinking and places it in center stage" (Throsby 2001:67). If this is in indeed the case, then we can expect both greater interest in the arts and cultur and in

finding some way of indicating their value so that efficient and fair resource allocations can be made.
The valuation methods discussed in this book set out some of the market and non-market methods currently in use in the valuation of cultural events, heritage, museums, libraries and monuments, amongst others. The benefits and disadvantages of each method from a practical as well as a theoretical perspective are considered.

Valuations based on market prices (economic impact) or on hypothetical markets (willingness to pay and choice experiment methods) are useful ways of indicating worth and can be effective in lobbying for public support. However, new and interesting work on more qualitative measures, including concepts like cultural capital, is also emerging. This field holds great promise because, although the "intrinsic" values of the arts will always be difficult to quantify, they do not generally have close substitutes and take into account the artistic aims of the cultural good. Recent shifts in economic thinking away from purely material measures of human welfare may make including qualitative cultural indicators as part of the value of cultural goods a reality in the future.

References

Anderson, E. (1993) Value in Ethics and Economics. Harvard University Press: Cambridge, Massachusetts.

Antrobus, G. and Snowball, J. (2004) The National Arts Festival Festino Survey. Commissioned by the National Arts Festival

Baumol, W. and Bowen, W. (1965) On the performing arts: the anatomy of their economic problems. American Economic Review 55,2:495-509.

Chesterton, G. K. (1941) In defence of nonsense. Stories, Essays and Poems: G. K. Chesterton J.M. Dent and Sons: London.

Grundy, K. (1993) The Politics of the National Arts Festival. Rhodes University Institute of Social and Economic Research: Occasional Paper 34.

Klamer, A. (2002) Accounting for social and cultural values. De Economist 150,4:453-473.

Klamer, A. (2004b) Art as a common good. Paper presented at the Association of Cultural Economics International, 13th conference: 2 – 5 June 2004

McCarthy, K, Ondaatje, E., Zakaras, L. and Brooks, A. (2004) Gift of the Muse: Reframing the debate about the benefits of the arts. Rand Corporation: Santa Monica, Arlington and Pittsburgh.

Schneider, F. and Pommerehne, W. (1983) Analyzing the market of works of contemporary fine arts: an exploratory study. Journal of Cultural Economics 7,2:41-67.

Seaman, B. (2003a) Contingent Valuation vs. Economic impact: substitutes or complements? Paper delivered at the Regional Science Association International Conference, North American Meetings: Philadelphia

Snowball, J. and Antrobus, G. (2001) Measuring the value of the arts to society: the importance of the value of externalities to lower income and education groups in South Africa. South African Journal of Economics 69,4:752-766.

Snowball, J. and Willis, K. (2006a) Estimating the Marginal Utility of Different Sections of an Arts Festival: The case of visitors to the South African National Arts Festival. Leisure Studies 25, 1:43-56

Snowball J. and Willis, K. (2006b) Building cultural capital: Transforming of the South African National Arts Festival. South African Journal of Economics 74,1:20-33.

Snowball, J. and Antrobus, G. (2006) The National Arts Festival Festino Survey. Commissioned by the National Arts Festival.

Snowball, J. and Webb, A. (forthcoming) Breaking into the conversation: Cultural value and the role of the South African National Arts Festival from apartheid to democracy. International Journal of Cultural Policy.

Throsby, D. (2001) Economics and Culture. Cambridge University Press: Cambridge.

Index